Just One Letter

By

Kirstie McEwan

Copyright © 2011

By

Kirstie McEwan

(2nd Edition – 2015)

Kirstie McEwan asserts the moral rights to be identified as the author of this work

ISBN **978-1-4709-1803-3**

All rights reserved. No parts of this publication may be reproduced, stored in a retrieval system, or transmitted, in any form or by any means, electronic, mechanical, photocopying, recording or otherwise, without the prior written permission of the publisher

Mum and Dad

May you both Rest in Peace

From your loving daughter

Kirstie

Acknowledgements

This is a true story. Names have been changed where necessary and the events are as I recall them and set at the appropriate time in my life. At no time do I mean to cause hurt or distress.

This has been a labour of love and I have many people to thank for their support and assistance in reading this more than once. My story could not have reached this stage without that invaluable help.

To David, my brother, I offer my unconditional love and thanks for his support throughout the latter part of my journey.

To Samantha, Katherine and Sophie, my daughters, I thank you for your ability to love and for having the capacity to live through a difficult time supporting me and to come through as stronger people.

Thank you to my college friends who have had to live this with me as I write; most notably Alison without whom the book would not have such an appropriate title and Linda for her unswerving dedication to providing constructive feedback.

Special thanks go to Steven Stahlberg, the creator of my cover image: "The Faery Queen on the eve of her wedding". A truly feminine image depicting freedom and happiness; emotions close to my heart at the end of my journey.

Last, but by no means least, to Dr Suporn Watanyusakul MD, without whose skill I would not now be living at peace, with body and mind in harmony.

PREFACE TO 2nd EDITION

It has been four years since I self-published the first edition of my life story. Sales have been, surprisingly, much better than I could have ever anticipated and the positive feedback has led me to believe that it has all been worthwhile. I set out to write my story as a means to help me to come to terms with what had happened in my life and, in that respect, it has worked perfectly. It was also a distant hope that it would help others to understand my choices in life and, most importantly, why I chose to live as I did for so long before making the decision to transition. The book appears to have gone some way to inform others and to help them to understand.

Why have I decided to produce a second edition? A lot has happened to me in the past four years. There are not sufficient events for another book, although some people seem to think there may be in another few years! I also don't think I have the capacity to focus so much energy on writing another book of this length. However, I do have the required focus to make the necessary changes, with help from a very important person in my life – Dawn, my wife.

I have been aware of minor errors (largely grammatical and typographical) throughout the book, since it was published, but it has never really worried me until now. No one has made any direct comment regarding this but I have always known about it and confess to being a little disappointed that I had missed these errors prior to publication.

This, the second edition, has therefore been re-edited and revised to eliminate these small, but nonetheless important, mistakes.

Additionally, I am now a qualified counsellor and therapist. Endings always lead into new beginnings and so I felt that it is now inappropriate to finish my story on an ending, as I did in the first edition. I now much prefer to finish as I started, with a 'New Beginning' – I have added a new final chapter. I hope you enjoy reading about my life as much as I have enjoyed living it – I now share this with you.

<u>Kirstie McEwan: November 2015</u>

Contents

Acknowledgements   4

Preface to 2nd edition   5

Chapter 1

Beginnings   9

Chapter 2

The early years   17

Chapter 3

Disappointment and tears   26

Chapter 4

Puberty, secondary school and a girlfriend   30

Chapter 5

A wonderful experience, Counselling and the future.   37

Chapter 6

Marriage, divorce and marriage again   50

Chapter 7

Moving on, a daughter is told and the last night out together   58

Chapter 8

The wilderness years   79

Chapter 9

Counselling; telling the children and my father and brother; I move out   92

Chapter 10

Wilderness and working as a male – the later years   114

Chapter 11

Learning to live as a female 24/7 and a holiday.   123

Chapter 12

My 'wake': goodbye to Ken forever. Good times and bad   142

Chapter 13

A special birthday card, Australia, unemployment and a disaster   161

Chapter 14

Thailand, the culmination of my journey: Outbound and reassignment   170

Chapter 15

Thailand, the culmination of my journey: Recovery and home   186

Chapter 16

Endings – Just One Letter   202

Chapter 17

New beginnings   210

Chapter 1

Beginnings

It was Monday morning just before leaving home for work when the realisation finally struck me; this had gone on for far too long. Our shared pain and unhappiness was too much to live with and I had to admit that it was my fault, otherwise one or both of us was heading for a breakdown.

"I know what's wrong with me and why our marriage has been a sham for so many years."

Jean, my wife of over twenty years, turned to me and stared, anticipation written all over her face as she would finally find out what it was that had gone wrong.

"What? Tell me." she replied.

I paused, took a deep breath and then just blurted out:

"I am transsexual. I was born in the wrong body and have finally realised I can't go on as I have done for the past fifty years."

Silence, for the few seconds it took for the impact of my revelation to sink in.

"Oh my God! What does that actually mean? Are you ill?"

She walked quickly across the kitchen to where I stood to give me a hug, the first in many months, perhaps even years, that really meant something between us.

I had agonised over it all weekend. The pressure and stress on me were just unbearable, as they were on Jean, who had to deal with my mood. After all, I knew what was wrong in our marriage; she had no idea. The weekend went as always, we did the shopping together but that was about all. We were two adults in the same house living entirely separate lives. We communicated when the children were involved but other than that there was little in common anymore. She had her own friends and spent as much time with them - and away from me - as she could. I had few friends and those I had I saw rarely. The children saw only that their parents were not getting on and did all they could to stay out of the way.

I suspected at the time that the years of silence from me had already done the damage to our marriage and that it would end no matter what. She, I believe, felt that there was still a chance; after all, who wants to start again in their 50's? The pressure had become too much for me and I was about to break in every sense of the word. I had no option. I had forced myself into a position of no return.

It was a conversation that changed the direction of my life forever. Emotions were high and tears flowed from both of us, although I am sure that my wife was unaware of just how much this revelation was going to change our lives over the next five years.

We had been married for over twenty years and had three daughters, Samantha, Katherine and Sophie, who at that time were twenty, eighteen and nine respectively. I was in a successful job, which paid well, and we had a lovely four-bedroom detached house with all of the trimmings. On the surface we were the perfect family. All was not well, however, and for the last few years life had been purgatory for us all. The children saw only that their parents were arguing and there was no open show of love or affection. I was moody, depressed and had no interest in family life, although I did my best to 'join in' and be the father that everyone saw and expected me to be. Although my family was unaware, my work was also suffering and my superiors had made comments.

There had been no intimacy in the marriage for a number of years; I was just not interested, to the point that we had attended Relate for marriage guidance, but to no avail. Deep down I knew what the problem was, I just did not have the personal courage to admit it; I was still in total denial.

"What do you do now?" she asked. We were both crying openly. My tears were of relief and happiness and hers just of relief in the knowledge that the issue between us was now named.

"I need to make a doctor's appointment and seek counselling".

I know that Jean thought that, with counselling, I would sort myself out and we could go back to our marriage as she felt it should be, and that everything would be fine. I, however, knew differently. This was the beginning of the end of our marriage and possibly our relationship. I knew that very few marriages could withstand the impact of a transsexual partner.

I also had not mentioned that essential word 'gender', when applied to counselling, as that was probably a step too far this early in the process. I was born in 1955 and had known from the age of six that there was something different about me. Obviously at that age I was not self-aware enough to know what and, without the internet, appropriate access to books, general acceptance and openness, there was no way I was going to find out. In the 1950's the concept of transsexuality was barely known about by the medical profession, let alone the general public. At my young age I had no idea that I was transsexual – just that it felt wrong being me. In fact, an American G.I. in 1952 had been one of the first people to come to the public's attention, when she changed her sex and her name, to become Christine Jorgensen. This was publicised internationally and, although others had preceded her, none had been publicly exposed. I, however, had no idea what it was to be transsexual, being born only three years later. Over the years I learned about the condition and, although it clearly applied to me, I lived a life of denial, doing all that I could to prove I was a man. However, by 2005 I had had enough of living the lie and all that this entailed for me and for those around me, whom I loved and cared for. Nature cannot be denied, no matter what we think we can do to confuse her; the burden on me, and on those around me, became too much and I just had to let it out.

I don't expect that anyone can imagine the release of pressure and emotion at the point where I finally was honest with myself. Behind the tears I was very happy in the knowledge that I was no longer hiding. I was me and it was public, well at least to one other, although I had been secretly exploring my femininity for many years at various 'dressing' services. I knew that there were many years of hardship and obstacles in front of me if I decided to follow the path, which I knew I would have to, and undergo transition from the male everyone saw to the female I actually knew myself to be.

I went to work happier than I had been in many months, as I knew this would be the first day of my journey to resolve the issues I had lived with for so long. The first thing I did on arrival at the office was to ring my GP and make that all-important appointment to discuss my condition and to commence my journey of self-discovery. Even then I was still in denial to some extent, as I was unsure of myself and my determination to reach the end point, which I knew would change me and all those around me forever. I knew from what I had read on the internet and other resources that my journey would be long, lonely and could lose me my family, my friends…everything. Did I have that personal commitment and self-determination to make the journey? At that time I had no idea, and to be honest, I didn't really care. I was happy for the first time in months and finally had a goal in life which, for me, would be the resolution to years of unhappiness. I was perhaps being selfish, as my happiness would mean unhappiness for others, most notably my wife and family. Yet I know I had no option, as I did not want the years of misery to continue affecting not only me but also everyone around me.

My doctor's appointment was made and I had my next milestone in sight. Life would now be a journey from one milestone to another until it was finished. I had no idea how long that would be but, as all journeys are one step at a time, I was content. My day at work was busy as always but this time I was happy, although I doubt anyone else really noticed the difference.

Going home that night was different. I was happy in myself, having taken that first step; however, I was also scared. How will she react? What had she thought about and what questions will I face? In fact there was little change from any other evening when I returned from work.

"How was your day? Did you make your appointment?" she asked.

"Boring as usual," I replied. "I made my appointment; it's next week."

"OK. What would you like for dinner?"

Jean was hoping that we could work toward a suitable conclusion of 'my problem', which would then allow us to carry on as normal. Life as she saw it – all happiness and roses - could continue as before. I, however, knew what was in front of me and that our future together was now on a countdown to termination, divorce and probable dislike. Despite this, I was happy inside as there was no longer any need to hide my feelings. I could see an end to a very long tunnel and I could finally be the person I had longed to be for so many years.

The story of the next few years is unique to me and it is my story. I will follow my development from childhood, through puberty, two marriages and parenthood, to the wilderness years of my adult life. During that time I totally denied my true self and lived, with varying degrees of difficulty and self – doubt, in the gender opposite to that which I really was. I will explore my work ethic and how my transsexuality affected me in the macho world of construction and development. On a separate thread I will go through the transition process from the moment highlighted at the start of this chapter to the culmination of my journey in Thailand and my Sex Reassignment Surgery.

It was not an easy journey, being full of pitfalls, joy, happiness, sadness and tears. There are many thousands of others who will take, and have already taken, a similar journey but each person faces different trials along the way. We each take this journey knowing the risks of all we can lose but we do so in the knowledge that we have to be true to ourselves and that, in the long run, it is a matter of personal survival.

The wait to see my GP was no more than a few days and I was very scared as I entered the consulting room to see her. The family GP had looked after us all for over ten years. I had been treated for depression and I suspect that Jean had also had consultations about our marital problems and treatment for depression.

One thing I am sure of, however, was that, after the usual introductions, she did not expect to hear the next few sentences. I explained the whole situation and went into some detail about transsexualism. I was very aware of the lack of knowledge that the average GP has in connection with this condition unless, of course, they had already been through the learning process with a previous patient. I was exceedingly lucky in that my GP was willing to listen and learn and did not just discount my feelings as fantasy. She listened to everything I had to say and then surprised me with her reply.

"I know very little about this and, as far as I am concerned, you are the expert. Tell me what you want or need to do and I will do my best to arrange it for you. In the meantime I will do my own research."

I don't know what sort of response I expected but this could not have been better. I had heard stories from other transsexuals about the dismissive attitude of some doctors; about how they felt desolate and without help for many years, until they could finally be registered with a caring doctor who would listen. Gender Identity Disorder, or Gender Dysphoria to give it the medical term, is a condition which is encountered only rarely by the medical profession. Indeed, the GP is most likely to be presented with a self-diagnosis by the patient, who probably knows more about the condition than the doctor. There is absolutely no test – blood, hormonal or genetic – which can prove or disprove the condition. Any of these tests would show that I was 100% male with all of the appropriate physical characteristics; having fathered three children that issue was beyond doubt.

The only route to a true diagnosis was counselling and the agreement of a psychiatrist/gender specialist that I was indeed suffering from this condition. So my next words were very clear,

"I need appropriate counselling for a diagnosis. Can you please refer me to the right person?" I asked.

"I will look into this and get back to you as soon as I can," was her answer.

I had mentioned the obvious route known to all transsexuals: a referral to the Charing Cross Gender Identity Clinic, which is where I thought I would be sent. However, I was prepared to let my GP help and see what was available locally; I put my trust in her abilities and left the surgery to await her letter, telling me the outcome of her research.

I was so happy. The first hurdle had been overcome and, to be honest, reasonably easily, due to the response from my GP. Had it been different and had I been dismissed with the comment that there was nothing wrong with me; then I cannot conceive what I would have done or where I could have gone. At least I was able to go home with a positive attitude and tell my wife that our doctor would refer me for further help, but it would just take some time.

At that time, of course, our children were totally unaware of my disclosure and of the likely outcome. Whether or not they noticed any change in their parents' relationship, I cannot say. I do think that there was, for a time at least, a lessening of hostility and an improvement in the general atmosphere at home. I believe that Jean felt that, with time, patience and appropriate help, I would be 'cured' and life could return to the happier times we had enjoyed when first married.

I knew otherwise: I was fifty and had had many years to search for information and to talk to others in a similar situation. The only 'cure' available to me, on the assumption that I was, in fact, transsexual, was to undergo the process of transition from male to female. It is not essential to have surgery in order to legally complete the process but I knew deep down that my final goal would be to seek surgery. I knew that I wanted to be as female as possible, in a woman's body, and with all the changes, within reason, that medical science could provide. I already surmised that the marriage was doomed to end in divorce, should I continue down this path. More importantly, I knew that I was gambling with my future and with that of my family and friends; I could lose everything, as had happened to many others who had trodden the path that I was now considering. The proper counselling, when I finally received it, would help in making this decision. I would be armed with the full knowledge of the consequences, should I turn away from transition and try to continue living the lie, as I had done so for many years.

I was not then, nor am I now, unaware of the hurt and pain this choice would cause to those I cared for dearly. My joy and happiness would come at the cost of their sadness and pain. Yet I had lived this lie for too long, and I could not continue as I had. If I did, they would feel a different sadness and pain, should I consider taking the ultimate solution by ending my own life. Suicide: it was not something I had considered in serious detail but I knew that it would raise its ugly head some time in the future as a solution, if I did not address as a matter of urgency the problem facing us as a family. I was only too well aware of the high suicide rates within the transsexual community. For those who simply cannot continue to live as they are, trying and failing to suppress the knowledge that they truly belong to the 'other' gender, or for those who perhaps do not have the determination, the means or the personal courage to take the journey, the option of suicide to end the inner turmoil, depression and unhappiness must seem all too attractive. We are, after all, individuals and no one else can really know what we feel or think and how we will deal with any situation. We all do what we think is best at the time; regrets, if any, come afterwards.

I could say that I then settled into life as normal, and waited patiently for the letter to arrive. That would be a lie. I know I came home from work each day with a mix of excitement and trepidation. The first thing I would do is check through that day's post for that all-important letter. I have no idea what Jean thought of this but finally I came home to:

"Your letter is here," she said almost as soon as I walked through the door. She was aware just how important this was to me and was doing her best to be as supportive as she could. I opened it eagerly and read that a referral had been made to the local mental health unit and that they would contact me in due course with an appointment. This was not as good as I had anticipated but at least it was another step forward; I just had to contain my frustration once more and wait for the next letter. I was desperate to run but was restrained to a walking pace; I knew just how long my journey was going to be and, now that it had started, I wanted to be off. Patience is a virtue but it was rapidly running out after waiting so long. Part of me knew that another few weeks, after so many years, was not really an issue but that did not stop me from fretting.

The letter finally arrived with the longed-for appointment at the local psychiatric unit. The reader may wonder why I had been referred to a psychiatric clinic. The answer is quite straight-forward; because there is no medical test for gender dysphoria it is treated as a mental health issue. As such, the diagnosis has to be made by either a psychiatrist or a psychologist, preferably one trained in some form of gender awareness.

I rang as requested and confirmed my appointment two weeks later and then settled down to wait. This was not easy to do, as this next step was perhaps one of the most important I would have to make. What if I did not make the right impression? What if I met a doctor who had no idea about transsexualism and just dismissed me as a waste of time? I had to trust in my GP and go to this assessment with an open mind and just tell the truth as it was, and explain how I felt as a person.

The day arrived and, as I always hated to be late for any appointment, (this one more so than any other in my life) I arrived an hour early and parked the car. I was nervous, scared and full of trepidation. Whatever happened in the next two hours would change the direction of my life forever and impact on everyone that I knew and cared for. I went for a short walk to find out where I was going, returned and sat in the car. I had a book with me but could not concentrate; I was, not unsurprisingly, just too worked up about what was going to happen. After fifteen minutes I gave up, got out of the car and walked to the clinic. Having already done this journey I knew I was going to be far too early but didn't care; I would rather wait and twiddle my thumbs in the waiting room than sit in the car and worry that I would miss the appointment or, even worse, get scared and leave.

The clinic was a large house in a residential area, but set back behind trees: just the sort of place to go if you want to enter privately and out of the public view. No one could have guessed that the man entering the building, dressed quite conservatively in a two-piece business suit, was in fact transsexual and desperately wanted to be other than he currently looked and acted. I was that man and this was to be the first of many episodes in my journey to become the real me. I remember the interior being drab and somewhat dark as I approached the frosted glass window marked as Reception. There was the usual bell push next to the window, which I pressed and waited for the response. A few seconds, which seemed like hours, passed and the window slid aside:

"Yes. Can I help you?"

"Hello. I have an appointment with Dr Smith."

"You are early, but please go to the waiting room and you will be called."

The glass panel closed. I was on my own again and went to the waiting room. I then spent the next forty minutes wishing I had my book. I could only read the wall posters and handouts so many times. There was not even another patient to look at or talk to. Finally the waiting room door opened, a nurse checked that I was the right person and asked me to follow her upstairs to the consulting room. My pulse rocketed: this was it.

Chapter 2

The early years

February 16th 1955 at Bryson Road, Edinburgh, Scotland: the traditional smack, a cry, and a baby boy was born to proud parents, Mary and Bernard. It was approximately 4:30 in the afternoon, deep snow had fallen and my elder brother had been banished outside to play for the duration of the birth.

It is impossible to imagine the relief and pleasure that my parents must have felt; I was perfect and apparently healthy in every way. There was no way to tell at that time that I was in fact not a perfect little boy but one who would grow up to realise that I was not what I appeared to be. That realisation was to take many years and my mother was never to know the truth as she sadly died before I had the courage to tell the world.

Every parent knows the joy and relief at being told, "Congratulations you have a perfectly-formed and healthy baby...." To my parents this was multiplied many-fold as I was in fact their third and only 'perfectly' formed baby boy.

My parents were both from small coastal towns on the west coast of Scotland, some thirty miles south of Glasgow. They had lived through the Second World War, my mother as a nurse and my father in the RAF, where he saw active service in the Far East. On his return to Scotland they met and fell in love, marrying in 1948 and moving in with Bernard's parents for a while, as they got down to the task of living together. My mother was soon pregnant and carried their first child to full term but sadly the child died shortly after being born. The baby was a boy, Dale, who was born deformed, surviving only long enough for the birth to be legally registered.

Mum fell pregnant again at the end of 1949 and my brother David was born on 20th August 1950. Worryingly for my parents, he was born with a bilateral cleft palette and double hare lip. Like his elder brother he was not expected to survive, being unable to suckle. He did however pull through and has become one of my greatest supporters during the difficult period of my transition.

Life was not easy for my mother during the early years of David's life. Much time was spent in hospitals, where he received reconstructive surgery at least once every year for the first sixteen years of his life.

It is not difficult to understand just how worried and concerned my mother must have been when she was again pregnant in 1954 with me. My brother was four and, although fit and through the worst of the birth difficulties, was still fragile and required regular medical treatment. The stress was compounded by the fact that her father was seriously ill and he, in fact, died on 17th February 1955 - the day after I was born. Her pregnancy while she carried me must have passed without mishap, as I am sure she would have been closely monitored in light of her previous history; I was delivered in a home birth, suggesting that all was well with her at the time.

I was perfectly-formed, fit and healthy: the culmination of my parents' wishes, despite their fears and worries. Clearly, though, mother had been under great stress during her pregnancy with me, both because of the issues surrounding David and the fact that her father was seriously ill.

Some current thinking is that stress in the mother at certain times during pregnancy can affect the foetus and its development. Clearly my mother was extremely stressed, which could have affected my development. It is quite conceivable that, at certain times, hormonal changes did not occur correctly, possibly resulting in my transsexuality. Physically and genetically I am 100% male; however my gender is, as far as I am concerned, definitely female. I am a woman born in the body of a man and I lived with this dichotomy all of my life until I was fifty, when I found the courage to finally admit the truth and do something to rectify the situation.

My life in Scotland was short. My father was a rising star in the field of exhibition cake decoration. His work was receiving national and international recognition, which would eventually lead him to be celebrated as perhaps the best in the world. It is an achievement that I will be eternally proud of. He worked hard and was absent for periods of time when he was preparing for an exhibition, but he always worked for the benefit of his family.

He was much in demand and, in 1957, was accepted for a new position in London, which required a family relocation. At the tender age of two and a half I moved down south to England.

We stayed in Enfield, North London, until I was eight and my early formative years are vague memories. This was the period when Dad was doing his best work and so he was absent for much of the time. He left home most days around 5am, before I was awake, and usually returned after my bedtime. Weekends would be the only time I would see him and he was usually busy doing things around the house, with improvements and those other tasks that husbands do.

My mother largely brought me up by herself and it's her influences that I recall most in my early life. I know my father loved me but he was driven to give his family the best and was making his mark in the world; that inevitably meant our time together as a family was limited.

Cuddles were not the norm, the family being what would today perhaps be called 'dour Scots'. Love was there, of course, just not in an open and demonstrative way. Mum still had a lot of her time taken up with David and his regular trips to hospital, the dentist and of course our annual holiday to the family in Scotland.

Some may say that I was strongly influenced by my mother in my very early formative years and that is why I have these feelings and consider myself to be transsexual. It boils down to the "Nature vs. Nurture" argument that is continually raging about transsexualism and its root cause. There are strong arguments presented by each camp and it is hard to decide which, if either, is actually correct.

Personally I am a believer in the view that Nature is all-powerful and will make the final decision on who and what we are. Nature can be strongly influenced by nurture, but in the end, it is my belief that nature is the stronger of the two.

David and I were never especially close mainly because of the age difference and also thanks to the fact that I always had to be careful during the normal rough and tumble of two boys growing up together. His face was very delicate and was easily damaged, particularly after surgery. Great care had to be taken so that there was no chance of any particular year's surgery being undone by a mistimed swipe or similar during play. I did hit him once, by accident, and ruined a years' worth of surgery; I didn't sit down for a long time afterwards!

I also believe that, although I was not an only child, I was almost in that situation; I became very self-sufficient and able to be on my own. The major difference, of course, is that I was not on my own and my parents shared their love and time between us, unlike a true only-child, who receives the love of both parents exclusively. Perhaps it was also weighted in favour of my brother because of the additional care needed to ensure he developed properly to enable him to live a normal life.

Hindsight is colouring a lot of my feelings, as I honestly believe that Mum and Dad gave me all the love and care they could. I most certainly was not neglected or starved of love, any more than any other second child in a family. All I am trying to express is that my upbringing was coloured by the environment in which I developed and that in many ways it gave me the ability to be on my own, to be a loner, self-reliant, self-sufficient and to survive the next fifty years of my life as a male.

How does a six-year-old boy know that he is different? This is not an easy question and, in all honesty, I doubt that there is an answer. It was 1960 and I knew that there was something wrong in my life. I had no idea what was wrong or whether it was a normal situation to believe that my life was wrong, it just was! There is no other way to describe the situation and the feelings that I had at that time. I knew I was not right and that I was in fact a girl; this is easily said now, but impossible to deal with at that age. I knew I could not speak to my father or brother about this, and I did not tell Mum who was, of course, the greater influence in my life.

Perhaps this anecdote will shed some light.

As a young boy I usually shared a bath with Mum; it was a treat and something special, which we did together. My brother would be at school and so I had Mum all to myself. It was when I was about six that I asked what was, to me at least, a very simple question. We were in the bath together and obviously naked. I looked at her and asked:

"Mummy, when will I have breasts like you? When will they start to grow?"

It was simple enough as far as I was concerned, because that was exactly what I wanted in life. It seemed perfectly natural to me but I am sure Mum was somewhat taken aback. Her reply was simple and direct:

"Don't be silly. Boys don't grow breasts like girls."

It was the last time we had a bath together.

An innocent question? I certainly thought so, but obviously it was not so for grownups and for my mother in particular. I was on my own, with no way of finding out information. There was, of course, no internet in those days and, even if there had been, at six years old I would not have been able to use it to search for what I needed. How lucky young people are today who have access to a world of information at the click of a button.

My mother was a glamorous woman and always looked after herself and presented herself to the world in the best light she could. I remember she always had nail polish and whenever I asked she would paint my nails when she was doing her own. I suspect she felt that there was no harm in it at my age as I wasn't exactly out on the town on my own. She would not do it when I went to school of course but otherwise she was accommodating in this request. I do think that Mum continued to indulge me where and when she could, so long as it was just between her and me.

My dreams and aspirations at that age were very simple; I wanted to be something I was not – a girl. Daydreams and thoughts before sleep were very similar and simple. I would find that 'magic' box of makeup and upon application would transform into the girl I wanted to be; and on its removal I would, of course, change back into the boy I was, so that I could live normally with my friends and family. If only it were so simple but, unfortunately for me, it was not to be and I forced myself to live a lie for many years.

Memories of my time in Enfield are naturally limited and hazy at best. I did start school at five and can remember enjoying my time there. I was, after all, young and had yet to realise the full potential and impact of my transsexuality; in fact I had no idea. I always found it difficult to make friends as I was shy and withdrawn but I do know I had both male and female friends. In fact I had my first crush on a girl. More likely I suspect because she was all I wanted to be – a girl, petite and blonde. That's about as far as it went at that time.

I do recall one incident very clearly and can still see myself in the playground dressed in a kilt. I was seven years old and it was a special occasion at school. As a Scot, and proud of it, my choice was to wear our national dress and Mum was able to borrow the full regalia for me. There were queries from the other boys about me in a skirt but in reality it was perfectly innocent, so there was no issue from the school or trouble from my peers. I know I felt happy that day and I feel sure that, as my memory of the event is so clear to me now, after fifty years, it must have been something more than just being in national costume. I can clearly see myself in the playground with the school buildings all around and other, faceless, children with me laughing and having fun as any normal group of children that age will. The kilt is undoubtedly a masculine style of dress; however, I feel that, to me at that age, it was perhaps more. Perhaps it was even my first introduction to public cross-dressing.

Don't misunderstand me: I still behaved as 'badly' as any boy of that age and got into enough trouble to ensure that no questions were asked about my personality and behaviour. Sexuality is not a word you can use about anyone of that age. Most notable, perhaps, was the day I pushed a creosote-covered paintbrush through someone's letterbox as a dare. Oh yes, and I ran away in time. However, when called back by the rightfully furious owner of the house I just turned around and went back for the dressing-down I rightly deserved. I did not have, nor do I now have, that final survival/killer instinct to run or to close down a situation to my best advantage. This failing was to show itself more obviously as an adult in my working life, which I feel is part of the feminine side to my personality. Obviously I suffered miserably at home after that incident.

November 1963: I was eight years old when we moved again, this time to Kent. Dad's exhibition days were over and he had been promoted once more and was to be based south of London. He had made it from a quiet Scottish west coast harbour town, working in a small family bakers, to senior management in one of the UK's largest companies. Along with that promotion came all of the trimmings: a company car, a beautiful three bedroom semidetached home in leafy suburbia and, of course, the salary. Mum and Dad were moving up in the world and got to enjoy the perks of his new position, such as invitations to dinner dances throughout the year held at the big London hotels. Mum was able to express her femininity and dress to the highest standards with the best that Dad could afford. She looked good and knew how to present herself as the beautiful, attractive woman she was. Dad, I am sure, was very proud of his wife as they mixed with the upper echelons of the baking industry and its suppliers.

Of course, with the promotion came responsibilities. Dad was away travelling the country for most of the week so, as before, we hardly ever saw him, especially in the early years as he established himself.

As for me, life went on as before. My mixed feelings and emotions did not change but I did have more opportunity to be what I wished to be – a girl. As I grew older I became more adventurous and willing to take chances. I had no sisters so the only available clothing I had was my mother's. It was not cutting-edge fashion for a young and developing girl but at least it was available to me and, as I grew older, I took every opportunity I could to dress as the girl I knew myself to be.

School was much as before, and my inner turmoil did not really impact on how I acted and felt when with my peers. I seemed to be able to separate the two parts of my emotions and wishes, something that was to develop into the ability to bury my true feeling for many years. I was a normal boy as I tried my best to join in with sports and social activities but was never any good, only making it into the house football team, for example, on the basis that only eleven of us were interested in joining.

Academically I was average and managed to keep up without shining. As for relationships, it was still too early for my difference to make its full impact known to me and I managed to get along with both boys and girls. The 1960's may have been the start of the sexual revolution, if we are to believe all that was said and published about that time. However, between the ages of eight and eleven I believe we still retained our innocence: the difference between boys and girls was only just beginning to make itself felt.

I was aware of my own difference but in a non-sexual way that was based on my own developing awareness and on how I actually perceived myself as an individual. My circle of friends was not large and was at that time mainly male. I was, perhaps, difficult to get to know. This was compounded by the fact that I had no school friends living close-by, such that I could go out and play with others after school. I had one local friend who lived a few houses up the road but, as he went to a different school, time together was restricted to weekends and after school hours. It was only when I reached the age of ten or eleven that I was deemed old enough to travel into town on my own to meet other friends. I was already growing up to be self-reliant, making my own entertainment and not necessarily needing the company of others. At home, however, life was far more exciting, as I could immerse myself in my daydreams and start to explore my femininity; perhaps this was another reason for my lack of external friendships, and may also have contributed to my ability to become insular and self-sufficient.

I had learnt all that I could about makeup and female clothing by watching my mother and looking in her magazines. Mum had no issue with me sitting and watching, while she got ready to go out. I would watch with quiet interest as she applied her makeup: it was, after all, the only way I could learn,

The drawback was that I could hardly ask for lessons, as any other young girl could. I may have innocently asked one or two questions but nothing so obvious that it would raise eyebrows. So there I was, soaking up as much information as I could from wherever I could. Television was not a great deal of use in the early years, as it was black and white and the advertisements had not reached the complexity and visual impact that we see today.

I finally reached the stage in my development where it was my turn. I did not use Mum's clothes when living in Enfield, so I must have been eight at least, and I suspect a year or so older. I cannot recall the first time or what it was that made me do it, I just did. I would not have been home alone at that age so I was taking a big risk in going into my parents' room and searching through Mum's clothes.

My explorations would happen after I went to bed. I can imagine a degree of fear that I might be caught, mixed with excitement at being able to explore my feelings. Added to this was the release of pent-up frustration caused by not being able to be true to myself. These are clearly my adult explanations being applied to my younger self, with hindsight and with the knowledge of self-awareness. At that age I would not have been able to express it in such terms. Mum would be in the house on her own and sitting in the lounge at the back of the house, with the door closed, so I knew I would not be disturbed. I could creep into her bedroom at the front of the house without too much difficulty or too much noise, which would have alerted her to my presence. So there I was in Mum's bedroom with one ear cocked to listen if the lounge door opened, so that I had time to rush back to my room without being found out. My early forays were short and not too intrusive but with time, and experience, these became more extensive each time, allowing me to release the feminine and just be a bit more like Mum than like Dad.

My first investigations were to look through the drawers and explore the sensation of touching the garments, the feeling of silk, nylon, satin and leather against my skin: sensations that I, as a boy, had never had. My early experiences would be with underwear such as knickers, a bra perhaps, stockings and my early favourites: a pair of kid leather opera gloves. These were items which could easily be removed and hopefully replaced without incident and without making Mum aware I had been there. These nightly forays were like a drug and I was addicted.

I have no idea how I managed to get away with this for over five years without being caught or Mum guessing what was going on. If she did, she never made an issue or mentioned it to me. It is almost inconceivable that I could search through her dressing-table, the wardrobe and, later on, her cosmetics and put everything back neatly and in such a way it was not noticeable. It was just not possible, especially in the early days. As I got older it is feasible that I became more experienced in my ability to be neat, and to remember where it all came from. But surely I would not have managed it in those early days, when the fear of discovery would be as much a part of the foray as the excitement in dressing. It was never raised in my hearing. Whether Mum was aware and spoke to Dad about it I will never know. I am sure she must have been aware of something but chose to keep it to herself. Perhaps the incident in the bath, so many years earlier, had remained with her; I don't know.

The early days, up to the age when I left primary school and entered secondary school (around the onset of puberty and all that that entailed) were still fairly innocent; I mostly restricted myself to touching rather than wearing the garments, although I tried on a few basics. In addition, I don't believe there was any sexual element to my early forays: that would come later.

As with the kilt incident, which I can so readily recall, there was one other similar occurrence, which remains firmly in my memory.

It occurred one Christmas at the end of term, during a play performed for our parents, staff and other children in our year. It was the final year at primary school, so I would have been ten and we were performing a pantomime. I was not in the cast but helping out with props as required. On the day of the performance one of the three fairies became ill, just before the start of the performance. Without any immediate replacement I was asked to step in and take over. It was all perfectly innocent but I would get to wear a dress and was overjoyed to accept this role, knowing full well that I would be ridiculed by my male peers. There was a problem, however: I was tall for my age and her dress did not fit; all I could use were the wings and the wand.

I needed a costume, and fast. My teacher obviously had a sense of humour and a good idea of comedy. He suggested we could make one – out of pink crepe paper. So I stripped down to my underpants and vest and he sellotaped me into a pink sheet of crepe paper giving me a skirt of sorts. It was not what I had expected but it was too late to back out now; I was in it up to my neck. The wings were attached, the wand thrust into my hands, and I was on. So what to do? There were no lines as such, just a song - and the whole class knew the words, so that was not an issue. The two other fairies were both girls and had lovely sparkly dresses whereas I was the comedy act in a paper dress, stuck on the end of the row. All we had to do was hold hands, dance on and sing our song. The play was about the princess who could not laugh and who had to stay straight-faced until the end of the play.

So we danced on. Had we walked on and stood still I am sure I would have got through the scene without mishap. However paper dresses and dancing do not mix and within seconds it had torn and started to unravel. Like a true trouper I just carried on, my supporting 'straight men' did the same and we had the place in uproar. I ended up with the dress in tatters and around my ankles, finishing in my pants and vest. Somehow I was not embarrassed; all I could think of was that the girl playing the princess was out of character, she was in stitches, as were the audience, the cast and everyone else in the room. I stole the show and was the star.

It was not quite what I had wanted or expected but in the end it was fun and I reveled in the applause. I remember little else of what followed but it does not matter. My foray into being a girl did not work out as I had wished but, then again, as I would learn many times in the future, not everything we wish for works out how we want.

Chapter 3

Disappointment and tears

I followed the nurse out of the waiting room and up the stairs to the first floor, with the usual inane chatter between us about the weather and how I was feeling, in order to try to put me at ease. She led me into the consulting room; this was it and I know I was both scared and apprehensive at the same time about what was going to happen.

It was not a large room, with one window, brown wooden paneling and dirty magnolia walls - more drab. The psychiatrist sat at an old wooden desk and there was a chair facing him, which is where I was directed to sit. The nurse sat on an old brown leather sofa behind me; there was nothing else in the room of any note.

The doctor explained that the nurse was a psychiatric support nurse and that she would be there to help and support in day-to-day matters. That was good I thought: someone I could easily reach, on the basis that the doctor would not always be available. So I sat and waited to see how this was going to progress, and to learn about how I was to be treated. This was perhaps not going to be as hard as I had anticipated and I began to settle down. The next half hour was a question-and-answer exercise about my life, marriage, mortgage, work, debts and finances; nothing, in fact, about my life and being potentially transsexual. He ignored the whole reason why I was actually there.

I was fully aware of all of the other issues that obviously impacted on my life, and of the fact that I was depressed, but these had nothing to do with why I was there. I began to worry where this was leading and was getting frustrated with his approach. We did not once talk about the reason for my being there and why I had been referred by my GP.

The session was drawing to a close and I was getting upset, not that the doctor even seemed to notice. His closure summed up the complete waste of time and, as far as I was concerned, his total lack of knowledge about what a transsexual is and about the condition of gender dysphoria.

"I note that you are being treated for depression and I feel it would be beneficial to increase your medication dose. I will write to your GP. If you want I can sign you off work for as long as you like. Do you think that would help?" he asked.

I was devastated; this was not why I was there and it was absolutely no help whatsoever. I am not usually a confrontational person and tend to shy away from this, so I just nodded and said the appropriate thank you. I did say that there was no need to sign me off work, as that was not a problem, and that I would discuss medication with my GP, knowing full well that there was absolutely no need to increase my medication. I was, in fact, desperate to have it reduced. I had far more trust in my own GP than in this total waste of time.

He finished with:

"The nurse will come down with you and make another appointment for a month's time and we can see how you are progressing. Please go down to the waiting room and she will be there in a few moments."

The nurse had, in fact, taken no part in the consultation, nor had she said anything, so I had no idea about what help she would be in the future. I left the room in total turmoil. My emotions were in overdrive: angry at the way he had treated me; anxious about what to do next; and deeply frustrated about the whole issue. I was devastated and as I walked into the waiting room on the ground floor I just burst into floods of tears.

The waiting room was still empty, so I did not have the added complication of embarrassing myself in front of other patients. This was not how I had imagined the first steps of my journey; all my hopes had been dashed in just one session, by a qualified psychiatrist who obviously had no inkling of how to deal with my condition and who did not have the honesty to admit this. He had picked on the one part of my condition that he was comfortable with, my depression, and that was all he was going to treat.

I was still sobbing when the nurse came in; she took one look at me and put her arms around my shoulders in comfort.

"I am so sorry, that was probably the worst consultation I have ever witnessed," she said. "He did not even consider why you were there and was certainly no help whatsoever. I will see what I can find out and contact you directly with the names of any local support groups."

"Thank you," I answered "Any help whatsoever will be much appreciated."

We just stood there for a while, with her giving me the comfort and support I needed until I got myself back under control again.

"Do you want to make another appointment? I would understand if you did not."

I thought about it and decided to give it a second chance, always optimistic! So a second appointment was duly made for four weeks' time. As I left, the nurse once more said she would call me in a few days with details of local support groups. I thanked her and left for the office to do some work for the remainder of the day.

That was it, my first consultation with a 'specialist' and I had come across every transsexual person's nightmare – a psychiatrist who did not know and, more importantly, did not seem to care about my condition, looking only for the easy diagnosis. I think he felt he was doing me a favour by offering to sign me off. That was the last thing I wanted. I was not sure exactly what I wanted or needed but it certainly was not what I received. I was unhappier than ever and felt really low. I told Jean about it when I got home and I received a kind of sympathy, but I don't think that she understood.

True to her word, the nurse rang me a few days later and gave me the details of some local support groups. I thanked her for her efforts on my behalf. I did not tell her that I was aware of all of the contacts she had given me and could probably have given her a dozen more she had not even come across. I knew that would have been unfair and a step too far under the circumstances, as to do so would be ungrateful after her help and sympathy. It had not been her fault for the way I had been treated. My GP had, of course, been right; I, like any other embarking on this journey, was already better informed than the average medical practitioner, no matter what speciality they practised. My own research was far in advance of my GP's knowledge and I was obviously a long way in advance of the psychiatrist's.

I can be patient when necessary and so I attended the second appointment with the psychiatrist. I was in a totally different frame of mind this time and was not prepared to take second best. I knew what help I needed and was damn well going to get it. The process was a repeat of the first time but without the nurse in attendance. I sat down waiting for him to open the proceedings.

My faith in human nature was sadly let down and my original feelings towards the psychiatrist were reinforced within the first few minutes. We started with a review of the last session and then went straight on to my depression and possible financial problems that, as far as he was concerned, were the root cause of my problem and which compounded how I was feeling. I wondered if he actually had my notes and letter of referral – it seemed as though he was treating someone else.

This session lasted all of five minutes before I had had enough. I refused to be treated like this and to waste another hour of my time. I stood up and told him what I thought of him.

"You clearly have no idea about my condition, or how to treat me, and you are likely to do more harm than good if this continues. This sad affair has set my progress back two months. I am leaving now and won't be back"

I turned and walked out. I don't think I slammed the door on my exit but I am sure it would have felt good had I done so; he said absolutely nothing.

I was back on the street and this time I was furious rather than the emotional wreck I had been on the previous occasion. I did the only thing I could: I rang the surgery and made an appointment to see my GP as soon as I could.

The next appointment was somewhat different to our previous meetings. I was upset and very annoyed at the waste of time and felt very let down. I explained the whole sorry affair and all she could do, of course, was to apologise.

"Please leave it with me and I will do further research and see if I can find a more appropriate referral," she offered.

We once more did not discuss the obvious referral to Charing Cross and I have never been able to work out why. I left feeling much happier and she promised to contact me as soon as she had found someone else to whom she could refer me. I do have to say that her further research proved to be very positive and in many ways speeded up my progress.

Chapter 4

Puberty, secondary school and a girlfriend

I passed my 11+ and made it to the local grammar school, where David was already a pupil. It was a school of 900, all boys, so my opportunity to mix with girls was non-existent. I would be growing up in an all-male environment and so had to do my best to fit in.

The school excelled at sports - primarily football and cricket. I was never really interested but always joined in just to be part of the mainstream, actually playing for the school rugby fifteen and hockey teams. In reality I was only selected for these sports because there were not enough interested people to have a choice to make up a good team. We never won anything and were massively overshadowed by the successful football and cricket teams.

With an older brother in the sixth form at school I was not picked on by the usual bullies so never really had to protect myself. I had had to do so at junior school on occasion and had learned at least to stand up for myself when needed. My circle of friends was never large but I did retain them throughout my school life, only slowly losing touch when I got married.

I therefore continued through life as before and learned to live with duality. At school I was Ken and did everything that any boy of that age and in that environment did. At home I did all I could to explore and expand my femininity. However, as the years went by, I would start to crush these feelings and deny my true self, in order to fit into the norms expected of a young adolescent boy.

Life at home was much as before: Dad was away a lot, David had reached sixteen and discovered the joy of motorbikes so we never saw him; it was just Mum and me most of the time during the week. As I got older Mum was prepared to leave me on my own for a while, such as on evenings when she went out to play badminton and attend other social events. This gave me a few 'safe' hours when I could indulge myself, as long as Dad was not home.

It would always be the same. I would wait ten minutes or so, just to ensure that Mum did not come back having forgotten something. Once the coast was clear I just indulged myself in my female nature.

If I had time, and with practice I could always judge it very well, I would either just use cosmetics or go all out and dress as well. I was now twelve, pre-pubescent and old enough to know more about what was going on in my life. I had an inkling of my 'problem' but still no formal idea of what I was. The papers had started sensationalising sex change, frequently reporting on April Ashley, for example, who transitioned in the early 1960's and who went on to become a famous model, photographed by David Bailey. Danny La Rue, a famous drag artist and entertainer, was often seen on television and was one of my mother's favourite entertainers. Cross-dressing was coming out of the closet. Dick Emery and Stanley Baxter were comedians who regularly played female characters. More often than not it was ridiculed rather than shown in a sensitive light but it was becoming more common. There were even documentaries, one of which, in later years, was to be the illumination for me of my issues and my way of life. I would always do my best to be around when one of these shows was on television and would sit with the family to soak in all that I could with respect to being female.

Over the years I had 'researched' everything I needed to know and do and, with regular practice, it all became so easy. To be clear, though: I could not apply make up to the same standard that my fourteen year-old daughter does now, as there was no way I could get enough practice. Similarly, my 'wardrobe' was limited but I felt right in doing what I did and it felt natural. I could look in the mirror and see myself as the girl I knew I was. There was always the issue of my hair, which was short and boy-cut. These were the days of Twiggy and her boyish look but it always felt false, no matter how I combed it. Then one day, wonder of wonders, my mother decided to buy a wig. I am sure I had more use out of it than she ever did! It was not a young person's style, of course, but better than my own hair: it completed the look.

I had also by this time entered into the realm of purchasing my own items. Clothes were out of the question but I felt that I could always go and buy cosmetics and similar for my mother or an imaginary sister. By the age of fourteen I had a small stock of items such as false eyelashes, which my mother would never buy. Saved pocket money and, regrettably, the odd pilfering from Mum's piggy bank paid for these. I stashed them in my room in the air vent high up on my bedroom wall, where no one would think to look.

One issue that I had failed to consider at my then age was local knowledge and gossip. We lived in a small town and everyone knew everyone. My mother, in particular, was well-known, as she worked in the local coal merchants and helped out in the community where she could. So, when I went into the chemist, where she certainly also shopped, and said I was buying something for my sister, the person serving me would clearly know it was not true. Nothing was ever said to me but I am sure that there must have been raised eyebrows at some time.

Initially there was no sexual need involved with my dressing. However, as puberty approached, the impact on me was as profound as on any other developing teenager and there was a need for sexual satisfaction during some of these episodes. I think it was quite natural to do so, just as any developing girl explores in her own way, I was doing the same. It was not like a cross-dressing fetish, which many men indulge in throughout their later lives. I had already experimented with feminine clothing from an early age and to me it was quite natural.

Timing was important and I always knew when it was time to pack up, so that I would be unrushed and could get everything back to just as it was when I started. Everything had to be folded and put back in drawers, put on hangers in the wardrobe and all without tears, smudges of make up or other incriminating evidence.

This was totally different to the male self, who just dropped clothes on the floor for Mum to pick up. Of course the odd accident did happen and there would be a few moments of panic. I learned to clean make up stains very well and, if not, it went to the bottom of the wash bin in the hope that Mum did not notice something she had not even worn being there. I even brazened it out and put things away with stains, hoping Mum would think it had not come out in the wash. I was pushing it at times and I still cannot to this day believe that she did not have some clue as to what was going on.

The last thing was always to remove every trace of makeup. This was perhaps the most important step of all, to ensure there was nothing which could be noticed. I can still remember clearly the shape of the bottle and the smell of Anne French Deep Cleansing Milk. It is one of those sensory memories that will never be forgotten. All tissues and cotton wool had to be flushed down the toilet carefully, so that I did not block it. I became quite paranoid in ensuring that everything was put away and cleared up and that I was spotless and back doing some innocent thing before Mum came home. As with the putting away of her clothes, I am sure that she could smell the cleanser but, of course, never mentioned it to me.

The best times were during the Christmas party season, when my parents would go to company dinner dances, leaving home early and not returning until the early hours of the next morning. I would be around thirteen at this time and they felt comfortable leaving me at home on my own. I then had the opportunity to 'get serious', changing clothes more than once but always being in bed and 'asleep' by the time they came home.

It was about this time, when I was fourteen, that the inevitable happened: I was caught.

I had never been caught before so, not surprisingly I started to take chances and push my luck. It was a Saturday afternoon and I had decided to take a bath. It was an opportunity when I could indulge myself with cosmetics and with the bathroom door locked could do so in perfect safety. Only, on this Saturday, I forgot to lock the door! I had by this time already started the process of burying my true self and my emotions. However, it was also the start of the period of 'Glam Rock' with Bowie, Marc Bolan and similar becoming national celebrities and well known for their outlandish life style. It was the beginning of 'gender bending', so I felt that I could continue as I always had, although the masculine was beginning to take charge. The edges between the sexes were blurring and so it still felt natural and acceptable for me to continue as I had for many years. I know now that I missed a perfect opportunity to express my true self and to come clean with the world in a 'safe' manner, just as many others did at that time. I, however, had chosen to deny my true self and continued to hide behind my male persona.

I had done the usual and had run a bath, while carefully applying my make up as best I could and then settled down to a long soak, just feeling that all was well and natural. Dad wanted to wash his hands and without thought, (he probably did not even realise I was in there), walked to the bathroom door, opened it and came in. Absolute mind-blowing panic on my behalf was the result. I can clearly remember sitting up and just plunging my head under the water, not that I could stay there for long. I came up spluttering, scared as hell and with the makeup smeared and running down my face. What would Dad's reaction be? What would he say?

I can recall a look of shock and disbelief on his face.

"What on earth have you got all over your face?"

I was embarrassed and petrified at the same time as I replied:

"Don't worry Dad, I just wanted to experiment and see what it was like."

A lame excuse perhaps but with the changing social mores the only thing I could come up with that I felt Dad might accept.

"Get that lot off and talk to your mother. I never want to see this again."

He turned and left me to my misery. Now, as an adult, I can totally see his point of view. After all he had no idea of my inner turmoil, as it had never surfaced anywhere before. What did I do next? The only thing I could: I cleaned up, got out of the bath, got dressed and I then went downstairs to face Mum.

I can still recall just how scared I was entering the living room, where Mum was sitting and reading the paper. Dad had gone out.

"What's this Dad tells me? You were wearing makeup in the bathroom? What's going on?"

She did not come across as angry; it was more like exasperation.

"It's nothing really Mum and I am sorry but just wanted to see what it felt like, you know David Bowie, like we see on telly," I replied.

It was the only reply that I could think of which would cover all bases but would not give away how I really felt.

"Och, don't be so silly. Dad is annoyed but he'll get over it. Just don't let it happen again."

My life could have been so different if I had taken the chance then and told the truth. However, it was not to be and my life direction was set from then on: I would be a boy.

That was the end of it. The episode was never spoken of again. The more I set down my memories of my early life, the more I realise that my mother could not have been ignorant of what was going on with me. She may not have realised I was transsexual, maybe even fearing that I was gay. Whatever she thought, though, she was my mother and she stayed supportive throughout my life, no matter what mistakes I made. As far as I know she kept her feelings and concerns to herself, never voicing them to me or another member of the family. It was to be our secret but one that we never discussed.

I was fourteen and my secret was out. It was not public but it was enough for me to be concerned in the family. This is perhaps the time when that five-year age difference between David and me became significant. I could not talk to him and in fact we rarely interacted. He was out with his friends most of the time, around and about on his motorbike and later in his car. His major influence was that, when I was old enough, I also wanted a motorbike but by the time that happened he had emigrated to Australia and it would be a long time before I saw him again. All news about his new life I received second-hand from Mum.

As I have previously noted, life at an all-boys school was not hard for me to live with, as I had the ability to release my tensions at home in privacy. I got down to the task of living, finally joining the school scout troop. I thoroughly enjoyed my time there and the companionship with others of my age. Puberty was arriving for us all and we were changing from young boys to adolescents, with all of the trials and tribulations that brought. As far as I was concerned, puberty passed me by in many ways, as I lived my dual life. My voice obviously broke and along came the body hair, with the eventual need to shave.

Like all boys at that age, the talk turned to girls and the inevitable top shelf magazine started to appear. Personally I was not really bothered, taking part in the usual "cors" and "wows" because that was what was expected. Little did anyone realise that I was more interested in the pictures from the neck up; how her hair was styled and how her makeup was applied. Not really the usual boyish fantasy, is it?

I was living a dual life, the boy at school and in outside situations but always the girl at home, however secret that longing was. I was a bit of a loner, largely due to this duality. However, I managed to join in enough so that questions were never asked by my peers about my behaviour and I was accepted as 'one of the lads'.

I think it appropriate that I stress the fact that I lived a dual life but was not a dual personality. I was not two people occupying the same body but one person living two separate lives, something I had to deal with again in the latter stages of my final transition. I found that I could separate my wish to be what I wanted and my need to be seen to be normal. It did mean that I was a loner at times and I did learn to be manipulative in order to protect my other private life. Most importantly, I learned to become very determined and to make my life what others saw it to be, instead of what I most wished it to be.

I was slowly building that impregnable cell into which I put my true self and it was where I was eventually to lock her away for many years, only letting her out on parole very occasionally and when the need was so strong it could not be denied. Of course this did not happen overnight. It was a long process, which slowly saw my adventures into femininity declining, and my masculinity taking over; I was, after all, full of testosterone by this time.

I did get my motorbike and later worked to save enough for my own car. I enjoyed the camaraderie of riding in a group, spending time stripping down engines and all that that entailed. Masculinity, and the fun to be had with peers, was taking over. But I could not be in a group to enjoy my femininity: that was always a solitary affair and was by now, in slow decline.

One benefit of being a scout was that the premises were on school grounds and the older members were allowed to congregate there; we could even hold parties. I am not entirely sure how official the party bit was but it did not stop them from happening. It was at one of these parties, when I was fifteen and just before I had a motorbike, that I met Pam, my first girlfriend. One of the lads had a girlfriend at a local girls' school and the word went out. No Facebook or the like - just word of mouth! So we had a party and there were girls present; they were not many and they were outnumbered by the boys, but that was the best that could be arranged in those days. There was no alcohol, of course, officially anyway, but I can recall the odd can of beer or cider being present. I was there with a friend and we met a couple of girls.

I was then, and still am, shy. I had no prior experience with a girl. The two girls knew each other and were at school together, so it was an easy pairing. It seemed to be the right thing to do and matched in with my masculine side, which was coming more and more to the fore of my personality. It was, after all, what boys were expected to do and by this time my feminine side was being slowly but surely put in the closet. Each of the two pairs went their own way and got to know each other. I think that my partner was also quite shy and we seemed to click. At the end of the evening she had a bus to catch home and I had to cycle the five miles home in the opposite direction. We agreed we liked each other and swapped telephone numbers. I also agreed to call her to arrange another meeting.

I do remember cycling home with a grin on my face and feeling pleased with myself. I had a girlfriend!

Chapter 5

A wonderful experience, counselling and the future.

In the months after I had told Jean nothing really changed at home. Obviously there was less pressure on us both but my inner feelings did not change. I knew it was the end; it was only a matter of time before I would be moving out and starting my life over again. As for Jean, I don't really know what she thought, as we never really discussed my 'little problem'. I am sure that she wished for it to be resolved and that we could rebuild our marriage and get back to a 'normal' family life; deep down though, I am sure she had her reservations and had an inkling of the likely outcome. She still had no wish to know more about my problems and lifestyle although she was willing to give me a little more freedom to explore further, so long as she was not involved.

Therefore, in November 2005, only a month or so after I had broken the news I made a request.

"The pressure on us both has been extreme and I am finding it difficult to hold my pent up feelings together. We both need a break. I need to go and express my female self in order that I can get my control back. I have not done so in many years and it shows," I began.

"How do you want to do that then?" she asked.

"I want to go away for the week-end, to a place that specialises in people like me. I want to live the life for a couple of days. In London, so I won't be too far away," I explained.

I could hear the resignation in her reply:

"Well, if it will help, I suppose you should. When will you go?"

"It should only take a short time to arrange, I just have to check availability, so a couple of weeks."

"OK. Let me know when and I will arrange to do something with the children," she replied.

The conversation I have just outlined would possibly seem very simple for what was a major issue in our marriage. It was, however, that simple: no questions, no recriminations, just resignation and a simple agreement to my request. The children at that time were still unaware of my situation and so were told that I was going away for the weekend. This was something I had been doing regularly with some friends to various wargaming conventions and events, a hobby I had taken up earlier, in an attempt to maintain the masculine front behind which I was hiding. There was therefore no question asked when I told everyone I would be away for the week-end in a couple of weeks' time.

By this time I had done enough internet searches to make a choice of which service I would use. I chose perhaps one of the best known in the UK at that time. Based in London, Image Works was run by the now sadly deceased Pandora. It had been so long since I had done this that I decided to ensure that it would be a memory to cherish for a long time and so I booked the top package, with an overnight stay. This would ensure that I was not rushed, could try as many looks as I chose, and could just revel in being feminine. I had, of course, dabbled in the past, but always in secret and always with a strict time limit.

As the weekend approached the excitement and anticipation continued to build; this was a first for me and I suspect many people would say it was a selfish act. However, it was also an act of survival: I needed to overcome the depression and the inner turmoil that had been building for a long time. Planning was minimal, as I was only going to London, a distance of no more than thirty miles.

I had no idea how Jean felt about this, as she made it clear that she wanted nothing to do with it in any way. We were once more drifting apart and things were to continue in this manner until our eventual separation. I also need to make it clear that I did not hold back when giving my family everything that I could. Yes they were material things, a good home, holidays and small luxuries. In a way it was a salve to my own conscience and perhaps to make up for the fact that emotionally I was living in a desert. They did not go without; and in that giving I was also denying myself. Therefore, in my eyes, I was not being selfish but was just giving myself what I needed most in life – the chance to be me for a change.

Saturday arrived and, as far as the family was concerned, it was no different to any other, with the exception that Dad would be away. However, this time I would be on my own, not with friends, and would, for a change, have the opportunity to express the feminine in me and to indulge myself in a way that I had not been able to do for such a long time.

Preparations for the day were more extensive than for my usual day at work. It started with a hot shower, a scrub down with an exfoliating body wash, and a shampoo. My hair was still cut in a short masculine style so that was in reality no different. I was also lucky: I was thinning but still retained a full head of hair, apart from a small area on the crown and slight recession at the temples. The hair loss due to male pattern baldness is a transsexual woman's greatest fear and nightmare. Hair transplants can deal with small areas and the hairline itself, but they cannot deal with total loss. To have to wear a wig for the rest of my life would have been dreadful. Had I lost much or most of my hair, I would have learned to live with it, as many others do, but I was to be lucky.

I then proceeded to a full body shave from top to bottom, taking great care not to nick myself anywhere. This is perhaps one of the most significant activities for a male still in transition to undertake. The removal of the masculine body hair is a very sensual process, leaving very sensitive and smooth skin in its wake. The subsequent application of body lotion just adds to that feeling and it is a very personal and feminine experience. My anticipation was continually rising as I carried out my personal preparations. The final act was a very close facial shave. New blades and absolute attention to detail were essential to ensure there were no stray hairs and no cuts. There is nothing worse than trying to deal with a bleeding cut on the face prior to the application of cosmetics; it can put a dampener on the whole of a subsequent evening out.

At that time I had not even considered facial electrolysis, which is something I now deeply regret, as I have to deal with it post-transition. Luckily my beard was already going white, so I did not suffer greatly from dark shadow after shaving, a blessing for which I am eternally grateful. No after-shave or any perfumed product was used. I wanted to go with a totally clean and blank canvas. Finally I was satisfied. Dressed in casual jeans and shirt I picked up my regular overnight bag, said the usual goodbyes and headed for the car. No one, with the exception of my wife, was any the wiser.

The drive into London was about forty minutes and the location was not hard to find. I parked close by and just sat there, thinking about the next twenty-four hours and just what a difference this experience - more so than any other - was going to mean to me. I was excited and also scared as I got out and locked my car, to take the walk of a hundred metres or so to the front door. It was a large, white-finished Victorian terraced house in a very pleasant and quiet area. I knocked on the door and waited, with my anticipation and excitement rising every second.

I did not have to wait long. The door was opened by a young blonde-haired man of average height and build. He introduced himself and welcomed me in, saying that Pandora was out till later but that he would see to my needs and look after me for the day. I was shown upstairs to my room for the night. He offered me a drink and a sandwich and said that I would have a short time to myself to prepare for later on. I had some fresh orange juice and then looked through the small library of books and DVDs. The room was not large but was totally suitable for my brief stopover. There were mirrored wardrobes on one wall and the double bed next to these. Other furnishings included a small chest of drawers, some bookshelves, a television and music centre. The window overlooked the secluded rear garden. I had all I needed. I browsed the magazines, which consisted entirely of transgender topics, from general interest to the more specific adult magazines. The DVD collection was much of the same and I was curious, never really having dipped into the more 'adult' genre. It is impossible to search the internet for transgender issues without coming across the 'adult' side of our lifestyle, so I was well prepared.

I was left to settle for a bit and to just relax in preparation for the afternoon ahead. I suspect that they were aware how much clients could be uptight on the first visit and, as I was here for a good length of time, an extra half hour was not a great issue. So I just lay on the bed and flicked through the magazines until there was a knock on the door and he put his head around:

"Right, Kirstie, are you ready?"

I had already assumed my female name, which I was to finally take by Deed Poll as part of my final transition. I was given a short cotton dressing gown and a pair of knickers to change into. I took off all my male clothing. I would not need it again for some time and put it to one side, pulled up the knickers and put on the gown. This was it!

I followed him out of my room across the landing to the main room at the front of the house on the first floor. It was a large room, being the full width of the house and at least half of the depth: I suspect somewhere around twenty-five feet by fifteen feet. Walking into the room, there was a wall of cupboard doors immediately on the right, all louvered and painted white. The wall directly in front was the exterior wall, with three large windows giving plenty of natural light. On the left the whole wall was once more cupboards but this time full height sliding mirrors reflected the natural light, making the whole room brilliant, as well as giving plenty of surfaces in which to view oneself. The wall facing the windows had a long row of dressers full of drawers and covered with the essential accessories of femininity and make up artistry.

The house was Victorian with high ceilings; the whole room was spacious with no feeling of claustrophobia. I was immediately at ease; this felt so right and I was looking forward to every second of the next few hours.

There were only a few pieces of furniture in the room: a comfortable chair and small table by the mirrors and a chaise-longue under one window by the louvered doors. A few small tables with flowers and a wall mirror added to the feminine feel of the room. My eyes were drawn to the centre of the room. A chair and a small trolley full of cosmetics sat there, waiting for the next occupant – me. This was just for me and it felt great, I would be preened and pampered for the next few hours; I felt that I was in heaven.

"Take a seat," he said. "You won't see anything till I have finished the first transformation. After that we can look at various outfits and looks as we take the pictures."

I sat down as he opened the various cupboard doors – an Aladdin's cave of clothes, shoes, boots and wigs of every colour and style imaginable was shown to me, just tempting my every whim and wish.

What could I say but "Let's get on with it, please."

I sat and let him work his magic over the next hour. I was facing the louvered doors and so had no idea what was going on. It is part of the whole experience and produces that WOW factor as the new person is revealed in all of her glory. We chatted about many things, mainly to do with the transgender community and, obviously. where I felt that I fitted in. I explained that I was new to coming out and that I strongly believed myself to be transsexual and would eventually transition.

As I write this, living as the woman that I am, I dress conservatively and live in leggings or jeans and tops. That day, however, I was looking for Glamour, with a capital G, and I am pleased to say I experienced that in every way possible.

A heavy foundation was applied to provide the perfect blank canvas. This was followed by the powders and paints of the consummate artist. False eyelashes were applied, followed by the final touches, after which he stood back and admired the finished effect. At this time I still had no idea what I looked like, having no mirror within sight. I knew that I just had to turn around to see the mirrored wall but to do that would spoil the whole experience, so I sat and did as I was told.

He then started to pull out various pieces of underwear from the drawers and, of course, the essential prosthetic breasts, which would fill the bra I was fastening.

"Not too big. I don't want to look top heavy,"

I replied, to the question as to what size I wanted to be. The final choice was enough to show, but not extreme. From current experience I guess it was a C cup.

"As you will be here for some time I suggest we don't use the corset for a while, as it will become too restricting," he continued.

I was willing to be directed by the professional in this matter and accepted his advice.

He then pulled out a gold, sequin-covered, off-the-shoulder dress for me to slip into, then finished off with a pair of black court shoes. He told me he had chosen heels which were not too high, until I got used to wearing them. He then asked me to sit down and put on the wig.

"I have chosen a short style for now and we can always change it but I think it makes the look."

I had no idea what to expect when he asked me to stand up and then slowly turned me to face the mirrors.

Well, I got the WOW-factor all right! There, standing before me, was a Glamorous woman, with that capital G that I had wanted. Yes, I turned and I preened and reveled in a few moments of being myself for the first time in far too long. Think 1980's Joan Collins in Dynasty and you will be close. To be absolutely honest, I was a bit subdued, as I did not like the short hairstyle, feeling it made me too angular and perhaps not as feminine as I had wished. "Don't worry," I was told, as I expressed my concern. "We can soon change that in a while."

I did as I was told; I am not naturally photogenic and, like many in this situation I suspect, a little unsure and self-conscious. I moved, I turned, I sat and did all that I should as he took picture after picture. I slowly relaxed and began to enjoy the experience.

After perhaps thirty minutes I was asked if I would like to change, which of course I wanted to do. That was, after all, why I was here. So began three hours of total bliss and self-indulgence. As I relaxed it became more fun and it showed in my expression and the way in which I posed. We changed the wig and moved on from the short style to a long, flowing, full-bodied, dark brown one which was more like my natural colour. The pictures from this part of the shoot are, in my opinion, some of the best ever taken and I will cherish them for the rest of my days. I am smiling, relaxed and the happiness just shines through.

It was approaching five o'clock and I still had all night; I did not want this experience to finish. However, it had to, for a while at least.

"We will have to finish for now; I have about ninety shots which I will put on a disc for you to take home in the morning. We are going out tonight and there are five other girls coming with us. They will be here soon to change and get ready to go. We haven't decided where yet; it will be either The Way Out or Club Rub. Do you have any preference?"

"No, whatever the rest of you decide I will go with the majority," I offered. I knew of The Way Out Club, of course: it was well-known as a major transgender club in London. I had no idea what or where Club Rub was, though. I was just glad that the day would continue.

"Well, you can go and have a rest, read or watch a DVD while we change the others. You can change later. Would you like to try a corset this evening?" he asked.

"That's fine by me," I replied, and went back to my room for a well-earned rest. I turned and posed in front of the mirror and just drank in my real female self, while the others arrived and changed into their feminine selves.

There was a knock at the door and when I called "Come in" Pandora entered and introduced herself. She was also carrying a large glass of chilled white wine for me, which was very much appreciated.

She asked how my afternoon had been and if I had enjoyed the experience. She had seen the pictures and complimented me on the result, much of which was, of course, down to the experience of her assistant. She then explained that the others were getting changed and that she would oversee my change for the night out. We were going to Club Rub, a BDSM venue near the city, and were aiming to get there around ten o'clock. A minibus and driver would be laid on, so there was no need to be concerned about being in public; everything would be taken care of.

I had no idea about the BDSM scene or what to expect so I just chalked it down to another first for me this weekend and looked forward to the experience with anticipation. She said that I would need to wait another half hour or so for there to be room for me to come back in to the main room; she suggested that I just enjoy the wine and relax, as it would be a long night. I sat down, flicked through a few magazines and was happy to follow her instructions.

True to her word, after half an hour Pandora put her head into the room:

"Kirstie, do you want to come in? Let's see what we can do for you tonight."

She had a knowing smile on her face and I just had the feeling that I was in for something special. I followed her back into the front room, where I was by now the only client.

Pandora quickly took charge:

"I know exactly the look for you tonight, so just leave it to me."

"I am in your hands," was all I could say. First I undressed and her assistant came forward, brandishing a corset with a grin. He slipped it around my midriff with the instruction to "Breathe in," which I did. Suddenly breathing out was more difficult! I had never been properly corseted before and the experience is quite unique, to say the least.

So I was now standing in my underwear but unable to see myself in the mirror, as the two of them discussed my next look for the evening out. My thoughts were in turmoil – What would I be wearing? How would I look? What would it be like in the club?… and so on and so on. I just let them get on with it.

Pandora sat me down and removed the wig, I had liked this look, and in some way wanted to keep it, but I had agreed to let her do it all, so shrugged to myself and let it happen.

My makeup was checked and touched up but not significantly changed. It was, after all, already quite heavy and glamorous. I put back on the dress I had just taken off; it was black velvet - already a favourite fabric of mine – and it followed my new curves rather seductively, even if I say so myself. The dress was full-length with a turtleneck and long sleeves, so very little skin was on show. It was, however, slit up to thigh level on both sides so my lace topped stockings showed through rather provocatively. I was then given a pair of black stiletto court shoes with five inch heels to finish the look. These were higher than I was used to but I was up for anything that night. I had had enough experience in heels to be able to cope, or so I hoped.

Pandora had already said that blonde would be ideal for the night and she chose two hairpieces, which she expertly put together to make one. This was long and upswept, with tendrils down below my shoulders. She seemed to be enjoying my transformation and took out a pair of scissors to trim the wig to her satisfaction. I still had no idea of the overall effect, as I was not facing the mirror and the anticipation was beginning to overwhelm me.

"Not long now. Be patient - it will be worth it, believe me,"

she said, as she preened and teased the wig into place. The final decision was on which jewellery I should wear. Obviously, diamonds on black velvet would be best. She had just purchased such a piece of costume jewellery and thought that I would be the ideal person to give it its first outing. She turned and brought out a rather large flat box and opened it for me. I could not believe my eyes when I saw what it contained: it was a magnificent, large diamante choker and necklace, with matching drop earrings. It was fantastic and would be the piece-de-resistance of the whole outfit. It was a high-necked choker with a triangular spread of diamante covering my upper chest and coming to a point between my breasts. It weighed a lot, spreading across my chest and, as she carefully put it on, I can remember her saying:

"The drops are quite heavy as well, so we will make sure they don't come off by gluing them on."

The things we do for effect!

I still had no idea what I looked like but could sense the pride that Pandora was showing by the smile on her face. Not only would I look stunning but I would also be a walking advertisement for her services.

Finally the look was complete and I slowly turned to the mirrors. I gasped - I looked absolutely stunning: Pandora's reputation for magic was well-earned. The woman, standing over six feet tall in heels, looked just spectacular….. and she was me! I was speechless for a moment, as I drank in the spectacle of what I had been transformed into. Not suitable for a trip to the supermarket perhaps; but for a night's clubbing absolute perfection. We went out onto the landing for some more memorable pictures which, as before, show the happiness and joy shining through. I felt completely at home, just being the female person I knew myself to be, both in my heart and in my head. The hairstyling, makeup, jewellery and all the other attention I had received was the icing on the cake so far and the night had only just started. As the excitement kept building I wondered what more experiences the night held for me. I could not wait to find out. This would be my first time in public as Kirstie and I was looking forward to the whole experience.

We then went downstairs to meet the others. It was not quite as easy as I had anticipated in the heels but I made it without mishap. Introductions were made over another glass of wine; there were six of us but I was the only one who would be returning at the end of the evening. The others were wearing their own clothes and wigs; they had come for the makeover and the chance to go out as a group.

Soon it was time for us all to get into the car which would take us into Central London. That first step out of the front door will be memorable for the rest of my life. This was it: out in public as Kirstie. It was dark and no one other than my companions could see me. However, that did not diminish that special feeling for me one iota.

The trip into London was uneventful and we all just chatted; the driver knew where he was going and would assist us all evening. This was also a new experience for me. Here I was going out at a time when I would usually be thinking about going home. This whole weekend was turning my life experience upside down and I just loved every second. Pandora would be joining us shortly; she, after all, had to prepare herself too for an evening out, as did her assistant. It was a dark and chilly November evening but at least it was not raining. The driver parked the car in a side street a few hundred metres from the entrance to our destination. This was it: I would have to walk down the street, not in hiding, but tall and proud - and I loved every step. It was chilly and I had no coat but I did not care. I stood, walked tall, and drank in the admiring glances from my companions and the few passers-by.

The venue was a pub, which had a large basement and was acting as host to the club. The theme for the night was uniforms and that is what I saw. Military, police, medical…every kind of uniform was there, in every kind of fabric: leather, rubber, satin and more. This was an eye-opener for someone like me, who had led a fairly vanilla life until this time. As transgendered girls we were admitted without any problem - after all, we were all in uniform.

Uniform was a topic that I had to discuss in some detail with my counsellor in later years. Unlike a transvestite, who often gains sexual gratification when wearing women's clothing, that is not the case for me as a transsexual woman.. Yes, on that particular evening I gained a lot of pleasure from the way I dressed but that was because it had been so long since I had been able to experience my feminine self. This was also an extreme situation. Now, living full time in the female role, clothes are simply a normal part of life, no matter what I wear.

I described female clothing to my counsellor as the putting on of a uniform, not necessarily for my benefit, but for the benefit of others, to help them identify me as female, and not as the male that I saw in the mirror. That seemed to be an acceptable description for my counsellor as to how I perceived myself and how I dealt with putting on female clothing: it is a means to an end and not the end itself.

I went downstairs to the club room which contained a bar, a large dance area and a dungeon. This was a totally new experience for me. Once we had all got our drinks we parted company; after all, we were all here for our own entertainment. For a while all I could do was look around at the people who were there, in all shapes, sizes and colours. Some were dressed and others were almost naked. I had never been to such a venue and I have to admit I loved every minute I was there. Pandora arrived about thirty minutes later with a stunning, and well-known, blonde as her companion. It was, of course, the male assistant who had looked after me all afternoon. We chatted for a few minutes and then she left me to explore.

The whole evening was a wonderful experience; I wandered through the rooms and talked to many people, all of whom complimented me on how gorgeous I looked. I, of course, just soaked it up; my ego was being massaged and I revelled in the experience of just being myself for a change. I was normally shy but I had no difficulty striking up conversations with anyone who would take the time to listen; many also came to me to talk. There are three memories from my time there which I can recall in detail. I am not in the least interested in this lifestyle but I learned a lot that evening.

The first was the public dungeon area. I had never been anywhere like this before. It was fascinating to watch but I must confirm that I was never interested in taking part. I don't intend to go into detail but needless to say I saw many things I had never expected to see 'in the flesh'.

The second was a conversation with a very attractive woman dressed in a military uniform. She had her male slave on a leash sitting on the floor beside her, not saying anything but showing nothing but adoration. We spoke of many things as she queried me about my choice of dress and lifestyle. I innocently asked where she came from and how she had come by her slave. She gave me a knowing smile: "He's my husband, of course." What more could I say?

Toward the end of my time there, it would have been about 3am, I went upstairs to the small bar. It was less crowded and much cooler. I was still wearing the corset and it was beginning to feel restrictive. In some way, perhaps, it was my introduction to bondage, although I can say that there were many there whose bondage was far more extreme than mine. I bought a drink from the bar and went to sit at a table. There was a couple sitting there, both dressed as American police officers, the only difference being that the uniforms were made of latex. We sat together and just chatted for a time. They told me that this was their first experience of an event like this and how much they had enjoyed themselves. They were just a typical suburban couple out for a new experience and enjoying it – just as I was.

I learned a lot about difference and diversity that night. Any prejudices I might have had about people and about that choice of lifestyle were dispelled. Everyone I spoke to that evening was polite and perfectly normal; they were no more abnormal than I was. The only difference was that they enjoyed something out of the ordinary in their lives. There was nothing I could find that was rude, unpleasant or even disrespectful and I enjoyed the company during my time there. I have to confess that, some years later, I went back with friends and found it just the same and I enjoyed the experience once more then, just as I had on my first visit.

The evening came to an end. I was the only guest returning to the house and we got back at about four o'clock in the morning. Of course I had to go through the reverse of the dressing process and remove the jewellery, clothes and make up. That was much quicker than its application and I felt both joyful for my evening's experiences but sadness that it had had to end. As I left the front dressing room at about 5am I chose not to look in the mirror – the 'loss' of my female image, and the return to my everyday male reflection, would have been very painful. I headed for bed and sleep; I was exhausted but extremely happy, with my batteries recharged and ready to face my drab male life once more.

I awoke later that morning at about eleven o'clock, still feeling tired but nevertheless rested. I was happy but also sad as I realised I had to return to male mode for an indeterminate period. I had no idea when I would be able to repeat my experience of the previous night but I knew I would have to at some time. I was elated; my depression had been lifted and I could face the world as Ken once more.

I dressed and went downstairs. I heard talking in the living room and knocked before entering. Pandora was there, chatting with the driver from the night before It was obvious that they had not been to bed and had sat up for the remainder of the night following our return. We talked for a while and I was presented with the disc containing the pictures from the night before. I thanked her, but after a while it was time to go. I made my exit for the return home.

I arrived home in the early afternoon of the Sunday, tired but happy. I knew it would not be easy for me to return to a 'normal' situation but had to do the best I could. The children were none the wiser and treated my return the same as at any other time. Jean was more subdued and made it very clear that she wished to know nothing of my adventure.

I was back to reality but knew that it would not be too long before the need to be myself again would arise. I had let the genie out of the bottle and there was no going back; she could not be returned to live in captivity. The taste of freedom had been experienced and I needed more.

It was shortly after this weekend that I received a letter from my GP. She had searched on my behalf and had found a consultant who was willing to see me and assess my condition. He was based at The Tavistock and Portman Clinic in London which, I have to confess, I had never heard about. I Googled the name and it transpired that the clinic was well known as a mental health clinic, with a gender centre specialising mainly in young transsexual patients and their families. It was not mainstream, like Charing Cross Hospital, but it was a specialist centre none the less. My appointment was arranged for January 2006, which was only eight weeks or so away. I was back on track and this time would be seen by someone who was gender-aware. I could not wait till the New Year and once more take a further step along the road to resolving my situation.

Chapter 6

Marriage, divorce and marriage again

I had a girlfriend and I was slowly but surely burying my feminine self, in order to conform to the society within which I lived. It was to be slow and painful but in time I succeeded, and entered the wilderness for almost thirty years - a wilderness where I denied my true self for most, but not all, of the time. There were moments when I had no option, as the pressure on me to open the door for a while was too much to bear. Release for good behaviour became more common towards the end of my wilderness time, as I gave in to the pressures of nature which, slowly but surely, became too strong to ignore.

This period of my life is perhaps the hardest to write about. My interaction with other people in an intimate and personal way is difficult to express and explore because they are still part of my life. In many ways I have hurt them once and don't wish to do so again. However, there is a part of me which also acknowledges that, if they ever read about this time, there is a chance they might come to understand a little about how I felt. With luck they might grasp what it was that drove me to lead the life of denial that I did for so many years; what it was like eventually to acknowledge my condition; and what drove me to do what was necessary to become what was, after all, my true self.

Is love at first sight possible? It is a question that many ask and one which, I suspect, never truly receives an appropriate answer. In my case, yes, I believe that it can happen; after all, there are two people involved so it is not a one-sided affair. Is it true love? Now that is a different question and one that I reflect upon when looking back as I write. I had never had a girlfriend before; in fact I had never even felt the need to have one, until I started to bury the feminine within me. As a teenager testosterone was running rampant and I suspect that this natural effect contributed to my feelings, although possibly to a much lesser degree than my male peers. They all seemed to be changing girlfriends as quickly as they changed their underwear. I, however, was content with my first.

We grew up together. I think that is an appropriate statement as we developed as a pair through puberty, into adolescence and then into adulthood. We grew and became comfortable in each other's company, much like a brother and sister in fact.

While my friends all changed girlfriends and had multiple relationships, we became 'The Couple' and were always together. I completed secondary school successfully and went on to do a degree in Construction Technology, gaining a second class honours degree. I had decided that I would enter the construction industry as, according to the school careers advisor, I seemed a very suitable candidate. I did not challenge this decision or think about how it would impact on my female personality. I had already managed to bury it deep enough for others not to see it and I was able to ignore it, most of the time at least.

I was already a very determined individual and I set my sights on succeeding in my chosen career. Determination was something I came to rely on, to enable me to ignore my feelings and to set them aside as I progressed through life. No matter what I actually felt, needed or wanted, I was determined to ignore it. A sad side effect of this was that I was also able to control and bury my emotions in a similar manner. I became insular and self-sufficient, traits that can be appropriate in the right place but which are also very destructive in the long term, particularly within a loving relationship. They are, however, defensive traits which enabled me to wander in my self-created wilderness for the best part of thirty years.

I know our parents were concerned that we were not behaving like normal adolescents and that we came to rely on each other so much. As Pam was unaware of my issues, so was I also unaware of hers. She has now also had many years of counselling, as an adult, to help her understand herself better. I feel that, at the time, we both used each other as a crutch to help us deal with our issues. Love was there, of course; no relationship can last as long as ours did without it being there. However, that love was perhaps tainted by the need we each had for support and was therefore doomed to failure.

On 30th August 1975 we got married: I was twenty and she twenty-one. It was a large wedding, with plenty of friends from her work and my college attending, as well as our families. There is no doubt that we were happy and that, at the time, we felt it was the best thing for us both. Pam had decided not to go into further education and went out to work to support us through the last two years of my qualification and training. We obtained a mortgage and bought our first home together. Everything was perfect; it was a struggle but we worked hard together to make it a success.

Life went on, I qualified and worked for a major UK construction company in the London and Kent area, commuting as required. I enjoyed work and fitted into the macho lifestyle of construction work. My trips into femininity had, for a while, more or less ended, as I did all I could to conform. Obviously the feelings I had had as a teenager were not natural and were clearly a passing phase; that is what I thought at the time, anyway.

No matter what I did, though, to lock the female part of me away, there was always a glimmering flame left alive as a constant nagging reminder of what I truly was – a female unwillingly locked in a man's body.

Even during my college years I had few friends and mixed with a limited circle of other students. Most of our friends were Pam's and I largely followed along to social events as requested. I had some school friends but we did not see them very often and, once we became a married couple, they began to drift away, such that I saw them even more rarely. As I travelled for work there was also little opportunity to mix outside working hours. I was actually happy with that arrangement, as it suited my feelings and allowed the defensive barrier that I built to continue to strengthen. I could not be myself so I would become no one in particular and would do my best to blend into the background.

I tried my hardest to ignore my true feelings, only occasionally slipping back into old habits. Usually it would be something very simple, like the application of a lipstick, which helped me through my crisis moments: the sensation of its application, its feel and smell reminded me of what I used to do. I very rarely went any further. It did occasionally become a crutch during more intimate moments and Pam obliged: after all, it was harmless, wasn't it?

I had locked my emotions away and found it impossible to express or discuss my needs. I suspect that this was slowly and persistently eroding our relationship, leading to its demise in a few short years.

We remained married for seven years, finally getting our decree absolute in 1983. I take the lion's share of the responsibility for the divorce. My lack of communication, associated with my inability to freely express emotions within the intimacy of marriage, was largely to blame. However, there were other issues that affected the marriage and ultimately my life as a whole.

As I have said previously, it is painful for me to put this down for others to read but in many ways it demonstrates the effect of my desperation to prove myself a man. That sounds a selfish act on my behalf, which in hindsight may well be at least partially true. However, at that time I was not fully aware of the impact of my condition or of the fact that the longer I did my best to contain and deny it, the more desperate I would become. At no time did I knowingly or willingly hurt anyone close to me because of my transsexuality. There were other actions, though, when people close to me were hurt and I take responsibility for those, as any adult should.

We had been married for about three years when Pam introduced me to a friend from her work. She was younger than us by some five years and, like us, had been married young. Her husband was similar in age to me and worked in computing. We all immediately became close friends and started spending all of our free time together, to the exclusion of our other friends. As a group we all had different things in common with each other, as well as many similarities; the dynamic was excellent and the friendships blossomed.

It was during this period that I came to fully understand what I was; it was now that the ramifications of my life-choice began to crystallise. I, however, did not have the personal courage to deal with it then, feeling that 'It was not really me' and I continued my life in the masculine wilderness. It is only now, looking back, that I can see how this could have been resolved so easily by being honest with those around me; I am sure they would have supported me however they could. Instead, I chose denial; and life became much more turbulent for a while.

It was a Sunday afternoon and we were all watching television after a lunchtime trip to the pub and a good meal. A documentary called 'George and Julia' came on; it was the true story of a young transsexual and the trials and tribulations she faced as she underwent transition from male to female. It dealt with her life and the hardships imposed by a society that did not then, any more than now, fully understand this condition. I could empathise fully with what was being shown because that was exactly how I was feeling, but I had been able to lock it away and live what I thought of as real life; as a man. I also know now that that was not the case. My whole life has been tempered by the female locked away inside; I was still working on the premise that I could deny nature and live life the way I thought I should.

It was a 'light bulb moment' and, although I am sure we talked about what we had seen, I made no comment as to how I was feeling personally. Next day I went out and bought the book, which I read from cover to cover in a matter of days. So I knew what I was and I knew what could be my future, but I did not have the courage to be honest with others and with myself. I had seen just how hard the journey was and, after years of denial, felt that I could carry on just as I was; after all it could not be that hard, could it?

It was like putting another lock on the cell door, such that, in later years I would have to search for the appropriate key to unlock it before freedom was obtained. I was my own worst enemy but did not realise it at the time.

I carried on being a 'man' and searched for every opportunity to prove that I really was a red-blooded male. I still had problems, however, as I hid my emotions very well and so I remained isolated, even in the close company we now had.

Eventually the inevitable happened in a group of people who enjoyed each other's company as much as we did. Pam and I were certainly inexperienced and the others were little better. We had all married young and now seemed an appropriate time to catch up on what we had missed all those years before. I do know that I struggled for a while, making excuses to avoid the inevitable, but I was still under the influence of testosterone and so gave way, willingly, in the end.

There followed a few years of excitement, pleasure and fun for us all. We enjoyed each other's company and lived for the weekends and whatever other time we made for each other. Deep down that flickering candlelight remained, keeping alive the female within. I did not allow it to surface very often but somehow it always did. As before, I would allow myself just a brief taste: I did not indulge to the extent I had as a young teenager, but it was enough to keep the longing under control.

The inevitable came to pass and we came to the realisation that we were slowly tearing apart not one but two relationships; we parted, to try to recover what was left of our respective marriages. It was not easy and we still met occasionally, but it was never the same again.

Could Pam and I have repaired the damage and resurrected our marriage to continue on as we wished? In truth I don't know; there are too many unknowns, not least my own transsexuality. I have no idea how long I could have continued hiding behind the façade I had built but, in the end, another event took over which made the decision for us. It was many years later, when we had repaired the damage and had become good friends again, that my now ex-wife, Pam, asked me:

"Why were you not honest with me? I am sure we could have done something to allow you to live your life as you wished. All you had to do was tell me."

Stable doors and horses come to mind; hindsight once more gave us, as more mature adults, the ability to be honest with each other. Perhaps we could have come to a satisfactory solution; we will never know.

The event which sealed our fate was to occur shortly before we had decided to break the ties with the others. I was working in Kent and drove there each day from South London, a journey of over an hour each way. Pam suddenly fell ill, so ill that the doctor had no idea what was wrong. She was admitted to hospital and was put in an isolation ward. We now believe that she had somehow contracted a severe case of scarlet fever but I doubt the truth will ever be known. As she was in isolation I, as her husband, was the only person allowed to visit; no one else, not even her parents could do so.

I was at an early stage in my career and could not afford to take time off work. I had to be there for an eight o'clock start and did not finish until at least six in the evening. With an hour's drive each way it was a long day, before I could even visit my wife in hospital. I was quickly exhausting myself and eventually could not cope any longer. Meanwhile, for most of her time in isolation Pam was delirious and was not even aware of my visits; she was living in her own personal hell. Eventually I reached the end of my endurance and became so run down that I fell ill; I could not even look after myself, let alone visit her in hospital. I moved back home to be looked after by my parents. Pam recovered and was discharged from hospital, to go home to her parents, as I was unable to look after her myself.

Pam had been so delirious that she could not understand all that I had been doing to provide her with support. All she knew was that I was not there when she came out and that she had to be looked after by her parents. This arrangement lasted no more than ten days before I felt recovered enough to move back home. With that I hoped we could try to continue repairing our damaged marriage.

It was not to be. We tried for another two years, even moving away to a new and larger house, but the damage was done. Unbeknown to me until much later, the seeds of distrust had already been sown. In her delirious condition Pam was convinced that I had actually poisoned her. She felt she could therefore trust me no longer. No matter how much we both wanted to make it work, we faced an impossible task. Now, all these years later, and as good friends again, we can see that there was no chance under those circumstances and that the developments that followed, although hard to understand, were in some way inevitable.

We slowly drifted apart and remained living together out of mutual need. My transsexuality was not to blame for the final breakdown of the marriage, as that had been well buried. I had kept in touch with the other party in our earlier relationship and in some ways had turned to her for support. Her marriage was also in a poor state and they had moved away from the area, but we did manage to see each other.

The relationship grew and we decided that we would leave our respective partners and start again, on our own this time. It was not that straight-forward or simple but the end result was the same. The decree absolute to end my first marriage was granted on 28th October 1983, and I married again for the second time on 29th June 1984.

Pam has since asked me:

"Why on earth, knowing what you are and what it means to you, did you leave one failed marriage and start a second, which has resulted in the same separation, unhappiness and divorce? I just cannot understand why. Please tell me."

The honest answer is that I truly don't know. Although I know that my female self was there, and that I was aware of her needs, it was also a time when my denial and self-determination were probably at their strongest. The needs of my male body were able to overrule the needs of my female self. I cannot justify what I did; in fact I see no reason for me to do so here and now. At that time, and in those circumstances, I simply did what I thought was right and proper, and what I needed to do.

As I have already said about my first marriage, it takes two to make a relationship work. Love was there in this second marriage, I am sure, and it made the world go around. After all, we had both left our respective partners and had started again. Life was not easy in the first few years; though I do not deny that the injured parties also had a hard time in coming to terms with this final result, after all that we had been through together. The other two went their own separate ways, remarried and, I am pleased to say, are still together with their respective second partners.

Hindsight proves that this second marriage was a mistake. Nature would eventually prevail over the life I had chosen and in which I made myself live. At that time, and in those circumstances, I did not listen to the inner female who was, no doubt, just as desperate to be heard then as in later years. I just did not take the time to listen or to make what would have been the right choice, both for me and everyone else. All I knew was that I was supposed to be a man and so I did all that I could to prove that to my family, my friends and my colleagues at work.

I cannot afford to have regrets about my decisions; I made them at that time and stand by them now. Had I not got married for the second time I would not have the three beautiful daughters that I now have. I would miss out on the love and affection that only a parent can know and understand. I have transsexual friends who made that tough decision early in life. Although they denied the feminine and lived in the masculine role for many years before succumbing to the force of nature, they never married and did not have the joy and love that only a parent can feel for, and with, their children. I know a number of them now regret that choice, even knowing that they would then be facing the pain that I had to face. Life truly is a double edged sword: you are damned if you do and damned if you don't.

I also had the love and affection of my wife, Jean. However, she also finally succumbed to the pressures of being married to someone who became isolated and unemotional. Once more I was fighting against my true nature, but my transsexualism at that time was not something I could properly communicate to her.

Please do not misunderstand: we did have good times together and we enjoyed the closeness and companionship that married couples have, especially during the early years. I remember the birth of each of my daughters with deep joy and happiness. I cannot allow myself to feel regret, otherwise I will not have been able to move on toward the future that now lies before me. I do, however, have great sympathy for the hurt I have caused to those close to me and who have had to deal with the outcome of my decision. I finally accepted what I was and decided to transition from the male I had tried, and failed, to be, to the female I had really been since birth.

My second marriage ended with the decree absolute being granted just six weeks prior to our twenty-fifth wedding anniversary.

Chapter 7

Moving on, a daughter is told and the last night out together

Life at home had been in a state of truce but with the occasional blow up. Kat, who was nineteen at this time, was training to be a hairdresser and was doing well. She, of all of my daughters, is the most like me and will call it how it is. We clash but get it over and done with and then move on.

She had seen her mother and me arguing and was getting stressed. Her older sister was away from home at university so she was dealing with it on her own. We did our best to protect Sophie, our youngest daughter, from the worst of the arguments but Kat was continually pushing and, in the end, I had no option but to tell her what was really going on, in the hope that she would stop inflaming the situation at home.

I therefore decided to tell her my secret and about why the tension at home was so bad. It was after a particularly bad row with Jean that I asked Kat to meet me in the pub after work. I reckoned that a public location would prevent any major outburst when she learned the truth.

So we met; she was obviously very wary as to why we were meeting and about what I was going to tell her. I bought us both a drink; I knew I needed one. I took her outside to the garden and we sat in a quiet spot to talk.

After the usual father/daughter pleasantries I opened the main part of the conversation with:

"I have asked if we could meet, to let you know the real issue between me and your Mum. It's not her fault. It is mainly my fault that we are in the situation where we are now," I began.

"And....?." she asked,

"Are you aware of TV's?" I asked, choosing to use the more commonly-known term used for the transgendered. My daughter was well-prepared and had mixed with a diverse group of people, so I was sure she would have an idea.

"Not televisions, then?" she responded, with a smile on her face.

"No," I replied. "I believe I am transsexual, a woman born in a male body". That was not easy for a father to say to his daughter, believe me, but it had to be done.

I explained what a transsexual was and how I had been different from a very early age. I asked if she would like to see a picture of Kirstie. I am sure that by this time she was scared.

"Yes," she said. "Show me."

So I did. I pulled out a page which I had previously printed with a few of the best pictures on it from my day at Pandora's. She looked, swallowed hard and responded:

"You look stunning Dad, but I need time."

I could understand that. I was relieved that I had not been shouted down and perhaps my choice of location worked to my advantage. I was to use it quite often over the next few months. I did not push the point as I knew and understood just how difficult this was going to be for her. She needed time for it to sink in and for her to work it out, to realise that I was the same person, no matter how I packaged myself. We finished our drinks and walked home together, each dwelling on our own thoughts.

Kat was the second person I had told. I don't think that even today she realises what a prominent position she holds in my journey of transition. I am, however, comforted that she eventually accepted what her father actually was; in her own way, after a period of deep reflection, she came to terms with my condition.

I know from her recounting of this event that she struggled immensely with my revelation and needed the support of her friends more than that of her family. She needed time and I, for one, was willing to give it to her. It was tough for her but she came back and told me that she would do her best to help and support me, whatever my choice was. I was so happy that the first of my daughters now knew and was prepared to help however she could.

She was also more aware of the home situation and that it was not necessarily her mother's fault that the atmosphere was so rough at home. She could also help her younger sister to try and cope, without letting on the reason why. She had promised that she would keep my confidence and that I would tell each of her sisters at the appropriate time and in my own way.

She seemed to take it well and I had showed her those pictures which went a long way to indicate how I felt and could look. She agreed that they were 'stunning' and, in her own words, which have since been published elsewhere:

"I had to admit you looked better as a woman than as a man."

She suffered with her conscience greatly over the next few weeks and needed the support and help of close friends to get through the shock of knowing that her father wanted to change sex. It took a few weeks for her to come to terms with the shock but we did talk and we did get through it.

Jean had reluctantly acknowledged that I could develop a small wardrobe of clothes, provided I did not 'parade' around in front of the children or our friends. She had even passed on a few bits to get me started, which had been a pleasant surprise. I could see that she was trying to understand and to support, but it was hard for her. I therefore agreed to her conditions, as I could still manage a dual life at that time.

Kat agreed to help me buy some clothes for my expanding wardrobe and a few weeks after I had told her my 'secret', we went to Milton Keynes Shopping Centre and spent my money. There was an advantage for both of us in going shopping together: Kat provided me with a degree of 'cover' in the fashion stores; and she probably guessed (rightly, as it turned out) that there might be something in it for her. It was too early in my transition for me to actually try anything on so we guessed the sizes and she advised me on style and colour. We also shopped for cosmetics for me. We did not hide that the purchases were for me but, there again, we did not go out of our way to advertise it either. Apart from the other purchases we eventually found a dress which we both liked so the shop made a double sale, at my expense of course, although the two dresses were naturally in different sizes. It was a risqué style but the whole process of discussing it, holding it up, and finally buying it was a lot of fun and we had a great time. She now realised just how good it was to go shopping with a dad who actually enjoyed spending time in the dress shops and was quite happy to do so all afternoon. Having a transsexual father does have some benefits.

Was she totally accepting of my situation? I doubt it, at least in the early days of being told. However, of my three daughters she was the one I believed most likely to accept. She was a hair-dresser, so her hair changed with her mood; she liked tattoos and piercing; and she had been quite a wild child only a few short years earlier. We got along and at least I had someone in the house who now understood some of the causes of the friction between Jean and me. More importantly, I had someone to talk to who would listen and possibly even give some advice.

I slowly filled the shelf in my wardrobe and one small section of the rail with my feminine clothes, wigs and cosmetics. Jean knew and, as long as it was not pushed in her face, accepted the situation however reluctantly. She was doing her best to understand and come to terms with what was, for her, a major disclosure and difficulty in our marriage.

It was towards the end of the year, and a month or so after my disclosure to her, that Kat and I found ourselves home alone on a Saturday night. Jean had taken Sophie to see friends for the weekend and we were at a loose end. We were bored, each doing our own form of nothing, when Kat suggested that I change and she would take some photographs for me. I could hardly refuse and so began a couple of hours of quality time together. We even reached a point where she borrowed some of my wigs to try out some new looks and I took pictures of her. We had plenty of fun and did not want it to end. I was dressed and feeling relaxed. She was also relaxed and enjoying herself, so I suggested:

"Do you fancy going out together? I can take you to a safe transgender club if you'd like to see a bit more of the trans way of life."

There was no hesitation.

"Great! Let's go!" she said. "There is no one here so it won't matter how late we are and there will be no one we know there, so it won't get back to Mum."

I had already broken the spirit of my agreement with my wife although I had dressed with the full knowledge and cooperation of my daughter. It was a moot point, but one I was willing to go with. As for going out, it would give me the opportunity to relax and be myself and it would not be anywhere close to home. I suggested we go to The Way Out in London, one of the mainstream and best-known transgender clubs in the capital. Kat was enthusiastic; she was looking for some adventure and a new experience. She was used to mixing with the gay community and going to gay clubs, as some of her best friends were gay. I knew of the club and where it was but had never actually been; this would be another first for me, as well as for her.

Once the decision was made there was no holding either of us back and while we finalised what we would wear I searched for directions from the internet. The biggest obstacle was me leaving the house and getting into the car without being seen as it was parked in the drive and Kat could not drive. It was approaching ten o'clock, so it was unlikely that anyone would be walking past the house. I turned off the security light and she went to the car and opened the driver's door and then got into the passenger side. I was wearing a red and black dress with black patent shoes with modest three inch heels, which I hid well beneath a long coat. The giveaway was the wig and the makeup, which I could not hide. So it was house lights off, head down and a quick walk to the car. No one was looking and in the shadows I doubt they would have seen anything out of the ordinary.

We got away with it and, laughing together, we headed for London, a forty minute drive; I knew the destination area quite well. Parking was not really a problem and we managed to do so right opposite the entrance to the club. We were still quite early. This was to be a second outing in public for me, this time in the company of my daughter, who was looking forward to a new experience.

I was excited and in no way self-conscious anymore; after all, this was not my first time in a London club. Having been to Club Rub only a month or so earlier this held no fear for me, as the clientele were very much like me. Many would be transvestite or 'she male', rather than transsexual, but we were all sisters in this life. Of course, being an adult club there would be the inevitable 'admirers' (a term used for men who like to go out with trans women, rather than with natal women) but I was sure I could deal with this and look after my daughter and myself. We got out of the car, locked it and walked confidently over the road and into the entrance.

We were early enough for there not to be a queue at the doors, so we went straight in and up to the pay desk. I paid for us both; a very pleasant and attractive trans woman took the money and directed us downstairs. No one was worried that I was there with an obviously young girl; my daughter was accepted, just as I was. We went downstairs and entered the club proper, which is like any other London basement club: low lighting, the bar running down one wall to our right, and the dance floor and DJ station on our left. The cloakroom was in the middle, with a small area at the rear laid out with tables and chairs. Light meals could be bought and eaten here plus it was, marginally, quieter.

It was quite empty at that hour so I checked in our coats and ordered us both soft drinks from the bar. We went to sit down and take in the atmosphere. We chatted as the club slowly started to fill and became noisier. We had seated ourselves out of the way in the back corner, so we had a good view of proceedings without being obvious. We had a few nods of welcome from others who were grabbing a light meal before the evening got underway.

We sat and talked about the future and my way of life. We also watched as more people came into the club, commenting on how they looked and dressed. A man and a woman, dressed as if they had been out to dinner, came in and sat down quietly beside us. They took note of the young woman with a transgendered adult, not knowing I was her father, and we struck up a conversation. I introduced Kat and explained that this was a first for her and, indeed, for me. We got along fine and it turned out that the man was, in fact, a well-known celebrity in the transgender community but, for that evening at least, was out in male attire.

My daughter was becoming a celebrity in her own right as others joined us and expressed their delight at her ability to support her father, who was learning to spread his/her wings.

The highlight of that evening was when we were joined by Ms Vicki Lee, the owner of the club, who knew everyone and who sat next to Kat. The two of them hit it off and just chatted like old friends. I was talking to all sorts and enjoying every moment myself. The music and bustle of the club melted away into the background and we were in our own little oasis of new-found friends; it felt so natural to me and I will never forget that evening.

All good things have to come to an end, though, and, although the club was open to the small hours, we had to get home. After all, I had to sneak into the house and it would not be appropriate to do that with the sun up.

We made our farewells to the new friends we had met and with whom we had spent a few pleasurable hours. Time had passed so quickly it was as though we had known them for years, rather than a scant few hours.

We drove home in silence; Kat fell asleep very quickly in the car. We arrived home some time between four and five in the morning, so the sun was not quite ready to come up, although it would not be too much longer. All the neighbours were tucked up in bed, so entering the house did not need the same tactic in stealth as when we had left.

We had had a great, and memorable, evening together. Once in the house we went our separate ways and each fell into bed, to sleep late. I, however, had to get up early enough to remove all incriminating evidence of our night out together, before my wife and youngest daughter came home.

My first counselling assessment was due in January, and the date could not come quickly enough for me. Before that, though, I had to maintain my role as the father of the household, especially over the Christmas period. Christmas, as always, was spent at home. My father would join us for a few days on his own, my mother having died some five years earlier, and we would be one big 'happy' family. I am sure my father was well aware that there was a problem with my marriage but obviously, at this time, did not know what it was.

The relationship with Jean had not really changed; she never brought up my weekend away and showed no further interest. The children did not see any change in the relationship and so we drifted as before. My time of wandering in the gender wilderness was slowly but surely coming to an end. I could see a small but bright light in the distance. It was to be a long journey to reach that place of freedom and internal peace but it was a journey I was prepared to make, however lonely it might be. Christmas that year was like any other: spend too much, eat and drink too much, and waste a lot. On the surface we were happy but inside, I suspect, we all had our worries and demons to deal with – I know I did.

The week of my appointment duly arrived and my anticipation grew as before except that this time I knew I was seeing an appropriate person who knew about Gender Dysphoria and who would listen to me.

I made the journey to London and arrived at the clinic with the usual time to spare. I have always hated to be late for any meeting and this one in particular was so important that I could not conceive of being late under any circumstances. I was at this time still living completely as a male. I was, after all, still married and the only person who ostensibly knew of my situation was Jean, who was unaware that Kat also knew the truth. Therefore anyone looking on would see no more than a man walking into a building; there was nothing special in that at all. I, however, was once more in a state of controlled excitement and, of course, a degree of worry accompanied that.

The gender clinic itself was an old converted Edwardian house, situated next door to a more modern building which housed the main clinic. In many ways it was similar to the clinic I first visited six months previously. I was, however, in a much better frame of mind as I walked up the entrance steps and through the large front door. I pushed the door open, walked into a bright lobby area and turned right to the reception window. I gave my name and the name of the consultant I was to see and was then directed to the adjoining waiting room.

"Please go to the waiting room. I will let the doctor know you are here. He will come down to collect you shortly," the receptionist advised.

So, once again, I was waiting to be seen by a psychiatrist in order to determine my future. At least this waiting room was brighter and had a friendlier atmosphere. The magazine I picked up to browse could not have been more than six months old: quite up to date as waiting rooms go. I sat down and looked through the pages without really taking anything in, and reflected on the previous months since I had told my wife.

I knew I was now on the right path; I had dealt with enough crap in my life, living as I had in total denial of my true self. I had wasted it all. No, I thought, that's not true either. I had made my outward life a success for many years and had fathered three beautiful daughters, whom I loved more than anything else in the world. I knew that my actions would inevitably cause them hurt and pain, with the eventual loss of their father figure if I chose to take those ultimate steps to transition. My actions would, for many, give rise to confusion, worry, loss, hurt and pain. I also wondered how my father would be able to deal with my choice.

Thinking about my life and the worries that I would soon face was, in a way, appropriate, in the light of what was going to happen over the next hour. I had no idea how this process would operate; after all, my previous experience was nothing to write home about, having been a total waste of time. I knew I was in a good place and that there could only be positive results from this and from the many other meetings I would have. I was unaware at that time that I would see the inside of this waiting room and consulting room every six weeks for the next two years.

The door opened and man put his head into the waiting room, smiling at me as the only occupant, and said "Kenneth?"

"Yes," I replied.

"Please follow me."

That was it. He seemed pleasant and open and I felt better, although still worried about what would happen. Would I respond appropriately? After all, if I got it wrong now and presented my case in the wrong way I may never get the resolution I desired. What if he felt I had been kidding myself all these years and was in fact not transsexual but just a crazy mixed up man.

I followed him out of the waiting room, up the stairs to the first floor and into the consulting room. It was not a large room and, from where I stood on entering the room, I could look down into a pleasant garden below. The room was bright and airy: just the opposite to my first experience of a psychiatrist's consulting room.

He smiled as he sat down and waited for me to sit and make myself comfortable. He then nodded to me as if to say, "Well? What do you want to talk about?" and then said absolutely nothing!

What happened to the nice cosy relationship? Where were the questions I was to answer, to prove I was transsexual? How were we to explore my history so that he could understand my feelings and recognise what I had done to myself over the years? Zilch, nothing, not one iota of help; he sat there with a pleasant smile and an occasional little nod of his head as the only encouragement I was going to get.

OK, this was it then. I swallowed hard, I faltered but I knew that it was all down to me now, and so I started.

"I feel there is something wrong with me. I believe I am a woman trapped in a man's body," I began.

I spoke openly and honestly about my past and my present, along with my thoughts, my ambitions and my wishes for the future. I did not stop for the whole of our fifty minute session. He sat, nodded and gave lots of non-verbal encouragement but asked me no questions whatsoever. I can now understand what was happening and how he was letting me explore my own emotions and experiences. He actually had no need to interject: I was doing fine all on my own.

My first session drew to an end. I was emotionally exhausted. I had no idea I could just talk about myself in such detail and with such feeling. The session ended as it began, quietly. He agreed the time and date for our next meeting and said goodbye. I stood and left the building, as I had come, none the wiser as to how I was received but in myself feeling already so much better. I rang Jean and told her what had happened, that I was feeling positive about the session and that I looked forward to the next. She responded encouragingly and I felt that she was supportive of how I felt. However, as with everything that surrounded my 'problem', she did not want to know any detail.

I went home happier than I had been in weeks, perhaps even since my earlier night out. Emotionally it was, after all, a comparable result, although through an entirely different medium. The first was a straightforward emotional high, brought about by sheer delight; the second was an emotional high but of an entirely different kind, being about my feelings rather than my actions. It was because I had finally reached a point in my life where I could perhaps see a glimmer of the future and come to terms with the condition I had lived with for so many years.

My next appointment was only four weeks away: I could not wait. My life at home and at work went on as before. No one was aware of the changes that were starting to go on in my life. I was slowly becoming the person I should have been from birth and I was now in a position to overturn the fear and doubt I had been suffering for so long. I could not have been happier with the result of this first session, even though I was the only person who actively participated.

The four weeks passed quickly and without incident. I was ready for more and desperate to just talk it all out. Prior to this I had had two exposures to counselling. The first had been with my daughter Kat, when family counselling had been recommended, but this had not been the greatest success. The second had been when Jean and I had gone to Relate. That was not very successful either but I have to take most of the responsibility for that, as I was not prepared to acknowledge and admit my transsexuality and the impact it was having on our marital relationship.

I duly attended the second session and that went exactly the same way. I sat down and I talked for most of the fifty minutes. It was much easier the second time. However, it was not until the third and last session with the consultant that I actually started to get some interaction. It was an exercise in clarification of everything I had said over the previous two sessions. At the end of this meeting we parted company. He did not enlighten me in any way; he just said he would write to my GP.

That was the end of it for now. I had been assessed by a consultant, who was knowledgeable in gender conditions, and I had to wait for his diagnosis. It was totally different to that first disastrous experience which was, after all, only six months earlier. I was impatient to hear the news from my GP.

It was around this time that I once more approached Jean, to try to get her to try to understand what it was that I was facing. There was a charity event in Manchester called Transfandango, organised and supported largely by the transgender community to help disadvantaged children. It was an annual event and the main patron was Richard O'Brien of Rocky Horror Picture Show fame. It would mean a night out at a charity ball at a swish hotel in Manchester. I was prepared to splash out on a new dress for her, and of course, on a new dress for me, too.

We had been getting on better; although I don't know whether that was because of the counselling going so well, or whether it was just that I approached the subject in a different way. I showed her the literature for the night out and we both agreed that this was a worthwhile event to support. We spoke in some detail and she agreed that she would be prepared to go and to meet with others, in an effort to better understand my condition. Tables were for six people, so we would be in a mixed group and she understood that this would be the case. She made the caveat, however, that if she ever felt uncomfortable in any way then we would both leave. I agreed to this as a reasonable request under the circumstances, as the potential benefit of better understanding was a prize worth having if all went well.

I was surprised but also pleased that she was willing to give it a try. Bravery was there but I am also sure that in the end curiosity also played a part. Rocky Horror had been a family favourite for years and Richard O'Brien also. The tickets were duly purchased, dates put in the diary and it only remained to do the shopping. The first stop for dresses and shoes for me was e-Bay. I successfully bid on, and won, a selection but when they arrived none was suitable for the occasion and of course some just did not fit properly. The few clothes I had purchased earlier with Kat were not suitable for this event, so we were back to square one.

I had promised a no-expense-spared event and so there was only one place left to go for clothes after the failed attempts on e-bay. Jean had previously shopped in a small boutique in town run by a lady who bought her stock, not from major suppliers, but from small family-run businesses in Italy. It meant that her clothes were almost unique, with only a few of each style available. The designs were influenced by her own fashion sense, which was exceptional, giving rise to some very feminine but also cutting-edge styles. On the few occasions I had shopped there with Jean for clothes I had always enjoyed the experience, just looking on as a casual bored male in attendance 'while the wife shopped'! This time I hoped it would be an exceptional experience for me; after all, I had never done this before.

This would clearly be a first for us both. I had never been to a shop for clothes for myself, always having purchased the few pieces that I did have either online or with my daughter. Most of those were usually purged and thrown away in short order. Jean, of course, had never been shopping with her husband to buy a dress for him. I have no idea who was the more scared. Whichever of us it was, the other was a very close second.

The choice of shop was not entirely down to its fashion range. Jean shopped there quite regularly at that time and had seen at least one other transgendered male shopping in there, without any concern from the owner. It was a transgender-friendly shop and that added to our safety net. Now, of course, I shop where I please and try on what I want without a second thought and without, in most instances, any questions or concern from the shop staff. This, however, was new, uncharted territory for me and I had no idea how to approach the owner or even what to do when trying on clothes.

As a man it's easy – look at the size, slip the jacket on, and it's done. Any longer than ten minutes and there was a problem that could result in no purchase at all. None of this going from shop to shop, trying everything on and then going back to the first shop to buy the first outfit you had tried on. It was to be an experience I will never forget.

Although we lived in an affluent area the shop was never crowded and very rarely had more than one or two customers browsing at a time. It was, after all, quite expensive and not for everyday clothing. We decided to go in on a Friday afternoon, on the basis that it was likely to be less busy as closing time approached. I was not sure that I could cope with shopping if other customers were present and I wondered, too, how my wife might handle it. Luckily, on that occasion, we had the shop to ourselves.

Anyone looking on would see just a bored husband following his wife into another dress shop. I was that husband but I was far from being bored; "scared and excited in equal measure" would have been a better description of my inner feelings.

The owner came towards us shortly after we entered the shop and she smiled in welcome:

"Good afternoon," she said. "How can I help?"

Not surprisingly, she had offered us a fairly standard greeting, as she would have done to any customers entering the shop, for we appeared to be no different. In that moment she did not realise quite what was going to happen over the next hour or so or how worthwhile it would prove to be, for her and for us.

I took the lead, as I suspect I was slightly less nervous and Jean was no doubt beginning to wonder what she was doing here.

"We are attending a charity ball in a few weeks and would like to buy two dresses, please," I volunteered.

The owner continued to smile; the penny had not yet dropped. Perhaps my wife wanted to have a choice on the night; perhaps it was a two-day event? How was she to guess the truth?

"Yes, of course. We have plenty to choose from. Do you have any idea of style or colour?"

She pointedly asked Jean as she turned away to lead up to the rear of the shop, where the gowns were.

"Sorry," I said. "Just to make it clear: that's one for my wife and one for me."

She turned with a smile.

"That's no problem. Let's go and see what we have."

Well, that was a relief! And I suspect it showed on our faces. She made the easy sale first and looked after my wife as I, with more courage than usual, explored the rails. I admit it was fun being able to rummage through the clothes, accessories and fabrics without feeling guilty! The shoes were another issue entirely and I was in my element.

It took Jean about thirty minutes or so to try a few dresses and choose the one she wanted. No questions asked I just said yes and then it was my turn.

"Do you know what size you are?" asked the owner.

"I think I am a fourteen," I replied with some trepidation. It was the first time I had ever had to answer that question out loud. My previous shopping trip with my daughter had given me a good idea.

"That looks about right," she smiled. "Let's see what we can find, and you can see what you like."

So began an hour of instruction, enlightenment and damn good fun. She had no problem with having me in her shop. The changing room was just a small circular curtained area toward the rear. The wall within was just one big mirror. She brought all types of style and colour and I provided the fashion show without any fear, especially once I got into the mood. Jean even began to lighten up and entered the discussion. I was clearly still very much a male, without makeup or a wig, and at that time I had a much more masculine way of talking. Later, speech therapy would largely iron out that problem, although never totally to my satisfaction.

It came down to a choice between two dresses in the end; she had shown me a number of two-piece outfits, none of which I liked. I was also in the throes of my rebirth and so still leaned towards the extremely feminine and perhaps more showy style, whereas my wife had chosen a fairly classic cream dress with a blue motif and lots of beading. At this time, of course, Jean had never seen me in a dress. She had not wanted to look at any photographs and I naturally never dressed at home as far as she knew. This had been a bit of an eye-opener for her as well.

The final choice was left to me so I chose a red dress. It had a halter neck top and was stretchy so it fitted me well. It was also similar in style to the dress I had worn when I had been at the fetish club the previous year with Pandora, having quite revealing splits up each side.

I was comfortable wearing it and felt I also looked good but clearly it would be much better with the appropriate additions of a wig and some make up. We decided not to look at shoes, as the dresses and the few pieces of jewellery I chose already added up to a considerable sum. We both left as we had arrived, I carrying my wife's purchases like the good husband I was. I am not sure how she felt but I was overjoyed; it could not have gone better and I was more than pleased with my purchase.

When we got home the dresses were put away: there was to be no more practice for me. Jean's feet were similar in size to mine and so she let me try on a few pairs of shoes, as those that I had purchased on e-Bay were not really suitable. None fitted or suited, so I suggested that I go back in the morning to get a pair that would go well with the dress. She agreed, whether reluctantly or not I don't know, but I had a plan and it was working out.

The next morning was a Saturday and, after doing the supermarket shop, I walked back to the boutique and went in without a care. There were a few other customers, none of whom took a second glance; for all they knew I could be looking for a gift for my wife or girlfriend. The owner approached as before but now she knew my secret so there were no worries as far as I was concerned.

"Hello. I would like to find a pair of shoes to go with the dress I bought yesterday. It turns out that there is nothing suitable at home." I explained.

"That's fine. What size are you?" she asked.

"I take an eight," I replied, smiling. I did not feel in the least apprehensive being there on my own and buying ladies' shoes. Her whole demeanour put me at ease.

"OK. Let's see what we have in your size. Sit down, please, and I will bring a selection over for you to try on. Would you like some of these to wear?" she asked, as she handed me a pair of black knee high stockings to slip on, after taking off my shoes and socks.

Once more I had the pleasure of taking part in my own fashion show, trying on various pairs of shoes and not worried about the other customers, as the owner was looking after me personally. They gave no outward obvious sign that they had registered that it was a man trying on the shoes. I, of course, did not care what they thought: I was having fun – again! Finally we hit gold, with a pair of medium-heeled black shoes, with four thin straps up the ankle. They were fabulous, and so easy to wear. The straps did not have to be undone, as there was a hidden zip running up the back. They were so easy and so stylish! What's more, they were mine and complemented my chosen dress perfectly.

I went home fully satisfied with my purchase. As with everything else my wife was less than interested, so the shoes were carefully put away in the wardrobe with the dress and left until needed for the event.

I also went online and bought a new wig which would be suitable for a night out. I had previously started to get a selection of wigs together, as my daughter had discovered, but I felt this occasion deserved something different and new. Over the years I actually bought some twenty wigs in different styles and colours, most of which were largely for fun. It was only toward the end of my period of living the dual life that I migrated toward the colour and style in which I now have my own hair cut and coloured. For the charity evening I chose a shoulder length dark red style with plenty of layers. I have always enjoyed being a 'red head': it suits my colouring.

The time from the shopping trip to the day of the ball passed without incident. I did not show Jean a full transformation, mainly because she did not wish to see one. She wanted the whole affair to be dealt with away from the marital home. If she did not like what she saw on the night then, as per our agreement, it would go no further. It was a gamble for us both, but a gamble we both seemed prepared to take with a reasonably open mind. I am not sure who had the most at stake, I at least had a good idea what I was walking in to; she, though, had no idea what it would be like and, perhaps more importantly, how I would look or behave. I do admire her courage in this, as it was a major step into the unknown for her.

When the Saturday morning arrived we each packed our own cases, then loaded the car and drove up to Manchester for what turned out to be our last night out as a couple. Yes, of course, we still went to the pub or out for family meals but never again for that 'special' night out shared by husband and wife.

The hotel was as upmarket as we expected, with all of the trimmings. We checked in, looked into our very well-presented bedroom and bathroom, and then went down to the bar for a glass of wine. The next few hours were potentially not going to be easy for either of us. We chatted as any other normal couple would; no one looking on would consider there to be anything out of the ordinary; we were just two guests enjoying a glass of wine and quiet conversation. We did talk about many things but avoided for the most part the reason why we were there. It was a large hotel and so there was more than one event being held but in the mid-afternoon it was not busy. We looked around but could see no other obvious attendees and began to wonder what was going to happen. It was due to start at seven-thirty so by five o'clock we realised that we ought to be getting changed. There was a lot to do and, for one of us in particular, a lot more than usual.

We went back to our room with, I am sure, a degree of trepidation and uncertainty. How would we deal with the change? I offered to change in the bathroom, leaving Jean the freedom of the bedroom to get dressed. In retrospect, that was me being the 'gentleman'! She had so much more experience in getting ready for these affairs than I did. After all, this was the first time I had ever had to get dressed to this extent for an event like this and on my own. I went into the cramped and dark bathroom, leaving her the freedom of the well-lit bedroom. I have no idea what she thought but she was ready far quicker than I was.

There is no other way of putting it: in the bathroom, I struggled. The dressing element was easy, for the dress was just one piece. The shoes were easy, too, and I had had a good body shave before we left home. The hard part was dealing with the makeup and the wig. I stood in front of the mirror and wondered how I should start. Although I had used cosmetics for most of my life, on and off, I had never before stood in this situation where I not only had to do it all for myself, with no help whatsoever, but also it had to be good enough to go out in public. It had to be right and I was getting very critical of myself; the more I fretted, the worse it got. I had learned basic shading and other principles from my time at Pandora's and I had a good idea what I wanted to do. However, I had never made myself up for public viewing, apart from my one night out with my daughter Kat, and certainly not with my wife as a potential critic.

I did the best I could. The end result was not bad but it was not what I would, or could, do now, with many more years of daily practice. In the end, time was against me and I had to make do with the final effect that I had achieved. I pulled the wig on and brushed it out. I turned and twisted in front of the bathroom mirror, which was not the best place to do this, but it was all I had. I felt I had to go back into the bedroom with that flair of a finished piece of work. I could not let myself down and feel inferior to someone who had done this a hundred times or more.

The next few moments count among the most fearful I have ever faced. I walked out of the bathroom to face my wife who had never met 'Kirstie' in all her glory before. I was worried, because I had not been able to have a practice before we came. I was relying on skills I had developed in private over many years but which I had never really had the chance to practise in public. I was well acquainted with the theory, but real life practice was a different challenge altogether.

I sheepishly walked out of the bathroom to see what reception I would receive. She had been finished for some time and was patiently waiting for me. She was poised and looking immaculate as I entered and stood for inspection. I tried not to overplay my pose and to be as natural as I could. That takes practice, believe me, and it was not an ideal situation for me but I did the best I could and waited.

"It looks good on you. I like the wig - it sets it off," she smiled, and I breathed a sigh of relief. We would be going to the ball after all – just like Cinderella!

We took a few photos of each other and then walked to the lift and went down into the ballroom. I was nervous: this was a first for me. I know that she, too, was very nervous, never having attended a function before with such obvious transgender and gay overtones. We had our tickets and the table plan directed us to the right table. The guests were a complete mix, from 'normal' couples supporting a good charity, to the totally outrageous drag queens. The majority of transgendered attendees were dressed quite normally for an occasion such as this and so we both fitted in without any problems. I think that when Jean saw just how many people were there, of all persuasions, she started to feel more at ease and began to enjoy herself.

Our table companions were another married couple and two single transvestites, all of whom were there to enjoy the evening. The other couple was in a similar position to us, with the major difference being that the wife fully accepted and supported her husband in his needs and future wishes. She had even trained in electrolysis so that she could deal with his facial hair at home. I felt a little envious, I have to admit, because I knew that I could never have that level of support and understanding.

Jean spent a large part of the evening talking to the other woman in our group but I don't think it changed her feelings towards me in any way. I hoped that she at least gained some insight into how other couples can deal with this situation. In one sense I was on my own, as I was the only transsexual at our table who had the goal of transition in sight.

Although I had still to receive a formal diagnosis, I felt that I knew what I truly was and where my journey was taking me. The other men at the table were quite happy living the dual life and would take their 'hobby' no further. In many ways that is what transvestism is: a hobby. It is an unusual one, of course, but little different to many other strange pastimes that people take up. The clothes are merely a uniform which identifies one aficionado to another. That is a simplistic definition, I know, but I hope it gives some idea of the diverse section of society which is known as transgendered. The spectrum is broad, with the simple male 'panty wearer' at one end and at the other the full-blown transsexual, who knows that he or she is in the wrong body and who will do all he or she can to rectify that situation. There are many, many variants in between. I felt that I was at that far end of the spectrum and that my table companions lay at different points along the rainbow.

It is important to clarify that I am detailing my feelings as a male to female transsexual. Let us not forget the other side of that same coin, that of the female to male transsexual. Their journey is just as difficult and has its own different pitfalls. In one respect they have one big advantage: no one cares about a woman wearing trousers and a man's shirt. It is accepted as normal fashion today. A man wearing a dress or skirt, however, is generally looked on as a freak or at least very unusual by many. The few attempts of the fashion industry to break that viewpoint have failed. Women are actually the biggest cross dressers in society, but they can get away with it, unlike their male counterparts. It is only fair to point out, though, that the surgical journey faced by female to male transsexuals is exceptionally difficult; the clothing advantage they enjoy pales by comparison.

Once we forgot about the fact that a large proportion of the attendees were men in dresses we got down to having a fabulous evening. I had my photograph taken with Richard O'Brien, who was wearing a fetching white sheath dress and blonde wig. He performed live later that evening, which is one of those special memories that we will keep forever.

The ball finished at about one in the morning and we migrated to the bar where we spent another three hours in the company of many others; I was glad to see that Jean had fun and let her hair down. By the same token we, the transgendered, are also just normal people and can have fun times just like any others.

We retired to bed at four in the morning, very tired, and slept late. It was hard for me to take it all off and return to male mode but I knew I had to. Jean had supported me in this and had met another spouse in a similar position to herself, but who had embraced her husband's difference and could live with it. We did not keep in touch so I don't know what happened but I wish them well and hope they are still together.

We had woken too late for breakfast so we just got up, packed our cases and checked out, like any other married couple who had spent a night in a good hotel. No one looking on would have known that the previous evening the husband had been dressed in a red, full-length dress, with red hair and full make up. It can be so easy to hide this condition if you are in a position to live a dual life and simply be happy as the male that you physically are, enjoying the feeling of being female when it suits. I, however, had been unhappy in the male role all of my life. I knew that I could not embrace that duality, even if my wife had been prepared to accept it in our marriage. But I knew she could not: she wanted a 'man's man', something I could no longer pretend to be.

The three hour drive home passed as any other car journey did: mainly in silence, listening to the radio, and each lost in our own thoughts. We spoke about the ball and what a good time had been had, but I could already sense the curtain was being drawn over the transgendered side of the evening. We did not talk about that again. She had done what she said she would and had supported me; she had had a great time herself but realised that she could not accept my true nature.

We looked at the photographs of the evening on our return home, but they were then stored away on the hard drive, never to be spoken about again. I have them now, and I still enjoy good memories of that night, but I know now, as I had surmised then, that it was to be our last night out as a couple. The end was in sight although, even then, we did not talk about it or acknowledge that it was hanging over our relationship, like a curtain just waiting to close.

I still have that dress but have never worn it again, even though I have been to events where it would have been appropriate; the wig I wore on many occasions and the shoes I still wear now: that's the benefit of buying good quality!

We returned to the everyday routines and life went on as it always did. The strain in the marriage was there; it was not going to go away. It would eventually get too much and the inevitable split was to occur eighteen months later, when we finally accepted there was no future for us as a couple.

It was not long after the Manchester event that I received a letter from my GP, asking me to make an appointment at the surgery. I knew that this would be about my recent assessment and so I made that all-important appointment as soon as possible.

I entered the consulting room with mixed feelings. What would I be told? What would happen next? Would I get that much-needed assessment of Gender Dysphoria? That diagnosis was required in order to open the gates and allow me to progress along my journey. I sat down with anticipation written all over my face, as we went through the usual welcome that occurs every time you enter a GP's surgery.

"I have received a letter from the clinic with your assessment," my doctor told me.

"Yes. And what does it say?" I replied, with an obvious tremor in my voice.

"The consultant has assessed that you are indeed suffering from Gender Dysphoria and are therefore potentially transsexual. The clinic is offering to continue with appropriate counselling, if you wish."

What relief! It was true! I had not been spending my life in 'La La' land. I really did have this awful condition, which I would not wish on my worst enemy. I had suffered for so many years and now it was strangely pleasing finally to be given such a potentially devastating diagnosis; to be told that I truly was that 'female trapped in a male body' (to use the commonly quoted phrase) was the news I actually wanted to hear. It was confirmation that my lifelong dislike of my male body had been for a reason: it did not represent on the outside the woman I always knew myself to be inside. Even after all my time in denial and doing all that I could to prove I was a man, to hear that it had been unnecessary was a load lifted from my shoulders. The relief was intense; I did not cry openly but my eyes welled up and I smiled:

"Thank you. To hear this is such a relief. I now have a goal in life. I can move forward and reach a point where I am comfortable with myself," I said.

She smiled and asked the obvious question:

"What do you want to do now?"

"I want, no I need, to continue with the counselling, to see if I can sort out this mess I have put myself and my family in."

So that was it. I did suffer from Gender Dysphoria and was officially transsexual. All I needed was to find out exactly where on the spectrum I actually lay. I, of course, knew but I had to prove it to a third party before I could reach that finishing line.

We arranged for me to contact the clinic and to make the next appointment for Gender Counselling myself. This was to take a further two years, but I did not know that at the time. It was a start and I would go as far as it required. It was to be a journey into the uncharted and I was to open so many locks and doors before I could view and release my inner being and emotions, and before I could reach the end and find the contentment I now have in life.

I went home on a high and told Jean what the diagnosis was. I don't think that she was as happy as I on hearing the news.

Chapter 8

The wilderness years

What is it like for a female to work in an all-male environment? More importantly, what is it like for a female who denied her true nature to be able to work in an all-male environment?

I really don't know how to answer the question, as there is nothing to which I can compare it. I had nurtured my own development to be a male and had managed to bury my true self, locking her away in that dark room where she lived and screamed unheard by me for so many years, while I pretended to be the macho male.

My marriage at the age of twenty was a signpost to the world that I was a man. Moreover, I had chosen construction as my career and was at that time in my third year of a four year degree course in Building Technology. I was indentured as a company trainee to one of the largest construction companies in the UK, so my future employment was guaranteed, for a while at least. This was 1976 and my female side was well and truly locked up and put away, out of sight and out of mind.

The wilderness years from twenty to fifty, that's thirty years, and more than half of my life, were spent doing something that was intrinsically the opposite to what was my true self. So what was I doing during this period? I was driven to become as successful as I could and to prove that I was just like everyone else.

Being what I call the wilderness years, there is in many ways little to write about my working life until the last few years, when I actually transitioned and Kirstie went to work instead of Ken.

My career was, in many respects not out of the ordinary. I completed my degree and became a 'site engineer', setting out and dealing with quality control on construction sites. I thoroughly enjoyed this period of my life. I was part of a team which produced a final result for each project upon which I worked. I also enjoyed working outdoors.

I was twenty-one and married – income became more important than the job so I found myself moving from construction to working for a Local Authority:

I became a surveyor in the GLC Housing Department. A salary increase eased the burden at home. Pam and I were getting on with life and we had met our friends, who were to have such an impact on us. For me, life as a man at the GLC was not too bad, as it was not a male-dominated organisation. For the first time in my life I moved in a mixed sex environment. Most of my time was spent out of the office visiting the many council estates throughout the London area.

I got on well with the female support staff as well as with the mostly male surveyors. I found I could chat easily with the women and they also with me. It certainly was not my macho charm at work, so I think it was more a meeting of gender, albeit unknown to the others. I was then, and always have been, more at ease in female company.

I, of course, was expected to bond with the other male surveyors and the contractors with whom I now interacted as the client. So it was that every Friday we would meet somewhere in London, usually in the east end, for a pint and a catch up - and of course to ogle the strippers; after all, that's what red-blooded men always did. One of us would pick a pub where strippers would be performing and the rest would drive there from wherever in London they were working.

Just as when I was a teenager, looking at the top shelf magazines, I now found myself looking at the real thing in much the same way. Sexually it certainly was not a turn on and it never has been. My compatriots were all commenting on "what a great pair" she had, and so on and I just joined in to be part of the group. I was actually still more interested in her hair and makeup, although it has to be said that, in this type of environment, the girls did not usually make a great effort, as after, all the audience was there to look at other parts.

Did I enjoy these times? I have to say: Yes, I did. After all, I was part of a group and we were all interacting as men. I learned how to become part of such a group and not to stand out; I knew how important it was never to decline such invitations, as to do that would make me seem odd. I was also actively denying my female side, so the more often I took part in these male bonding situations, the more 'natural' I felt I would become. This type of exercise was to be repeated throughout my working life as a male and I always participated to the best of my ability.

As with all things in life the good times come to an end and, with the impending closure of the GLC, and with my department being dramatically reduced, we all moved on. I joined a small contracting company which had worked for me and I then, in turn, started working as a contractor, with what remained of the GLC as my client. This time it was my turn to be the contractor and my turn occasionally to entertain the client. It seemed to suit everyone and no one thought any the worse of me. I was managing to operate quite successfully in the all-male world where I had chosen to live.

It was during this period that my first marriage came to an end and no one at work thought it unusual. I had already lost the ties with my college friends and with most of my school friends. As would happen often in my life, I was on my own, with no one to talk to or with whom I could really express my true feelings, except my potential new wife and her friends.

My brother was in Australia and we hardly communicated, except for perhaps one air mail letter a year. My parents were confused but always stood by my decisions and supported me. I did not move back to my parents' home, nor did I move into a flat on my own. I moved straight in with my new partner. Perhaps if I had taken time out on my own, to think through my decisions and the reality of my life, the course I took may have changed. However, that was not to be; I still had to prove I was truly male. So, as far as my male work colleagues were concerned, I had an affair, left my wife and moved in with my new girlfriend. What could be more normal? At the time everything just seemed to be a natural progression and I retained the masculine façade as always. It was not planned, and certainly not the cold-hearted manipulation which it may appear to be. At that time, it felt natural to behave in the way that I had.

My feminine side was buried and locked away although, as I now know, she was continually influencing my subconscious self and trying to direct me to be honest with myself. I turned a deaf ear and did what I felt was appropriate for me to be seen as normal in society. Affairs, divorce, living together and second marriages were far more acceptable to society as a whole than the idea of a man wishing to have a sex change which was then, more so than now, such a rare occurrence.

Even now, in a more open and accepting society, being transsexual and undergoing reassignment is considered strange by so many. Those who are open and informed see it as a courageous step, as well as being an unusual one; they don't prejudge or discriminate. They are, however, still a minority, so back in 1980 it would have been a step too far for me to consider. I have every admiration for those transsexuals who, back then, made the decision to transition, despite the views of society and the limited support from the medical profession that was available. They are the truly courageous ones, paving the way for others, like me, who did not have that spark of courage.

The positive view I can take from my decision not to let nature take its course is that, thirty years later, when I finally took those essential steps to transition, society and the medical profession were more aware and more accepting of this unfortunate condition. Furthermore, advances in surgical technique meant that my final result is far better than I could have ever experienced then.

My knowledge of my true condition at that time, when I was in my mid-twenties, was in many ways still in its infancy. I did not know where to go for help or whom to approach and, without the internet, it was very hard to meet others in a similar position. I had made myself move into a male-dominated industry and so my opportunities were severely restricted. It was actually easier to deny my true nature and to continue with the pretence, which is exactly what I did.

There was a recession, which always hits the construction industry hard and, with the imminent closure of the GLC, my employer put me on notice of redundancy. This was quite a shock but I was aware enough of the economic situation not to be surprised. I applied for a position in the building and development department of a major UK retail company, and was immediately accepted.

This came with the perks of working for a major company, an increased salary and a company car being the most evident. It was, however, a UK company with outlets throughout the country so I, like my father before me, would be travelling all over the country. I spent the next four years establishing my credentials in the retail development sector and totally ignored my inner self. I threw myself at the task and ignored my feminine nature in order to become someone who knew what his employer wanted and needed, and made sure it happened, no matter what the cost to others.

I know now that, even then, my approach was tempered by the less confrontational female within, when I compared myself with my peers. However, the 'clout' that my employer carried within the industry meant that this aspect of my personality was rarely noticed and I always seemed to be able to 'negotiate' my way through problems.

We worked hard and therefore we played hard. The parties and events occurred throughout the year and Jean thoroughly enjoyed herself and the kudos of being in such an environment, with all of the perks that it brought.

My inner female was still there, of course, and although I never allowed her to surface I was always interested in the latest fashions, colours and styles, although during this period I never indulged myself. I still noticed how a woman was dressed, her makeup and hairstyle. It was a passing interest and I believe for a while an unconscious one but it was always there, niggling in the background.

This was a stressful job and playing hard with the others was the only way to let off steam and de-stress ourselves. We enjoyed nights out, always with too much food and the obligatory alcohol, and we stayed up till the early hours, knowing that we also had a very early start to get to wherever the site was. I never mixed outside the company of my colleagues, our suppliers and consultants. It was a totally male-dominated situation and I had to fit in so I did what they all did, no matter what the cost to health and wellbeing; I was a man!

I was well-established and enjoying my position in life. We moved from London up to Bedfordshire in 1983 and bought our first house, having lived in rented accommodation since our respective divorces. I married for the second time in 1984.

My eldest daughter, Samantha, was born in 1985. I was present at her birth, just as I was at her two younger sisters' subsequent births. Was I a proud Dad? Of course I was! How could I not be? I have loved and cherished each of them from the moment they entered the world, and I continue to do so now as they grow and mature into adults.

My second daughter, Katherine, arrived in 1987 and then there was a gap of eight years until 1996 when Sophie, my youngest was born. I love them all and I was the best dad I could be to each; I believe I still am. They, like everyone, have had difficulty with my transition, but they have come through it, each in their own way, and I believe we are all stronger for having done so.

Life at home fell into a routine. On the surface we were the perfect family but the stirrings of later problems were already showing. I really had no interest in intimacy although could obviously do so when required – three daughters testify to that. Our close friends all lived in the village and, for the most part, were our neighbours. We mixed well, and baby monitors had range enough to reach across the road, so we could go out and the babies were always safe. Our friends took as much time in looking after the children as we did and were happy to walk across the road or next door if the monitor indicated any distress. It was a perfect mutual arrangement which suited us all.

We had parties or just met socially and always had barbecues in the summer. It was an idyllic time in many ways. I was always on the edge of the group, however. I could laugh and joke with the rest of them; I did innuendo very well and had learnt a cutting sense of humour from a master, my then boss. Yet I was never totally part of the group and was usually the first to leave, normally on my own, as my wife would follow later after I had gone to bed. Later on, when I left home and started my transition, many friends said:

"It all fits now. I can see why you were always on the edge and never took part in all that was going on with us as a group."

This is so very true and is perhaps a testimony to how well I managed. It could also be a sad indictment of what I had become and of what I did to myself for all of those years.

We lived in the village for thirteen years and it was towards the end of our time there that I earned some parole and was able to let my feminine side out of her cell. It was not just a parole - I had been in denial for so long that the stress and internal tension were becoming too much to bear. I was edgy, quick to get angry, and in some ways I was showing irrational behaviour. It was a critical time and I knew I had to do something about the female inside, which I had ignored for so long.

My position at work had moved on, this time due to a company merger, and it was no longer the same environment. A good friend and mentor persuaded me that I should become a consultant in my own right and he helped me to start out on my own. I will be eternally grateful to him for giving me the push I needed and for the financial and emotional support in those early days. Sadly he developed leukaemia in his mid-50's, (he was twenty years older than I), and passed away very soon after. I often think of him with a great deal of fondness and wonder just what he would have thought of Kirstie. Sadly I will never know but I would like to think that we would have remained friends and that his support would have continued no matter what.

I continued working in retail development, this time under my own steam, and worked hard to survive and develop my own business. I also found that I had more freedom, although the pressure for me to perform was just as fierce. My inner self was shouting continually. After all, I had denied her for the best part of twelve years by this time and her voice was becoming too much to ignore. I also realised that it was necessary for me to let her out again, otherwise I would crack.

I wondered how I could find a way to release the tension in me. I could not dress at home and at that time knew no other transgendered person whom I could ask for advice or with whom I could share my distress. It was 1987, long before the internet became available. Perhaps surprisingly it was the weekly magazine Exchange & Mart which came to my rescue. The back few pages were almost entirely given over to the transgender and gay communities. For those of you who don't know of Exchange & Mart, think eBay before the internet and without the element of bidding. People who had something to sell or a service to offer would place an advert in this weekly paper, now defunct as a printed title, but which still continues as a website. The publication had no editorial or articles: it existed only as a vehicle for display and classified advertisements. Most commonly the paper was used for the sale of cars and vans but, as time went on, the scope of offers expanded, such that you could find almost anything for sale if you looked hard enough. Slowly but surely the back pages started to include advertisements for sex aids, fetish-clothing and other goods and then finally 'personal services' were included.

So I started looking and finally came across a number of adverts for transvestite dressing services. There was no address given; just a brief offer of dressing and a telephone number was all that was generally included in the advert. Now on the internet you will find sites offering these services, which would include a selection of photographs of satisfied customers, much as I have already described about my trip to such a service provider. Back then, though, the whole thing was a pretty risky affair but I was so desperate I was prepared to take that risk.

Twelve years is a long time to live in almost total denial. My second daughter was on her way, life at home was already beginning to turn awry, largely due to my continued suppression of my true self, and at work I was heading for major stress. I had been working long hours and travelling all over the country, all without any back up. I was originally working from our spare bedroom but with the impending birth of our second daughter I had to move out and find a small office.

I shortly had that office, a business phone line and, most importantly, an address where I could receive mail without the knowledge of others. I also started getting the trimmings to go with a business. One vital item was a car phone, mobile phones being far too new and large for most of us to carry. I had also treated myself to a Polaroid instant camera. There were no digital ones at that time but I could take pictures which developed privately, without the need of a third party. Taking pictures of my female self, which would have to be developed and printed by a commercial company, was a risk too dangerous to contemplate.

Working on my own meant I could also manage my time and occasionally give myself a few hours to do as I wished. So it was that I rang one of the numbers in Exchange & Mart to book some 'me' time. In those days there were no 0800 numbers or similar. All numbers were for the district in which they were located and the geographical location could therefore be identified. I chose one which was based in North London.

In addition, I knew I had to have a female name; I did not want to go to this sort of place and still be called Ken. I suppose I could have done so but I felt it was about time that my female self had her own identity. So it was that I became Karen. Why Karen? At that time I chose it purely because it was a christian name with the same initial as my male christian name. That meant I could have post delivered to the office addressed to Ms K... and most people who shared the building would not notice any difference from the usual Mr K... a simple printing error.

I was eventually to take this further in later years and had my credit and debit cards identified without the prefix of Mr or Ms. They were genderless and I could use the same card in whichever gender I was dressed. It saved so much time and confusion, as I did not need to keep separate accounts for my female and male spending.

I rang the number and made an arrangement for a few days later. I was given an address and I knew it was going to cost me twenty five pounds for a two hour stay; there were no other details needed. I was asked to telephone on the day to confirm my arrival because so many made an appointment and then failed to keep it. My 'hostess' did not want to go to the trouble of dressing herself, which took time and effort, if it was all for nothing. This seemed a sensible arrangement and I duly agreed.

That one telephone call was a life-changing milestone. It was an acknowledgement that no matter what I did, or how I presented myself to the world, my feminine need was still alive and had her own needs which had to be catered for. This was entirely new territory for me, never having done anything like this before. I had been in denial for so long that the internal pressure would soon blow if I did not take the time to give my true self some parole. This was both an exciting time and also a time of reflection. I knew that in many ways this was a crossroads in my life but one I would still do my best to navigate safely. After all, if I could learn to live a dual life and only be female at times of stress or great need, then life would continue as before with no one any the wiser. As I now know, this was wishful thinking, but at that time it was a solution I was prepared to consider and develop.

On the agreed day, I said goodbye to Jean and headed out to work, or so she thought. My appointment was for two o'clock and I made the call to confirm my arrival later that day. All was set; I just had to get there and so I set off south to London at a suitable time.

My destination turned out to be a typical red brick block of council flats. I parked as close as I was able and took the short walk to the entrance. I was determined to go through with this; I had no idea who would open the door or what I would find inside. The voice I had spoken to over the phone seemed pleasant enough so I was as well prepared as I could be.

The door was opened by a young woman of medium height, with shoulder-length dark hair. She was wearing a blouse and skirt with low heeled court shoes; all quite ordinary in fact, except that I already knew she was transgendered, for we had spoken on the telephone. The voice is our greatest hurdle and one which we all strive to perfect as soon as we can when transitioning. Some manage better than others and some don't try too hard, as they know they will never pass because of height or build. We are all individuals in this matter. Contrary to popular belief, the addition of female hormones to the male body does not affect the voice, whereas our counterparts, the female to male transsexuals, find that the addition of testosterone to the female body will lower the voice.

She invited me into her home with a pleasant smile and welcome. Unlike similar services today which are run on a more commercial basis, in those early days most people worked from home as a means to improve their income. Then, more than now, a transsexual had a great deal of difficulty in holding down employment and in making ends meet.

We sat in her living room, got the exchange of money done with, and then she asked what sort of look I was seeking and if I had any specific requirements.

"Nothing specific, just day to day wear," I said, as I went on to explain that this was my first time and that I was unsure of my true feelings and what I wanted in life.

She smiled:

"No problem. I will tell you now, though, that you will either hate this and never do it again or you will love it and can never give it up. Be warned. I have clients from many walks of life, so do not feel that you are on your own."

This was exactly what I needed: some advice and general knowledge from someone in the know, from someone who lived the life and who was willing to help and offer advice – for a price, of course, but I felt that the next few hours were going to be worth every penny. In fact I recognised her, having seen her in a recent late night documentary. I mentioned this to her and she just laughed. Even now, over twenty years later, I can clearly recall her name; it had made that much of an impact on me. Of course, I had had no idea when making the booking that I would strike so lucky and meet someone who truly understood the life of a transsexual, being one herself.

"Yes it was me, something I did nearly a year ago. It took its time getting onto TV!"

We chatted and broke the ice but I was aware that the clock was ticking; I had paid and wanted to get on with it. She obviously picked up on this and led me into a bedroom which had been converted into a dressing room.

As in later experiences the room was sparsely furnished, with the obligatory wardrobe along one wall with sliding mirrored doors. A chair and small table were set close to the mirrors and there was also a chest of drawers and a dressing table. I was happy to be there; I knew it could have turned out so much worse.

I had decided that my first excursion back into my femininity should be simple and quite basic, so I let her get on with it. She opened the wardrobe doors, checked my size and told me which area I could choose from. We discussed what wig I would like to try and we settled for a dark, straight, shoulder-length style. I chose a blouse and skirt, and tights with black patent court shoes to complete the ensemble. The heels were higher than I had ever worn but I was sure that I would manage.

She left for a few minutes, while I changed my clothes. The wig was to remain off until the makeup had been completed and then, as always, I would face the mirror to get the effect of the transformation in one breath.

Taking off my male clothing felt like I was removing all of my woes and worries. A great weight was lifted from my shoulders and I was free. I had, for a few short hours at least, opened the door to my self-constructed cell and let the real me, the female within, out for some fresh air and to live a bit. This freedom was necessarily short but I intended to make the best of it before I would have to shut that door and turn the key once more.

The dressing was just the reverse; it was an uplifting experience as it happened so infrequently and had been denied in total for the past ten or so years. There were no tears but a smile creased my face and I am sure that it must have showed when she walked back in to apply the makeup and finish the transformation.

The required look was quite low key and we were not looking for high quality photography afterwards, so the application process was quite simple and quick. She stepped back to check her handiwork and then picked up the wig, which she brushed through and then fitted to my head.

"Looks good," she said, as she had me stand and then turned me to face the mirror so I could see the result of her ministrations.

"Yes; it certainly does," I replied, as I looked at Karen for the very first time ever. In all of my previous twenty-five years of cross dressing I had never seen myself presented in this way. Staring back at me was just an ordinary young woman who could go into the office any day.

In all of my early years of dressing at home I had had to use my mother's clothes - an entirely different generation - and my own application of cosmetics was, to say the least, basic. Even as I grew older and became more confident and able with the application, I could never have matched the appearance of that young woman in front of me. Of course, having a totally feminine, and young, hairstyle for the very first time made an enormous difference and I am sure that my pleasure at the final effect showed through.

"Thank you so much," I said, as I turned and looked at myself from every angle, just drinking in what was in reality my true self, no longer hidden within the drab clothing and outer façade of a male. I was so happy.

As she had so rightly warned me at the outset, I would either hate this or love it. I knew which camp I so willingly and ecstatically belonged to. I could not and would not give up this wonderful feeling of freedom and emancipation that I now had.

"The flat is yours to wander around, for as long as you are here. You can read some magazines or I can make a cup of tea and we can chat. It's up to you."

I walked up and down a bit to get used to the heels; after all, I had not worn any in a long time. My wanderings always seemed to take me back to the dressing room to review the young lady that I now was. Yes, I did it all: I turned left and right, looked over my shoulder, played with my hair…. and I loved every second.

I had that cup of tea and we chatted about the transgender life that she already lived and which I still did not have that determination or courage to follow. She was also very clear to explain just how hard it was to survive at that time. The two hours went far too quickly for me but I respected the fact that it was her way of making a living – I could not drag things out just because I was enjoying myself. Before I had to change back we did take two Polaroid shots of me in two different wigs. The first picture was with the dark and straight hair and for the second picture I chose longer hair with a bit of curl. These are the only two pictures of me prior to my time at Pandora's, almost twenty years later. I have lost one of them over the years but still have a cherished scan of the second; it has many happy memories and is the first image of my true self.

I put back on the male clothes I had arrived in, with the instant burden that went with them, and made my farewell with mixed emotions. I was happy because I had allowed myself the time to be me; but I was also unhappy, because I had had to lock her up again and become the man that the world expected to see. I also had to go home and maintain this entire episode in total secrecy; no one could ever know.

I returned to the life of an everyday man, knowing that there was always a part of me that would hate it and want to be given her freedom again. I was never so cruel to myself again as I had been over those last twelve years, and I promised to give myself that little bit of time every now and then. Not often enough, I would say now, but it was enough to keep the lid on and to keep me from breaking down until that fateful day in 2005. Each time was an event in its own right. There was, however, one common factor throughout; each time was such a great release of tension and such an uplifting experience that it gave me the strength to carry on.

There is one other significant event which happened during these mid-years of my wilderness period. It was the second time I had let Karen out into the light of day, this time at a location in Manchester, which was more commercial and had a shop on the premises.

I had been browsing in the shop and picked up a transgender magazine. Its contents were quite informative, with articles about, and pictures of transsexuals; it lacked the more usual pornographic elements of its shelf-mates and for that reason I bought it and took it home.

Sam was at secondary school, Kat was approaching nine years old and Sophie was nearly two. As with many couples, intimacy, or lack of it, was back on the agenda for discussion with my wife. I was struggling to deal with this and felt that the introduction of my more feminine side may well help. So it was that one Sunday morning, as we were lying in bed, I introduced Jean to the magazine in much the same way, I hope, as other couples try to introduce an alternative, to spice life up a bit. I was in uncharted waters and did the best I could at that time.

Jean at least looked at the magazine, wondering why I had brought this up. I was perhaps looking at introducing a little cross dressing but was really looking for some way to keep my dual life in control. It was not to be. She ridiculed it all; she could not understand what on earth made a man dress or behave in that way and could not imagine being in a relationship with such a person. I was immediately confronted by my wife ridiculing what was an inherent part of me and what made me the person I was. There was absolutely no way I could continue to explore this, or admit more openly how I felt, in the hope that it would allow me to continue my life and to help rekindle our relationship. I knew I could not raise my needs again; there was no possible way that she could accept or grow to accept these, so I just added a few more locks on the door of the cell, shrugged my shoulders and continued as I had done for the last few years. I never did mention cross dressing or associated issues ever again in our marriage until that pivotal day in October 2005.

I did not perhaps realise it then but that was, in its own way, the start of my long, and lonely, journey of transition.

Chapter 9

Counselling; telling the children and my father and brother; I move out

The two years 2006/07 were in many ways the busiest time for my transition. There were a lot of preparations and changes to make as I told others about my wishes and slowly made my way through the maze of detail that would be required in order for me to reach my goal.

Life at home was once more deteriorating. The further into my journey, the happier I was becoming, and Jean could clearly see this. I was not interested in being the husband any longer, although I continued to be the best parent that I could.

It was a very difficult time for the two children still living at home, as the breakdown of their parents' marriage became so obvious. Sam was away at university and so she saw the breakdown through the eyes of her sisters and of course during her visits home.

My father and brother were also aware of my home issues, although initially it was never openly discussed. I know my father was concerned and only saw a marriage that was 'on the rocks'; he had no inkling of the real reason behind the breakdown. It was not a pleasant time for any of us; but in one respect at least it was a happy time for me, as I slowly made progress in coming to terms with myself and seeking my goal in life.

Counselling was to be the way forward for me and it was to take two years before I was to satisfy the counsellor, and myself, that I was a stable and happy person and that transition was the best solution for me. Of course the counselling might have helped me decide that I could, in fact, live a dual life and that transition would be a mistake. I felt it would be unlikely but that option was always there for consideration.

A lot happened in my life over the next two years, leading up to that major hurdle in the life of all transsexuals – The Real Life Experience, which I eventually started in April 2008. The standards by which practitioners in Gender Dysphoria operate are known as The Harry Benjamin Standards of Care, named after the doctor who first identified the basic needs and essential stages for treating transsexuals. These were first set down in 1979 and have not changed a great deal since, although minor amendments have been made over the years. The standards of care require a period of twelve months as a minimum for the real life experience. However, the NHS in the UK has extended that to twenty-four months before surgery will be sanctioned.

It was in May of 2006 that my first counselling session was organised and after that I went every six weeks for almost two years. It was at the same location as my assessment and I would be seen by a psychologist who had specialised in gender issues. I was on track and moving forward at an ever increasing speed. I knew where I wanted to go, I just had to follow the directions laid down by the NHS and I would reach my goal. Impatience became something that began to gnaw away at my inner self as I wanted it to all happen at once. It was the essential ticking off of each box before I could move on a step that began, over time, to drag and to make me impatient. I am sure that those around me began to notice a shorter temper and less tolerance although, at that time, none knew the reason.

I am a very determined individual but I also have an innate sense of fair play and therefore do not, often, break the rules or go off on my own track. The rules governing the issue of feminising hormones to a transsexual, for example, are very strict, especially within the NHS. Shortcuts can be made if a patient decides to take the private, although costly, route where there is more leeway, although the basic principles of the Benjamin Standards of Care are still followed. There is also the route that many take and that is to self-medicate, which in my opinion is extremely dangerous and a route that I personally was not prepared to consider. Female hormones introduced to a male body are extremely potent and can be life-threatening if the dosage is too high or is misused or is not properly monitored.

I started my counselling without knowing how long it would take before I would actually be able to move on and start hormone treatment. I was by then sure of my ultimate goal and where I intended to go in life. I was already becoming aware of the issues that I would have to deal with in relation to my family, friends and, of course, at work. These were issues that I was to discuss in detail with my counsellor, in order to ensure that I was totally aware of my condition and of the impact it could have on those around me.

My assessment sessions were purely that: an assessment by a specialist to determine where I lay on the transgender spectrum and, as was appropriate in my case, to offer the diagnosis that I suffered from Gender Dysphoria. The assessment did not go into the detail of how, why, where or when. These issues were to be dealt with in detail as I progressed in my transition - a process which had now formally begun. It was made clear at the outset that this type of counselling was not time-limited; I could attend these sessions for as long as I required and until I, or my counsellor, decided that there was nothing further to be gained by meeting again. I had already proved the principle of my dysphoria; I now had to look at the detail and ensure that I was fully aware of what would happen, depending on which route I decided to take.

There were still many options open to me at this time. I could decide that, with appropriate counselling, I could learn to live a dual life and perhaps maintain my marriage and family as it was. I could also decide that I could dispense with my feelings and continue to live totally as a male. That would not have been the best outcome, I think, as I had already tried to do that for so many years and it was unworkable. I could decide that I would transition and live life in the female role but without the need for surgery. Many transsexuals find that they can live in this situation contentedly. Finally, I could decide that the only solution that would enable me to live life fully and at ease with myself would be to transition into the female role and to have the same life-changing surgery that many others choose.

The counselling examined each and every one of these options alongside my own feelings and emotions. We looked at the alternative solutions if I did or did not make a particular decision and how each option would affect those around me. These sessions were emotional and intimate. I knew I had to be totally honest with myself, otherwise I could make the wrong decision for me, never mind those around me. The wrong decision on whether or not to have irreversible surgery is a massive challenge: get it wrong and there is no returning to life as it was before. It is for this reason that the route of transition from male to female (similarly for female to male) and its associated surgical intervention is so closely monitored. For those of us on the journey, though, it seems to take forever.

Each session was a journey into the unknown and I enjoyed each of them with relish. I left emotionally drained but with anticipation for the session that would follow. We interacted; I was challenged often about why I felt the need to do what I was doing. Some questions were extremely difficult to answer and many had no answer at all: only feelings and emotion seemed appropriate. It was more about how I felt, how I perceived my life and how it could be changed for the better. I do know that I cried more than once as we dug deeper and deeper into the depths of what made me the person I was. During each session I imagined myself undoing one or more of those locks I had put on the cell door which contained my inner female self. I was breaking down the barriers I had built and had hidden behind for so many years. I was slowly but surely escaping from my self-imposed imprisonment – it felt good.

It finally boiled down to a choice of two directions. The first was to remain as I was and to make the best of life without change and to be the male that everyone already perceived me to be. The second was to transition and then to look at how I would feel and what impact it would have on those around me.

It was not an easy choice but, in the end, I decided it would be better for all if I followed the route of transition; this I knew was the only route that would satisfy my own needs. I would certainly feel better but it would obviously adversely affect those close to me. However I would be there to support my children and it is that fact alone that helped me decide. If I chose the alternative and continued as I was, I would fall deeper and deeper into depression and unhappiness. We discussed suicidal tendencies, as it is all too common a solution for some who cannot come to terms with this condition. I had not reached that stage but could see all too clearly what may happen if I decided to brazen it out and continued to live the lie and remain the male that most people saw. I could not in fairness follow that road, either for myself or for those I loved. I had no alternative but to transition, to become the female I had always been. That way I could be there to pick up the pieces of shattered lives and wishes for those I loved and help them come to terms with my actions.

I cannot begin to condense two years of counselling into this narrative. Needless to say it was a journey of exploration into self-awareness. I could not have continued on to my final transition without undertaking this important journey. I realise just how important this step is in that journey for, without it, there is no possible way that the right decision can be made. It assisted me in making a decision and that was to transition from male to female and to undergo that final step in seeking to have SRS (Sex Reassignment Surgery) and become physically, as far as current medical and surgical procedures would allow, that which I knew myself to be – female.

There was one very significant finding of my counselling sessions. My mother died in 1999 and she was clearly a significant influence in my life. As we have seen already, she was surely aware that something was different about me and we had reached that stage so many years earlier of having a secret that we never discussed. I had kept my side of the bargain, as well as I could, for all of those years but with her passing I felt that I could be free from our unspoken pact and be myself again. It took a while for me to get the courage to do so, and I did have a few years of denial to overcome. However a few friends have said that I started to change after her death and I can agree with that observation. So there is that unconscious potential that I was released from my unspoken agreement with Mum. She was no longer there to be hurt and I could be myself.

As a family we had moved out of the village nearly eight years previously but had moved back again, feeling that our roots were there and that it was where we had been at our happiest. Both older girls had gone through secondary school and Sophie was well-established in primary school. The move was only a few miles and she was able to stay at the same school, although we now lived in a different county. We felt secure in the knowledge that she would follow the route of her older sisters and would move on to secondary school in the same catchment area. This, however, was not to be the case as we now lived out of county and the rules had changed.

We did eventually get her into the school of our choice but it took an appeal process to achieve it. It was perhaps the one time Jean was glad that I was transsexual, as we used that as the basis of our appeal. The appeal relied on the need for my daughter to have the support of her peers who were transferring to our school of choice. She was initially offered a place at a school ten miles away, where she would know no-one. This was totally unacceptable to us as parents and to her as a pupil, even without the introduction of my imminent transition.

The argument was that, although at this time she was unaware of my condition, she would have to be told shortly and certainly before she transferred to secondary school. She therefore needed the support of her peers, with whom she had been at school with for the previous five years and without which she would be totally unable to cope with life at home. The argument was successful; no school authority could deny her a place when that was taken into consideration.

We were back in the village where we started and had felt so comfortable, although now in a much grander house. We had moved a few rungs up the ladder of success. A lot of our friends had moved away but there were some still there and we felt that it was best for us all to be back where our roots were. With our two older daughters no longer at secondary school we felt it was time to move back. There was also a secondary reason: we wanted to try to rebuild our marriage, which was deteriorating fast.

The new house was at the edge of what I could reasonably afford but in some ways I was prepared to take on the debt, guilt perhaps playing a part in that decision. I wanted to try and make it right for my wife and family although, in reality, that was to prove impossible.

As a couple we were leading separate lives by mid-2006 as I slowly but surely became more at peace with my life-changing decision and explored the female within more openly. My wardrobe was small but growing and I made use of it more often during this period. It was always away from home and always with the knowledge of my wife. My weekends away came more often as I visited clubs for the transgendered: safe places where we all start, before venturing into the real world with confidence. I met others online and my own circle of friends and acquaintances expanded quickly, allowing me to find out more and more about my condition. Added to the awareness coming from the counselling, this helped immensely with my decision to continue my journey, now that I had started.

My family is immensely important to me and I knew that I had to tell them all before they heard anything from a third party. It would be totally unacceptable for them to hear gossip and incorrect information from others. That is one reason I had been so careful and always went out away from home, the only exception being that night out with Kat, but even then we had been very careful. So it was that I started planning how to tell my immediate family. I knew that the two hardest would be my father and my youngest daughter so I planned to leave them till last; that left my eldest daughter, Sam, and my brother, David.

Sam at this time was living away from home at university. She was only twenty or so miles away but it was enough for her not to be affected on a daily basis by the issues at home. She knew, of course, that there was a major problem in her parents' marriage but not what was behind it. Kat, true to her word, had not broken her promise to me so it was left to me to give Sam the news myself, which was only right.

Telling Sam was, by comparison, a fairly simple situation. She is my first and eldest child and the bond between a father and first born daughter is strong and very important. My transsexuality does not affect this bond: I am, and always will be, her dad. I was well aware of the shock and hurt I would cause but the success with her younger sister Kat gave me the courage to face the task with a positive attitude.

It was a Saturday afternoon and I was at home on my own when Sam dropped in for a visit from university. We were sitting in the lounge with a cold drink and had chatted through her university issues and the usual student problem of 'no money'. We were talking well and had spoken about the difficulties at home and about what was going on between her mother and me. I felt that this was an appropriate time and so took the opportunity to be honest with her about the problems at home.

"Sam, I know that you are worried about my relationship with mum and about our marriage. I think it's about time you knew the truth," I began

I could see the worry and a degree of curiosity cross her face as she turned to look straight at me.

"OK, Dad. I'm listening."

I am sure she was expecting me to tell her about one of us committing adultery, or about an extreme debt which would require us to sell the house; something that at least was in her scope of comprehension.

As with every other previous, and subsequent, occasion, what she was to hear was the last thing she ever expected.

"As you are well aware, relations between your mum and me here at home are poor, to say the least. There is a reason behind that, which I think you have to know."

Sam sat back expectantly and said simply: "OK."

"Sam you know I love you all but I have been living a lie for all of my life and the hiding is killing me. I can't go on. I have to be honest and truthful with you all. I know it will hurt."

I then just blurted it out as she recoiled back in astonishment.

"I believe I am transsexual; a woman born in a male body. I am moving forward and will eventually have a sex change so that my body matches my true feelings."

I sat silently as I watched the shock cross her face. She also sat in silence for a few minutes as she digested what I had just said.

"I can't really understand this, dad. Are you saying that you are a woman?"

"Yes, in many ways that is what I am. I just unfortunately have a male body and obviously have the ability to father children. You three girls are testimony to that. It is very complex and not easy to explain without a lot of detail. Just believe me when I say that this is the hardest thing I have ever had to deal with. Mum is aware and obviously is not happy with the likely outcome. At the moment she is doing her best to be supportive but it's not easy and I don't know how long it will last. Ultimately we will divorce. All I ask of you all is that you do your best to support each other and of course Mum."

"This is hard and will take time Dad. Who else knows?"

"I told Kat a few months ago because she was dealing with it at home. You being away from home meant that you have been cushioned from the worst of it. I don't know what she has told you."

"Nothing. I knew there were problems but had no idea about this."

"How could you? It is not a common situation. Please believe that I love you all and will do my best for you. However, I have no choice in this; my path is set and I must follow it or the consequences are unthinkable for me."

"OK, but I need to think about this. It's a great shock. I love you but it won't be easy to deal with. I need to talk to Kat and get her take on it. I won't talk to anyone else. Does Sophie know?"

Her care for her younger sisters showed through. It was hard for her so how must it be for Sophie and Kat at home?

"No. Sophie does not know and I don't want her to be told until the time is right. She is too young to understand."

"Yeah, I think that's right. I will talk to Kat and maybe a few friends if that's OK with you. I need to sort this out."

"Of course, if you need to know anything else just ask."

"Thanks Dad, I love you but I think I need to go now and see Kat."

"I understand. I love you."

We stood and hugged before she turned and left to sort it out. It was a shock for her, much as it had been for Kat and her mum, but I had confidence that she would come to deal with it. I was to be proved right in time, although it was not easy for her; after all she would soon lose the father figure in her life. I sat alone in the house after she had left, just thinking about what I had done and, more importantly, about what I was soon to do to my family. I also knew I had no alternative: the die was cast and I must move on.

David was a different matter entirely. He lived 12,000 miles away in Queensland, Australia, and for many years we had hardly communicated. That began to change following the death of our mother but it was still hard, certainly for me, to open up and exchange e-mail regularly. E-mail had at least made life a bit easier: I just could not deal with air mail letters, they were far too much trouble. I was still receiving most of the family updates from Dad who exchanged family news with David every week. David was aware that my marriage was in decline but, like everyone else, had no idea why.

I had to tell all to those I loved before they found out from third parties. It was also something that had to be done face to face; it was not, in my opinion, something that could be done at a distance. David travelled extensively and would visit the UK on business quite often. Whenever he did he would add a few days' holiday to his schedule and visit Dad; they would then both make a family visit to see me. One week-end in June 2006 he brought dad up to visit. I knew that this had to be the moment of truth and that I had to tell my brother everything that was going on in my life and most importantly why.

These visits were always a family affair. The three girls would be in attendance: they never missed seeing their Grampa if it could be helped. My father was a major influence in the lives of all three. He loved them all and was always there to help in whatever way he could. Visits would always involve a full family roast meal and Jean and I always did our best to put our differences to one side for these events. Clearly, no matter how we behaved the stress would show through and I know Dad was very worried for me and the way in which my life seemed to be heading for divorce, with all that it entailed.

It was still too early to break the news to my father and I also knew I would need David's support to help him through what would be a major shock. So it was that, shortly after their arrival and the usual welcome and pleasantries, I asked if David would take a short walk with me to the local pub for a chat. I had not told Jean that I was going to do this but it was clear from her reaction that she guessed what I was about to do; she was far from happy about it. There was never going to be a good time as far as she was concerned and by this time I was more or less working to my own agenda; our relationship had become so bad that we did not communicate well at all anymore.

Whatever he thought, David kept it to himself and simply agreed to my request. I suspect that he thought I was going to tell him that my marriage was over and that everything would change shortly. This was partly true at least; but the main reason behind it all was unknown to him. It was a warm and sunny day in June so we let Dad know we would be out for a while and left for the short walk to the pub. It was only about eleven o'clock so the pub was almost totally empty. I ordered a coffee for my brother and a large white wine for myself; I knew I would need it. We sat down at a table in the corner away from the staff and any other customer who might enter, giving us a degree of privacy. The pub was to become a common thread in all of my episodes of telling my secret. It was a pleasant pub, well-used in the village and, it being a public place, I hoped it would limit any major reaction from whomever I told. I was well-known and no-one would think it unusual for me to be talking privately to others. It worked well, just as it had done when I told Kat that first time.

So we sat and exchanged news about work and family; after all, I had not seen him in over a year. It was all so natural until I changed direction:

"I have something to tell you," I started, "but I am not sure how to go about it so please be patient."

"Fine. In your own time. I will listen to whatever you have to say without comment, until you finish." He smiled, thinking he knew what was about to be disclosed.

So I told him everything that was going on in my life, that I was transsexual, and that I would eventually seek sex reassignment surgery. Just to clarify: my brother is in the ministry and is well-used to talking to others about issues which may not be common knowledge. In his own words after the event:

"I remember being rather unsurprised by it in the end and it was certainly no great trauma—too many years of pastoral ministry to be totally surprised by most things I guess."

That was it. I can't remember him being shocked or even at a loss for words. He was my brother and would be there to support me on my journey. He agreed that our conversation would remain confidential until I said otherwise and that he would be there for me when I told Dad. We both agreed that this was not the best time and that it would be another hurdle for me to jump in the future.

He was not even curious: his love and acceptance were there and that is all that mattered to either of us. We finished our drinks and walked back home in the knowledge that Jean would be far from happy at this turn of events and that Dad would certainly be worried and wonder what was going on. It was a frosty return home, for me at least, but we continued with lunch as normal. The poor atmosphere was no longer unusual so I don't think that Dad was any the wiser and the girls would have taken it in their stride by this time – Mum and Dad were simply not talking. The older two, now at least, knew why but, for the sake of Sophie, played along and did the best they could to make things seem normal for her.

Jean was furious with me and did not hide the fact, once our guests had left. There was little I could say or do so I took the verbal beating and carried on as usual. I know that David told Dad that we spoke about my marriage and the troubles I was going through. He made no mention, though, of the real reason and, as it fitted in with Dad's expectations, there was no further need to expand on his behalf.

The disclosure on my part was a massive release and it allowed both my brother and me to become closer than ever. We started regular email communication which, I am pleased to say, is as active now, four years later, as it was then. I sent him the pictures by email shortly after his return home and he acknowledged their receipt and reaffirmed his love for me as his sibling. That, for then, was more than enough for me and the knowledge that I had his support was an immense help to me over the months to come. I knew I could be honest now and could vent my feelings if needed and that I had someone who would listen and give me honest feedback in return.

It was at about this time that I also made the decision to tell someone outside the immediate family. Surprisingly perhaps to many, it was Pam, my first wife. We had made contact a few years earlier and the friendship was rebuilding. Initially Jean was part of the re-established friendship but that was to deteriorate over the months, until it was only I who remained in contact. I had taken up war gaming with her husband, in an attempt to widen my own limited circle of friends and it had been another means to maintain my male façade. I enjoyed the whole gaming fraternity and made many friends during that period, some of whom I still stay in touch with as Kirstie, although I have given up the gaming itself.

I broke the news in much the same way as I had with the few family members who knew at this time. I arranged to meet her and her partner for lunch at a pub in their local town. Once more the public venue made me feel less exposed than if I told my story in the privacy of their home, where I could be cross-examined more easily. I recall the lunch-time crowd making it very noisy so I felt that I could talk quite openly, without being overheard by others. Having done this a few times now, my speech was well prepared and I knew exactly what I would say to them. What I had not factored in was the element that we had been a married couple and that we knew each other so well. Her husband had also become a good friend and I knew I did not want to lose that friendship. Their response was wonderfully positive: of course they would support me in my journey; my change would make no difference to our friendship; this was nothing as far as they were concerned; I was a friend and that was all that counted.

Pam became a staunch supporter, even doing her own background reading to better understand my situation. I have been able to talk openly with her about my issues and have always received honest feedback in return. She had, in her own way, also become a surrogate aunt to my children: she had helped them in the past and had always done so in a confidential manner. Whatever they told her stayed with her, and they knew it. I know that they did talk to her, once my situation became public knowledge, and that the support she gave was an essential part in the way that they were able to deal with my transition. I am eternally grateful for that help then and now as we remain the true friends and confidents we became all of those years ago, when we first met at fifteen.

As for me, I was continually exploring and expanding my own boundaries. I was going out to clubs and meeting people there and online. The more I learned, the more I became confident in my own self and in the knowledge that I was doing the right thing. The counselling was progressing, which was adding to my self-awareness, and I was gaining in confidence. I was also getting impatient to progress faster and I started to consider looking at the private route to transition. The cost of this route was an obvious bar, as I knew that divorce was going to be expensive for me. However, I felt that I should still examine it as an alternative.

I therefore made an appointment to see a gender specialist based in London. The doctor is well known in the transgender community, being a female to male transsexual himself. Part of my reasoning was to obtain a second opinion, which I clearly did not actually need, but also to test the waters for private medication and support as an alternative to the long NHS route I was following at that time.

It was October 2006 and I was in a private room on Wimpole Street in London for a forty-five minute consultation. This was not like the earlier assessment by the psychiatrist, when I had to talk about myself without guidance, but an assessment by a medical practitioner who has specialised in gender issues; it was a straight-forward question and answer session. The fact that he was transsexual himself made me feel more at ease and more comfortable in these circumstances. I felt that I was talking to someone who could understand how I was feeling and could therefore empathise with me.

The meeting ran smoothly. We explored my family and my personal history; we discussed how I actually felt; and we talked about how I had managed to live my life as a man, feeling the way I did.

I received an immediate response from him on completion of the consultation. He felt that I was suffering from Gender Dysphoria and was probably transsexual; it came with a recommendation for appropriate counselling to further resolve my issues, of which there were many. What was important about this occasion was that I also received a copy of the assessment that was sent to my GP. It is an important letter and the first that I had personally received. It was the start of my own medical file, which I have to stress is very important for those of us undergoing this journey. We must be able to prove that we have reached the various milestones along our journey in order to progress; the earlier the file starts the better. In the end I decided not to pursue the private route, as the cost was prohibitive for me. I therefore planned out my own path to transition and settled down for the ride.

This was a period of exploration and escape from my self-imposed imprisonment. The more I got out into the real world as Kirstie, the more people in similar circumstances I spoke to or exchanged ideas with on-line, the better and freer I became. The bonds were dropping faster and I was happy but those around me were not doing so well. Jean could see my happiness increase and her own decrease at similar rates. I was sympathetic to her situation but she wanted nothing to do with my transition and so there was no longer any common ground. My guilt at what I was doing to our relationship and to my family increased at a similar rate but, in the end, I had made my decision to transition and I was not for turning back. My reasoning was sound: I would be there for them in the future but there were bound to be casualties along the way, the biggest and most obvious being my marriage of nearly twenty-five years.

I researched all that I could about my condition. I was already well-read on the subject and had proven myself to be more knowledgeable than some members of the medical profession. It was during this time that I took up the reins for a large online transgender support group and became the moderator. I learned a lot about myself and my condition and was also able to offer my own experiences and knowledge to others. I was also learning from those who had finished their journey or were travelling it much as I was.

I was still living my life primarily in the male role. I had not gone far enough to live even part-time as a female, let alone full time. I knew that I was progressing toward a time when I would leave the marital home to start my life over again. That was a scary thought and one which I tried not to dwell upon too much until it became inevitable. Although we shared the same roof, my wife and I were living separate lives. In that sense I was well on my way to starting my new life, but to have started living in the family home as Kirstie would have been more than a step too far.

At about the time of my private consultation I had been exchanging information online with Linda from Norway. She visited the UK quite often to live in the female role for a few days and asked if I would like to meet. I was open to new ideas and meeting new people and we seemed to get along well enough so I agreed. It was to give me the opportunity to live entirely in the female role for four days and something I looked forward to. I had experienced the real world enough times now not to be too concerned when her first request was to collect 'him' from Stanstead airport! I thought about it and the risk was not that high: after all the arrivals hall would be crowded. I even thought that if I did not like the look of my companion for the next four days I could just 'miss' him in the crowd and go back home.

I had already learned that it was far easier to pass in a crowded place than in a quiet bar or restaurant. People in crowds don't look or take a great deal of interest in others: they just pass on by. It is most likely to be another woman who picks up on a transsexual in public; they just sense the difference. I have often walked past a woman and noticed the slight smile as she picks up on something out of the ordinary. It's a fact of life for a transsexual to be 'read' at times and it is best ignored.

The worst time to be 'read' is usually by teenage girls; they show absolutely no mercy. I can clearly recall to this day a lift ride in a department store with two girls who just laughed and sniggered the whole time. I could do nothing but try to ignore them as the lift rose just one floor. This was in the early days when I wore a wig and was not so self-assured and is a reminder of how cruel the world can be to those of us who are slightly different. It was no use trying to explain that it was an acknowledged medical condition that I suffered from; it would have fallen on entirely deaf ears. So you learn to swallow hard and just look the other way – it's hard to do in a lift but I managed.

There was no way I could dress and leave the house as Kirstie. Instead I arranged to visit my friend Sarah on the way to Stanstead Airport; she would let me change at her place before collecting Linda from the airport. I had also met Sarah online a few months earlier and had visited her for an evening. I had arrived as Ken and then changed to spend the evening as Kirstie. It was a pleasing encounter as I met another transsexual as well. After several hours of chat, a light bite to eat and just getting to know each other I once more had to go and change as, unlike my hostess and her friend who lived as females, I had to return home as I had left: as Ken.

As I was leaving Sarah gave me the greatest confidence boost imaginable:

"You know you are not a transvestite; you are most definitely one of us. You are just a natural woman; of that there is no doubt. Your whole demeanour and personality changed from the miserable male you came in as to the woman you transformed into. You are relaxed, and confident, and you behave so naturally: you fall into the female role with ease. Believe me, it takes one to know one."

She said it with a glint in her eye and a reassuring smile. I left and drove home feeling so happy. Not only had I met some new friends but they had recognised the real me. The compliment I had received gave me a far greater boost than any assessment from the medical profession. It was the start of a long friendship, lasting to this day, which included us both going to Thailand at the same time and having our SRS within four days of each other.

I had taken a few days off work and told Jean I would be away. I gave her no details, as by this time we were no longer a partnership but were two individuals living in the same house. I travelled north and stopped over to change. I would not need any male clothing for the next four days and had chosen my wardrobe carefully. This was not party time, although our itinerary did include a visit to two clubs. I would be out in public and needed to ensure I would blend in as best I could, so I chose a sweater and jeans with sensible shoes. My wig was a blonde, chin-length bob, much like my natural hair now, and my makeup was light. I still needed to cover some beard shadow but it was not heavy and I could get away with daytime coverage.

As I drove into the airport car park I started to worry. What the hell was I doing meeting a complete stranger and then spending the next four days exclusively in her company? I was transsexual and she was a transvestite; there could be nothing in common. However, the chance to live my life as a female for four whole days was too much of a draw. So I parked and plucked up the courage to walk into the busiest and most public area I had ever experienced. The Arrivals hall was as busy as expected but as I had surmised I was just another face in the crowd. After my initial concerns and worries I settled into the role and started to enjoy the whole experience.

I recognised my friend from the photo she had sent and went over; after an initial assessment of each other we embraced and left together for the car park. It was that simple. We had exchanged enough information online to enable us to gel quickly and without too much effort. I spent the next four days entirely as Kirstie. On the first night we went to a TS club. The next day we took a trip to Southampton for a photo session and a night out. We followed that on the third evening by returning to London for a night at The Way Out Club, staying at a hotel located just around the corner. Aside from the 'safe' places, such as the clubs, I had to use garages for fuel twice and went into a number of shops. We also used a restaurant without there being any raised eyebrows.

Linda was older than me by some five years; her wife knew about her hobby and seemed to accept it. In addition, she had sufficient finances to enable her to do these trips three or four times a year. There was a degree of envy from me but also I knew that I still had major challenges to overcome; I was, after all, transsexual. She, as a transvestite, was happy living a dual life and could cross the boundary from male to female and back again with some ease. I, on the other hand, was finding that change back to being male harder each time.

I thoroughly enjoyed my few days living as a woman and that experience was to be the first of many where I learned to live in the real world and not just in safe transgender locations. I was glad that I had taken the risk and we both enjoyed our time together as friends. We still exchange mails occasionally but have not repeated the exercise again. To be honest, I don't expect that I would enjoy it in the same way, now that I live my life full time in the female role. There is no longer any surprise or benefit to me in duplicating that type of journey although for her, or someone similar, the chance to experience a few days in the female role will always be a major draw.

I took her back to the airport, said my farewell and then I went to Sarah's to change back into my male clothing. It was becoming harder to do so each time that I experienced life as the female I truly was. I knew that the time for me to break the ties with my male self was rapidly approaching; I needed my freedom.

Life at home continued much the same, with both good and bad days. We did our best to keep things as normal as possible but it can't have escaped out daughters' notice that their parents were approaching separation and divorce. Divorce does not carry the same stigma now as it would have done twenty years earlier. In fact it is common for there to be as many children from broken marriages in a class at school as there are those from stable situations. Sophie still had no idea why this was happening and was unhappy but could do nothing about it. Her two sisters did their best to be supportive, knowing what they did, but they could not and would not tell her the underlying reason.

Christmas 2006 was much as before. My father joined us for a few days and we did our best to show a normal front for others to see. It was not to be: we had gone too far along the road of separation and were living separate lives. There was very little in common any more apart from our children and the same address. Talking to David later on I now know that my father was extremely worried for me and for his grandchildren, whom he loved dearly. Jean did try to understand and come to terms with my condition, trying at times to take part with online forums. However, it did not work and we continued the downward spiral.

The New Year, 2007, started much as any other with the exception that this time I knew I had to move on in my journey. I could not continue to live as I was, hurting everyone around me. I was still being treated for depression, which was hardly surprising under the circumstances. I wanted to move on with my life and to do what I could to regain some happiness. I began to plan how I would move out of the family home and put my life on track, yet I still had the challenges of telling my father and Sophie and this formed the foundation of my plan.

In order to tell my father I needed the back-up of my brother and so I waited till he visited the UK once more on business. As usual, he arranged those few extra days' holiday to stay with Dad and to visit me in June 2007. The weekend of the family visit duly arrived. Life at home was at a low ebb and, unbeknown to Dad, I had moved out of the house in a low key manner the previous Thursday. I had stayed within the village, to become a lodger at the home of an old friend whom we had known since we had first moved to the village all those years ago. I had agreed with Jean not to tell Dad prior to his visit at the weekend.

A couple that we had known had separated and the divorce was going through. The female partner, Christine (Chris), had remained in the marital home and let out a room to supplement her income; she was looking for a new lodger. It was an ideal situation. I would remain close to my children - the walk was less than 5 minutes - and I would be staying with someone I had known for a long time. Of course I had to let her into my secret before the final decision was taken.

I broke the news to her in the time-honoured way in the pub. It seemed to work well and I was getting quite good at doing so.

"Chris, I have something to tell you before I move in and it may influence your final agreement."

I could see the shock on her face as she went through the permutations, most of which I have subsequently learned revolved around terminal illness.

"I am transsexual; it's the reason that my marriage has come to an end and why I have to move out."

She thought for a moment and then replied:

"I thought you were going to say that you had cancer or something similar. Not that I know much about what you have said, so please explain."

So I did, much as I had already done with my children. I showed her the pictures that illustrated what I was talking about.

"Not a worry," she said reassuringly. "I have known you for over twenty years and will always be your friend. It makes no difference and it may even be fun as I have only had male lodgers for some time."

That was it; once more I was astonished at just how easily my situation was accepted by another. Jean was even in agreement and in some way happy that I had found somewhere to live so easily, with an understanding friend and still close enough to my youngest daughter to make visiting easy. Sophie at this time still had no idea what was planned; that would come later.

We agreed that I would move out of the marital home into my new lodgings in July. That left a short time for me to tell my father and my daughter. Luckily David's visit in June fitted into the timescale and I gave him adequate warning about what had to be done.

We were exchanging emails regularly by this time and he warned me how difficult it would be to tell Dad but that he would be there to help us both. I was naturally worried about how my revelation would affect our father but also knew that I could not progress any further without telling him. The phrase "Trapped between a rock and a hard place" came to mind and I just had to deal with it as best I could. Telling Dad would be painful for us both but, whereas I was prepared for this, he would walk into the revelation totally unprepared. It was not a fair situation but there was no choice; it just had to be done.

Sunday lunch was arranged, much as it had been almost a year previously, when I had told my brother. This time Dad would accompany David and me to take that short walk to the pub. They duly arrived at coffee time and, after the first round of greetings, I asked if they would come for a walk, as I had something to tell dad. I could see the worry on his face: he was clearly concerned for his youngest son and, of course, for his grandchildren.

He was expecting me to tell him that I would be getting a divorce and moving out and in many ways he was not wrong. It was not a great situation for him but one he was well-prepared for as he had seen my marriage disintegrate over the previous few years. He prepared himself for the inevitable as we walked to the nearby pub. He still had no idea of the bombshell I was about to drop into his life.

David kept his own counsel. I have no idea what was going through his mind but I know he was prepared as I told Dad the news. I ordered two coffees and a large white wine, and we settled into the quiet corner of the pub as I prepared to tell Dad that he in fact had a daughter ….. he just never knew it until now.

How do you tell an eighty year-old man about being transsexual? It's worse when that man is your father, believe me. I did not want to hurt him in any way but knew also that the next few minutes would be a devastating revelation to him. I was so glad that my brother was there to support him. This time was to be different to previous revelations: there would be no pictures and I would limit the detail to the minimum necessary, unless he wanted to know more.

"Dad, this is not going to be easy for either of us. I have something to tell you which will be a bit of a shock."

I could see him swallow hard and perhaps even see his eyes glass over a bit as he realised that this was it: I was going to finally tell him about my divorce.

"Go on son, I will always be here for you, no matter what. Don't worry."

Of course I worried; who would not in these circumstances? I knew I had to go on, so I did the easy part first.

"I am moving out of the house shortly, and will be getting a divorce. My marriage is at an end."

That hurt him but at least he was expecting it. He was concerned about my living arrangements and how it would affect his relationship with his granddaughters. He did not want the break down to stop him seeing those young ladies who meant so much to him. I reassured him on this before I continued:

"There is more Dad. What you need to be aware of is the reason why this is now happening."

Whether he was expecting me to say that one of us was having an affair, had debts or whatever I will never know but what he then heard was the last thing in the world he would have anticipated.

"Dad, I have been diagnosed with an unusual condition. I am transsexual and will be looking towards changing sex in the next few years."

Perhaps I was not quite so direct but the gist of the matter remains the same. I could see the shock cross his face and then, worst of all, the guilt.

"I don't understand. What did Mum and I do wrong in bringing you up?"

It was the obvious response from someone, particularly a parent, who was not aware of this condition. He immediately assumed guilt; he wondered what he and my mother had done wrong; he questioned whether all this could have been avoided if they had brought me up differently.

I reassured him as best I could. There was nothing that could have been done differently under the circumstances. Life was different fifty years ago, when no one fully understood this condition and when there was certainly no way I could have spoken out about how I felt. I am so glad that David was there to reassure our father and to reinforce my statement that he and Mum were not at fault. He helped explain to Dad that I had an acknowledged, but unusual, medical condition and one that required a similarly unusual and very obvious treatment to resolve.

It was perhaps the most difficult thirty minutes of my life. I had upset my father in a way that could not be contemplated or imagined. He took it as well as could be expected. I am sure it took some time to sink in and I am forever grateful to David that he was there for the next few days, to support our father in this time of distress.

"I don't understand. I need time for this to sink in. But please be assured that I love you and will do the best I can."

I could ask for no more than that, and at least he had not disowned me, something that I knew happened all too often. We finished our drinks; I could see Dad thinking and I know he was hurting inside, as he had no point of reference to work on. My revelation had come out of the blue. It was something he had never even considered, nor could he have been expected to do so. I was sure he could deal with the divorce, but the underlying reason was beyond his knowledge.

The subsequent Sunday lunch was a quiet affair, with Dad and my brother leaving earlier than usual. They had a lot to think about.

I do know Dad struggled that night, as David has recently told me:

"I remember when we got home that evening; Dad could not settle as the news really devastated him and we spent several hours talking about it. We went to bed quite late and then he woke me about 3am, as he could not sleep and was struggling to breathe, so we got up and had a cup of tea in the kitchen and talked it all through again."

I still feel guilt at what I had done to my dad but also know there was nothing else I could do. I could not keep it secret from him and continue on my journey; he had to know. At least he was not alone that first night and was able to talk it through with David, who helped him start to come to terms with my condition. Most importantly, he was reassured that neither he nor our Mum was in any way to blame for this.

My dealings with Dad over the next few years, prior to his death, were always carefully controlled. I never wore overtly feminine clothing, always dressing in a plain blouse, jeans and flat shoes. I never wore make up or jewellery in his presence. I was always referred to as 'son': what right did I have to correct him in this, after so many years? Much as my daughters have always called me 'Dad' it is a fact of life and a compromise I have always been willing to make.

There remained one last person in my life to tell and that was my eleven year old daughter Sophie. Jean and I could never agree on whether or not she should be told at this time. I felt that, as with my father, there was no option. I was soon to start living a dual life and she needed to know beforehand otherwise she would find out from someone else who would not be so kind or understanding. Jean went as far as to suggest that I put the whole thing on hold until Sophie was eighteen, not starting my transition until then. She clearly had no idea how I felt, or otherwise I am sure she would not have made what was in fact a preposterous suggestion. She was, though, deadly serious at that time but I could not even consider that as an option.

We could not agree and so it was that Sophie was told that her parents' marriage was finished and that we would divorce. Yet she was not told the reason why. Of course she was upset, as any child would be when her parents separated; but at least I moved out on a friendly basis. Jean and I had by that time come to terms with the end of our marriage. She was pleased that I had found a safe place to be and that I was close enough for our daughter to visit easily. She even helped me to move.

However, there were still the emotional elements of blame and recrimination in the background, which go with most divorces. I also added guilt to my side of the equation. Nevertheless, we did our best for the sake of the children to remain friends for as long as we could.

I was not prepared to leave it much later before I was to tell Sophie, she had to know the truth before Kirstie was seen in the village, which was to happen all too soon.

Chapter 10

In the wilderness and working as a male – the later years

We moved from the village into our new house in 1996 and settled down as any other outwardly normal family. My relationship with Jean was already strained as there was no intimacy - I just was not interested. I wanted to be myself but there was no way I could, so I continued as before, hiding behind Ken and being the ordinary man everyone saw. I did what was expected and improved the house, we had the holidays and did what was required to fit into society; it was all a lie.

When both of the eldest girls got on with each other life was great but when they fell out, which they did all too often, life was hell for us all. Sam managed to get through these years without too much trauma. Kat, however, made up for this in spades. She became the original wild child, with no respect for her elders at home, at school or in fact anywhere. We were in regular contact with the school and, I am sorry to say, the police. She just did not want to fit in or conform to any rules. This just made relationships with her sisters even worse and added to the general disharmony at home. With hindsight I can see that she was able to read the real situation all too well: she knew there was no love in the marriage and that there were significant issues between her mother and me. I am sure her older sister was also aware; she just dealt with it differently and left for university at a fortunate time.

In many ways this period of my life was uneventful as far as my gender identity was concerned. Life went on as usual, I went to work, came home and did my best to hold the family together. Kat was our greatest challenge at this time, especially when she moved to secondary school, from which she was eventually permanently excluded. She even ran away for a time; I can still remember well the night we received the call from the police to say they had found her in Skegness. They asked if we would go and collect her; it was a long journey but worth it, as we had our daughter back and she was glad to see us.

Life was predominantly about keeping Kat on track, which was difficult enough, and about limiting the effect this had on her sisters. No matter what differences there were between my wife and me at that time, and later, we always stood as a partnership when it came to the wellbeing of our daughters. We always showed a united front whether it was to the school, the police or the counsellors we saw as a family. Together we saw Kat through this difficult time and kept the family together, no matter what adversity we were forced to face.

My ability to dress and be Karen was, for those few years, totally denied, as I had more than enough to deal with in keeping our daughter alive and in one piece. This was our life for almost six years until that fateful night when we almost lost Kat to a broken bottle, stabbed into her neck after an argument in the local park. It was a wakeup call for her: she knew she had gone too far and from that night the change in her was obvious.

We decided that we could no longer stay in that house, with all of its bad memories, and felt that we would be comfortable back in the village where we had come from. It was, after all, close enough to ensure that our daughters did not have to change schools, although Kat had by this time been permanently excluded. She was in limbo for a while but decided to go to college to learn design. She then changed once more, to train as a hairdresser, which is the profession she follows to this day.

I thought that a fresh start in a new home would once more let me put my troubles behind me and that I could continue in my denial. It was not to be but I was at least satisfied that I had done the best I could for my family. We moved in to our new house during November 2003, just a few short years before our family life came tumbling down and I left to start my new life as Kirstie.

I was still working throughout the UK, travelling a lot but not staying away from home quite as often, as I now had staff working for me. I was still a loner and had trouble fitting in to the all-male environment. I know also that my work began to be affected, as I was just not coping with the life of living a lie anymore. The doctor had prescribed antidepressants, although she had no idea of the real reason behind my problems, putting it down to stress at work and marital difficulties. My work began to suffer as I lost interest there too, after coping for the last thirty years as a male but desperately wishing to be the female I was inside.

I was a member of the senior management and so was often invited to networking events or, to give them their more informal title, 'Boys' Weekends Away'. One such event happened annually and I attended twice in consecutive years. It involved leaving on a Friday morning and returning on the Monday morning – the destination was Palma on the island of Majorca off the coast of Spain.

It was a typical itinerary: after check in at two o'clock at the hotel, we would be in the bar an hour later and continue drinking till the wee small hours, with food fitted in somewhere to suit. We were a party of about twenty each time and there was plenty of opportunity to mix; I did the best that I could. It was not an environment I was comfortable in and I am sure it showed, particularly on the first time out.

There are two experiences, from the different trips, which remain firmly in my mind. They are poles apart in content and one now brings a wry smile and the other memories of deep peace and contentment; I think it will become obvious which is which.

This was to be my first, last and only trip to a brothel! As a group we had divided into two parties and I went with the people I knew best but without realising the ultimate destination. I remember someone asking the taxi driver where he recommended and that is where we went. I was just one of the group and could not back out at this stage so, even though I had no interest in this excursion, I felt that I had to go along for the ride.

I have nothing with which to compare it, so can only describe this instance as best I can. It was supposedly one of the best, according to the taxi driver at least, and located in a quiet back street. The taxi deposited us at the front door where two bouncers were standing on guard and we were escorted into a small brightly lit bar area. One of our group had taken on the role of spokesman and told the attractive woman who came forward what we were all here for. I was glad when someone handed me a beer and we settled down for a chat and to look at the wares on offer from the girls in the establishment. After all, in many ways this was to be a shopping trip where we were expected to choose the best girl to 'enjoy' for the short time we were to pay for. At this stage one of our more wealthy members, whose idea it turned out to be, offered to settle the bill for us all. You could see the sparkle in madam's eyes! I was also relieved, as I can categorically state that I had not budgeted for this in my weekend's pocket money.

It was a comfortably lit lounge area with quiet background music. With such a large group of men now in the lounge, the number of girls slowly increased to give the customers some choice. It was like going back to my early days at the London strip clubs so I at least had an idea how to behave and joined in with the chat and discussion. English, of course, was not spoken; we had not come to a tourist trap but to one of the better Spanish establishments. However, language was not a barrier in this case, as my colleagues quickly managed to make their choices by pointing and smiling; alternatively those of us not as quick on the uptake were chosen by one of the girls, which is what happened to me.

Hell! What was I to do next? I am not now, nor was I then, particularly sexually active, now knowing myself to be asexual. More specifically, I really had no interest in the experience I was about to have. I was one of the last to leave the lounge.

I stood up, smiled and then followed my 'date' to our room. It was dimly lit, so there was little detail to be seen or retained. There was a double bed, a basin and little other furniture and no windows. I was in a closed box. I had no idea what was going to happen or what behaviour was expected and of course we could not communicate because of the language difference. I am sure that any red-blooded male would have taken charge. I knew the biology of course and what I should do: but I had no inclination or wish to do so. It just was not in me. I had had enough to drink so that I at least tried to be the man but it just did not happen and, to be honest, I am sure she realised my heart was not in it so she did not help much. Basically, we gave up: we sat around for a while, but of course we could not chat, so we sort of just dallied. After all, I was in no hurry to be first back: I still had to keep up appearances!

After a respectable time I followed her back to the lounge where some of my colleagues were already sitting with a drink, each with a smile and lost in his own thoughts. One by one each returned to the group, ordered a drink and started chatting. No one spoke of what went on behind the closed doors so, for all I knew, everyone had had the same experience I did. I remained deep in my own thoughts as the lounge filled up again and the girls came back in to keep us company, as they waited for new customers to arrive and we prepared to leave.

A taxi was called and we moved on to the next bar, where we broke up into smaller groups. At no time did anyone make any comments about what had transpired earlier apart from the basic: "She was a great fuck." Of course there was no romance: it was pure animal instinct and something I could not relate to at any level. I found it all quite strange and degrading.

I was not a typical 'red-blooded male' and was certainly different from any of my colleagues, as I am sure many were already becoming aware. I had no interest in sport, football or any of those other male pastimes. I had nothing in common with the people I spent time with except work and an appreciation of good food and wine. I could pass the time and communicate at one level but I could not bond with men my own age and I was finding it harder as time went on. I was not a 'man's man' - I was something totally different. I was an undiagnosed transsexual, suffering from extreme Gender Dysphoria but still unwilling to acknowledge this; I was already on a downward spiral.

The second incident, a year later, was far more in keeping with the female inside me, although it did gain me some kudos from my male companions. The itinerary was the same as before; this time, however, I made sure I stayed away from the more adventurous of my companions. I was still there to enjoy myself and this time I knew what to expect and so could arrange the Saturday evening to suit myself.

I did not go out with the majority as I had done previously, instead spending more time on my own exploring the area and just enjoying the balmy weather. My colleagues did not miss me. I came across others in our party at various bars along the seafront and we sat, had a drink and chatted. Unlike the previous visit, however, I did it my way and regularly moved on.

I finally met a colleague some time after midnight and we decided to go and have a final drink prior to returning to the hotel. We walked along the seafront and heard loud music coming from a small club. It sounded great, a salsa beat, and we went in. I cannot express the emotion and sheer sensuality of watching young people with natural rhythm performing this dance in its true form. We ordered drinks and just watched in sheer awe.

The patrons were not locals: they were generally from North Africa, out for an evening's enjoyment before starting work again the following day. The holiday season was closing and this was one of the last nights they would party like this for some time. English was spoken by many, so we could communicate, insofar as the loud beat would allow, and had a wonderful time. We stayed till the club closed and left at about four o'clock into the pleasantly cool pre-dawn morning.

As it turned out we were almost next door to the hotel, so did not have far to go to get to our beds. I, however, was still on a high and really did not feel like returning to the room I shared, just to lie awake and listen to one of my companions snoring loudly. I knew I would not sleep anyway, so said I would go for a walk and said my farewell as my colleague made his way to get a few hours' sleep.

The next few hours will remain as one of the most beautiful experiences I have had in my life, one which, to me, is a testament to my inner true feminine being. I looked around the bay to see Palma Cathedral in the distance, overlooking the old town and the sea, and decided I would make that my destination. It was a good two or three mile walk but I knew I was capable. Pre-dawn is a wonderful time to be alone and to just think; walking along the coast with the cool sea breeze in my face just added to the experience; I was entirely on my own.

This was a complete contrast to the sensuality of the club I had just left. There was almost total silence except for the quiet rush of the sea on the pebble beach to my right. I was left to my own thoughts and drifted with the rhythm of my steps as I drew closer to my goal. I had my second wind and certainly was no longer tired; the whole experience was like a stimulant to my tired and jaded system. The stars in the clear sky slowly extinguished as the dawn lightened and I made it my goal to reach the cathedral in time to watch the sun rise over the blue Mediterranean Sea.

I finally turned left and entered the old part of the city. Narrow streets enclosed me as I started the walk up the steep hill toward the cathedral and I lost sight of the sea, although the slowly brightening sky could still be seen overhead.

The yellow stone walls of the cathedral eventually rose beside me as I continued my journey. I still had the streets to myself, the odd cat being my only companion. I walked around a corner into a small plaza and there before me I could see the sea again and the clear blue grey of the false dawn. There were a last few glimmering stars which were slowly extinguishing as the sun awoke; I had made it in time.

I walked across the last few yards of the plaza toward the parapet wall surrounding the perimeter of the cathedral, overlooking an almost sheer drop down to the coastal plain and the sea. The sun had not yet risen although the whole of the distant horizon was alight with the promise of its impending brilliance in a cloudless sky. The parapet was low and wide so I was able to sit on the top, draw my knees up to my chin to protect against the chill of the incoming sea breeze, and watch in awe as the sun slowly appeared, bringing a new day to life.

My only companion was a small black and white cat sitting on the parapet a few yards away, also catching the first warmth of the day. We communed silently for about half an hour as I just sat in silence with my own thoughts and let the stress, depression, worry and hurt I was dealing with wash away. It was like a cleansing ritual, a once in a lifetime occurrence, a new dawn and a fresh start as the warmth from the new sun slowly relieved the chill of the early morning.

The city behind me was waking as more people started the day early. The cathedral area was deserted apart from me and the cats; it was still too early for the first service of the day. The sun had risen and it was time I collected myself and went back to my companions, although most would still be fast asleep. The walk back was pleasant but did not fill me with the peace and contentment

I had felt earlier. I was journeying back to the reality of my life as it then was and to the pressures of daily living. On returning to the hotel the cafe next door was open and one of my colleagues was there having coffee so I joined him. It must have been about 7am, so not an unreasonable time to be up for those of us who were early starters at work.

He smiled as I told him of my adventure and wished me luck in staying awake for the rest of the day and into the following night, when we had booked a table at a good restaurant. I was spiritually refreshed but physically tired and knew that the next twenty-four hours or so would be hard. There was no way I could go to bed now, so I had to do a full forty-eight hours awake. I managed the challenge and slept the whole way home on the aeroplane the next morning. That was to be my last trip, as work politics, my own state of mind and perhaps the realisation of my colleagues that I had serious problems meant that I was not invited to attend again. I am so glad I had the opportunity to have that experience on the parapet; I often wonder how the cat felt.

My mother was still alive at this time and so I still felt bound by my promise so long ago about my dressing and about never doing it again. Of course I had done it: I could not deny my true self. I had, though, kept it almost entirely to myself and, barring a few special exceptions, had not been seen in public. I felt I had largely kept to the spirit of the promise. Life was getting harder for me to deal with and I was heading for a breakdown, as I slowly but surely realised I could not continue living a lie and would have to do something about it.

The sunrise had refreshed my spirit and gave me time to contemplate my future and what it was that I had to do to get back on track. Mum died a year later, allowing me then to make those decisions and finally to take the first steps on my journey toward inner peace and a new life.

The family enjoyed my success, particularly in the early days. We had holidays abroad, enjoyed eating out, the house was well-decorated and the furniture of good quality. Yet we were missing one major element to be a completely happy family: love and affection between the parents. I was cold and emotionless, and it showed.

My life from 1999, when my mother died, until 2005 when I took those first steps to freedom, was quite miserable. Mum died suddenly at home, after a long illness, and it affected me deeply. My relationship with my mother was always one of distant love; we were never a touchy-feely family and rarely cuddled; however, there was deep love and affection between us. She may not have agreed with many of my life decisions but she always stood by me; after all, it was my life and I lived by my own decisions not hers.

I know both she and Dad were concerned about how young and inexperienced I was when I first got married but they kept it to themselves. I also suspect it was the same when I moved directly from one failed marriage into the second relationship without a break. I am sure she was only too well aware that there were deep emotional troubles in my life, following on from what she knew about my childhood. It was something we had never spoken about as adults and I will regret that forever. She never knew Kirstie and I would like to think that she would accept and love her daughter as much as she loved and supported her son.

She died at home in her favourite chair, sitting next to Dad, and was finally at peace after a long and draining illness. Dad was, of course, devastated when he called me. I left home immediately and drove the eighty miles to meet him at the hospital, where we said goodbye to mum together; it was a sad and emotional time for us both.

I took a final few minutes on my own to make my farewell. I never saw her again, as I did not go to the funeral parlour when she was 'laid out'. Unlike David I am not a religious person and do not acknowledge openly a holy presence, God if you like, but I do feel that there is something there about which we know little. I did not voice my feelings to her but they were in my thoughts. I would like to think that she was now aware of the troubles in my life and at this unique time knew what was going on. I know she was there in some way and was happy that I would eventually reach my own place of contentment. I am sure she still looks over my shoulder even now and is, I believe, happy for me.

David flew over from Australia to officiate at Mum's funeral. She was only in her 70's and so many friends and family were there. It was the most beautiful ceremony I have ever attended and was also the first time I had heard my brother in his official capacity.

It was not a conscious or immediate decision, after mum's death, to then make the changes in my life that I did. I cannot say for certainty that I was actively aware that I could move on after making that unspoken promise to Mum all those years ago about my cross dressing. It was only later, after comments from friends, and when talking to my counsellor, that the pieces finally fell into place. I was free from that promise when Mum died and could openly make those decisions in my life that I had buried so deeply within.

This, of course, left Dad on his own to eventually meet his daughter and I regret that only too often; I am sure that, with mum's help and support, he would have found it easier to come to terms with my transition. Sadly I will never know how that would have worked out.

Chapter 11

Learning to live as a female 24/7 and a holiday.

I moved out of the family home a few days before I told my father what was to happen. Jean was glad to see me leave, although at that time she was still being as supportive as she could. I had spent the last few months sleeping downstairs on the pull-out guest bed and had turned the dining room into my room as best I could.

The children were accustomed to the fact that their parents were now leading totally separate lives and that they no longer shared the same bedroom. It had not been an easy few months for any of us and there was some relief that, at long last, the decision had been made and that I would move out.

My move was a simple affair: I took just a suitcase with my clothes, both male and female, together with a few other essentials. I left almost everything behind, although I had agreed a list of articles I would take when I was able. I did not have far to go: only a few hundred yards to a house four doors down from where we had originally lived in the village. In some ways it was a homecoming for me as I knew not only the area but also the house into which I moved, having spent many evenings with friends in the living room there just a few years previously.

Jean and Sophie helped me to move in, as they also knew the house, and Chris was a mutual friend. It was as simple as that: no trauma or tears; those had been shed months previously. It was a time of calm acceptance, which was to change over the months as the sordid details of divorce and realisation were to creep into the equation. For now, however, I was glad that we were finally at peace – a peace which lasted long enough for Jean to finally meet Kirstie in the local pub only a month or so later.

My new home was just a double bedroom large enough for the bed, a wardrobe and chest of drawers, with a little room to move round the furniture; it did not take too long to get it all sorted out. At least I was in a house to which I was no stranger and where I had free rein. Had I moved into a stranger's house, I am sure it would have been much harder and I would have confined myself to the bedroom. This, however, was familiar territory and once we had opened a bottle of wine and had sat for a while in the lounge it felt no different to being in my own space. My wife and daughter stayed for a while but soon realised that this was now my home and that I had to settle in with Chris, my new landlady.

I agreed to contact them shortly and confirmed that Sophie was always welcome, although it would be best if she let me know when she intended to drop in. We adults were aware why this was necessary but she still did not know that it was Kirstie who had moved in and that I would now be leading the dual life of a male at work and a female for the remainder of the time. I could not afford to be found out by accident and so had to make it a priority to tell her.

I had agreed some basic ground rules with Jean. I would not be seen in the village dressed as Kirstie until we had resolved the issue with Sophie. In addition, I would always appear as Ken when she visited until the issue was resolved. These were not unreasonable conditions and I readily agreed; after all, Sophie's wellbeing was of the highest priority.

I sat chatting with Chris for some time as we sorted out the living arrangements. She was looking forward to me staying, as she had known me for so long and there was no strain in our friendship. She told me that she was looking forward to the new experience and to having a female friend and lodger for company.

The reason for the move out before actually telling Dad was simple and required a small but essential deception; Jean had no option but to agree with it for his sake. I had seen my GP in January and had requested that she refer me to the Charing Cross Gender Clinic, as I felt it was the right time to move on in my journey. The counselling had settled the matter in my mind and I was now sure what I had to do. I had received the initial letter from the clinic and my first appointment had been set for 14th June; it was my intention to attend as Kirstie and not as Ken. I knew this was not an essential requirement as far as the clinic was concerned particularly for the first appointment. I, however, was anxious to start my journey and felt that this was the appropriate place to do so.

My appointment was actually on the Thursday before I told my father the following weekend about my condition and about what I intended to do in the future. I could not 'officially' move out before telling him and so planned the small deception to make it as easy as I could for his sake. Having gone this far it seemed silly to drag out my last few weeks in the family home and so the decision was more or less made for me.

Thursday 14th June 2007 was a pivotal day in my life. I would take another huge step forward within the NHS system towards transition and, ultimately, reassignment surgery. Although, even at this stage, I knew that my surgery would be carried out elsewhere if I could possibly afford it. I needed various supporting documents to reach that stage, plus the appropriate guidance for my GP, so that she could prescribe hormone treatment for me. Alternatively, I could take a short circuit and follow the private route but had already determined that the expense would prevent this. I therefore had to take the NHS route and follow the directions and requests of others to ensure that all of the boxes were ticked, so that I could reach my final goal.

My appointment was for the early afternoon, so I had plenty of time to get myself prepared for this first, very important, assessment at the Charing Cross clinic. I had already been diagnosed with Gender Dysphoria so did not anticipate any real problems but still had to be careful in how I presented myself. I was still attending my counselling as a male and so this appointment was doubly important, as it would be the first time anyone in the medical profession would meet Kirstie.

I had changed my chosen name from Karen to Kirstie some years previously when I commenced my journey. I knew that I would eventually have to change my name by Deed Poll and live with it for the rest of my life. Karen had too many past memories and so I had reconsidered and changed to become Kirstie. Another more mundane reason was that my initials remained the same and therefore I could still use my credit cards and use my normal signature, irrespective of how I was dressed. It was a simple solution to a complex issue and I was happy with my choice. How many children hate the names they are given by their parents? At least I could now choose a name that I liked and with which I felt comfortable.

I took the day off work to prepare for this important occasion. I had been out in public before but always in company and at 'safe' locations. This would be a first, on my own and on public transport, as I would be using the train and underground to get to Hammersmith, where the hospital is located. It was scary but I knew I had to do it, otherwise I would remain in the closet forever and that was not an outcome I was prepared to consider.

I had already assembled a small but useable wardrobe of day clothes and a good quality wig. I was a red head in these early days and now had a workable knowledge of the application of cosmetics. I would be moving in the normal day-to-day environment of people who probably had never met a trans woman or even had any idea about the transgender lifestyle. I had to be seen to be as natural as I could.

I still had beard-growth to cover so a close shave was essential. I then dressed quite conservatively in a black business skirt suit with a white blouse. My hair was shoulder length and I applied minimal makeup. I took my time and eventually stood back to look in the long mirror. I was satisfied with the result; in my opinion a passable, middle-aged, smart business woman looked back at me and smiled. How I would pass in public was probably a different matter and I would find out in the next few hours just how good, or bad, I was.

It was mid-day when I left the house, so most people were at work and the street was empty. I had parked the car in the side drive, although I had to walk out of the front door which opened directly on to the street to get there. I stood at the front door for a few moments to gather my thoughts and to build up enough courage to walk out into the street in the village where I lived. I trusted to luck, took a deep breath and opened the door to my new life as I walked the few yards to the side of the house and into the drive where my car was parked. No one was around and no one saw the unfamiliar red haired woman walk out of the house where, as far as anyone knew, she had no right to be. It could have been extremely embarrassing had I been seen, as I still had to be formally introduced to village life as Kirstie

I was heading for a number of 'firsts' and each one was to be a challenge that I had to meet head on. I had just completed the first which was, in many ways, the easiest. It was how the rest of the world approached and dealt with me that was the great unknown.

My second challenge was the railway station, which was only a short drive away. It was busy so I ended up parking at roof level and then walking down the four flights of stairs. I was not wearing heels that were too high and managed this with some ease; practice, after all, makes perfect! I had not met anyone I knew so my confidence was slowly building as I became more comfortable with how I was dressed.

There is a massive difference between dressing to go into a safe transgendered venue compared with walking out in the street. I was nervous but knew I had to see this through on my own. Others I knew made this first journey with a confident friend to offer support; I had no one.

As I walked across the car park toward the station entrance I was becoming more self-conscious, wondering what others would see and think. The station was not too busy and I could avoid using the ticket office, where I would have to speak with someone, as automatic ticket machines were available. Getting the voice right is one of the greatest hurdles a transsexual will face. We are born with male vocal chords and even speak in a different manner to a woman.

Hormone treatment does not have any effect on the male vocal chords and male-to-female transitioners require speech therapy to learn to speak in a more feminine manner. I had not even thought about therapy at that stage and so still spoke with my masculine deep voice. It was my greatest concern and I did all I could to avoid speaking to others until I had become more confident and less concerned about what others thought.

I had no wish to put on a false high falsetto as in my opinion that just pointed directly at me, rather than allowing me to blend in, never mind the damage it can do to the vocal chords if unsupervised.

The sliding doors to the ticket area opened automatically as I approached so I just continued on as if this were the most natural thing I did every day. Of course no one turned to look: I was just another passenger entering the station. I walked to the ticket machine, purchased my ticket and walked through the barriers onto the platform to wait the ten minutes or so for the next train. Even the simple act of standing in one place, waiting with a few other passengers for the train, took on the nature of yet another test: would anyone notice, or say something to me?

I don't know about anyone else but in situations like this I like to 'people watch' and observe who or what is around me. I could see the middle aged man on my right doing just that. He paused as he looked at me, while I stood still, looking straight ahead so as not to turn and stare him out; I did not need any confrontation or unnecessary embarrassment. He looked a bit longer than just a passing glance and then turned away. Had I been clocked or had he just noticed an attractive red head on the platform with him? I would like to think it was the latter but somehow, at that stage in my transition, I doubt it.

The rest of my journey was more of the same. The trains and the underground were not too busy, and people were looking around, but no one took much notice of me. There were no double-takes or sniggering behind a hand, actions I would have to deal with in the months ahead as I learned to move in the real world. I was to make many mistakes with my wardrobe and presentation but did my best always to learn from them and, I have to say, I have had a smooth transition compared to others I know or have heard of. In many ways I would like to think it was due to my confidence and determination to succeed. I did not hide but instead just did my best to brazen it out and call the onlookers' bluff: in most cases it was they who turned away rather than me.

I learned that it was safer to be in a busy environment, where people just get on with what they are doing and take no notice of others around them. I was to prove this to a friend later on, when she asked me to accompany her out for the first time. She was scared to do it on her own and felt very self-conscious.

She asked if I knew a quiet place we could go and have a bite to eat. I explained that in quiet places she would be looked at and people would be curious so I asked her to trust me; she agreed with some trepidation. It was a Friday night so we went somewhere I considered safe (other than a specialist transgender venue or club) for a first time out. I suggested we go to Covent Garden in London which was, of course, packed with tourists and others out for a good time.

She thoroughly enjoyed herself after the first few minutes of fear and was in her element as we went window shopping and stopped for an Italian meal next to the opera house. She walked tall and proud, even gaining admiring glances. It worked, and I was able to prove that crowds are safe; it was a lesson learned. The only downside to that evening was that I had inadvertently parked the car in a 'Residents Only' space. It cost me £110 for the release fee and a one hour wait! Never mind: her happiness more than made up for the loss.

I arrived at the clinic in good time, without any mishap and feeling very pleased with myself. My first solo trip out in the world was over and I felt confident that I could now do it anytime and anywhere. The clinic is separate from the main hospital, located on the first floor above a shop, with its entrance in a quiet side street. I walked confidently to the door, pressed the bell and waited while the CCTV checked me out. I answered the call point with my name and the time of my appointment and was buzzed in.

I checked in at the reception desk and then made a quick visit to the ladies; I had to ensure that I was presentable enough to make a good first impression. I sat for a few minutes in the empty waiting room before being called in to see the psychologist who would assess my needs and my present location along the journey to transition.

The fact that I had already been in gender counselling for over a year was a great bonus and, as I had arrived dressed as my feminine self, I showed I was serious. The route was explained, as were all of the various stages I would have to complete before being allowed to progress. The good news was that my transsexual status was in no doubt. Before I could go much further within the NHS system, though, I would have to change my name and all of my documentation. Even then I would not be considered for hormone treatment until I could demonstrate that I had changed my way of life and was now living and working as a woman. I then had to live and work in the female role for a minimum of twenty-four months before I would even be considered for surgery.

All this was in accordance with the international standards of care, with the exception of the requirement in the UK for a twenty-four month 'Real Life Experience'; the international standards only require a minimum of twelve months but the NHS sets the bar even higher. It was a lot to consider but I was determined and I knew it was the right decision for me.

I was glad that my GP had sought help elsewhere in the first instance. I was also happy that I was already seeing my gender counsellor every six weeks, as each appointment at the clinic would be about six months apart because of the long waiting list. The clinic was very busy and had limited resources, so it was made clear that to miss an appointment without good reason or prior notice could lead to me losing my place on the programme. If that happened I would need a new referral from my GP and would have to start again. The rules are quite strict and there are many serious decisions to consider. In one sense it is no wonder that so many choose the self-medication route and take other short cuts where they can, but this was not the way I wanted to go.

The meeting with the psychologist went well: we looked at my life history and discussed in some detail the nature of my feelings. My next appointment was set for November, five months later, when I would see the head clinician and psychiatrist. The clinic insists on at least two assessments before a formal diagnosis is made. At that stage I should then receive the confirmation that I was indeed transsexual. That would enable me to make further progress within the system. As our meeting ended she did say encouragingly that she saw no problems as far as I was concerned. I was given a piece of paper and directed to go to the main hospital for a full blood screening, to provide base levels of my hormones and other important information.

Relief washed over me, followed by the realisation of just what this journey was going to entail. There were so many hurdles I had to jump successfully before I could progress. I could understand why some take different, in some ways riskier or more expensive, routes through the transition process, and do what they can to avoid the NHS 'red tape'. I, however, am different and if I decide to follow a path I tend to stay on it without too much deviation.

It was to cause me some distress in later months but I am glad that I did stick to the 'proper' route, at least until a much later stage of my journey. The challenges are there to protect those taking this journey; we have to prove in every way that we are being true to our nature, and that our decisions about our future plans are not only genuine but also carefully thought-out. In the end the surgery cannot be reversed and, if a mistake has been made, the results on an individual's physical and mental health can be disastrous. On the other hand, for those who truly need to achieve the congruence of mind and body, who need to match their physical appearance with what goes on in their heads, then the ultimate goal of sex reassignment surgery can alleviate a lifetime of misery.

With all the checks and balances which are built into the international standards system, it is possible to stop at any point; the individual can step off the path for a while if the future looks too difficult, for the transition process is truly daunting and uncomfortable, incurring many material and emotional losses. Getting back on track after a pause can then be difficult, but it is not impossible. Some even decide that the journey is actually not for them; they decide to return to living in their birth gender, which may well have been the right one after all. It is better to opt out like this than to go through with surgery in too much haste, and then to regret what is irreversible for the rest of one's life.

The red tape is also there in an effort to weed out those who, for example, try to avoid proper medical supervision, or who hope to obtain hormone treatment without needing or intending to go further; there are those who take cross-sex hormones to satisfy a fetish or other sexual desire. These people live in the 'grey' areas of our transgendered spectrum and are not in reality transsexual.

After my meeting with the psychologist ended I left the clinic and walked across to the hospital for my blood test. It was a good half-hour wait and I perhaps drew more looks here than anywhere else I had been all day. I was getting tired: it had been a long and emotional day and I suspect that the strain was beginning to show. Nevertheless I made it through and was pleased when the lady taking the sample called me "Madam"! I suspect she was well-used to transsexuals arriving for the initial blood test and it was second nature for her; the paperwork, after all, still showed my sex as male.

The journey home was much the same as the journey there, just a bit more crowded. I made it out of London before the rush hour proper, for which I was very grateful. I could not imagine standing inches apart and face-to-face with some man on the underground; too much could go wrong it that instance. I got back to the house in good time before the street became busy with homecoming workers.

The whole experience had been a wonderful eye-opener. I discovered that I could easily pass in the street without incident and realised I actually had little to worry about.

Of course I still had to tell my father at the weekend and that was a difficulty I did not relish. However, as I have already described, it was not as bad as I feared and was put behind me. I had already moved out into my new home, leaving that final and perhaps greatest challenge: telling Sophie. I really was not looking forward to that but knew it had to be done very soon.

I settled into my new surroundings quite quickly and easily. Being with someone I had known for many years made it so easy. I still went to work as Ken; it was far too early to consider changing at work and, like many before me, that would be the last major obstacle to cross. I came home and, more often than not, changed into comfortable female-cut jeans and a blouse. Of course there were times when I wanted to enjoy my freedom and I would dress in a skirt and blouse, put on a wig and some make up but these occasions were not the norm. I also had to think about visitors to the house and especially about Sophie, who could drop in unexpectedly.

Chris was happy to call me Kirstie, allowing me to begin my new life relaxed and contented. This dual life, as Ken at work and Kirstie at home, could not last for long though. I soon had to start living in the real world as Kirstie, not just behind closed doors. I had to get to the point of telling Sophie very soon.

I chose my moment and spoke to Jean about telling our daughter. At first she refused to let it happen, expecting me to wait another seven years until Sophie was eighteen, and could make up her own mind like her sisters. I, of course, could not agree to this. Another seven years of living a lie, and of maintaining a dual life, would certainly be my downfall into massive depression or worse. I argued my case and eventually she gave in, acknowledging the fact that it would have to happen before I was seen and the gossip started. My landlady, Chris, was totally trustworthy but we had neighbours and I would inevitably be seen sooner or later.

It was towards the end of July, only a few weeks after I had moved out, when I found myself walking the few hundred yards back to the family home in the evening to talk to Sophie. I had no idea how I was going to do this but knew for certain that it was not going to be easy and would likely end in tears or even worse. What if she disowned me and never wanted to see me again? That was the worst I could imagine.

I knocked at the door and Jean let me in. Sophie was out in the park with her friends. I was left in no doubt that Jean disagreed with this but she realised that I also was not for turning away from my goal: I had to be true to myself; I had to be Kirstie in the village and elsewhere in public. Perhaps she felt backed into a corner, or that I was being unreasonable staying in the village. Part of me feels that she may have had a point; but we had discussed every aspect so many times and I felt I had already made concessions. I was determined to stay close to my daughters and to be there is they needed me, no matter how hard the early stages would be. I rang Sophie's mobile:

"Hi, it's only me. Could you come home for a bit? Mum and I have something to explain to you."

I felt I could sense her fear as she replied:

"Yeah. Be back in ten".

I sat in what was no longer my living room, on furniture that was no longer mine, and waited. Jean sat opposite me. Her fear, impotence and anger at this situation I had put her and our daughter into were almost tangible. I, though, knew in my heart that it would work out in the end, no matter how tough the journey. I had to do this, and most likely hurt Sophie, before I could make it better for us all.

Sophie came in and sat down next to her mother, looking for support and comfort; after all I was the one who had left. There was silence as she looked at me expectantly; wondering what was so important that we should ask her to come inside on what was a glorious July evening.

"I have to tell you something about the reason why mum and I have separated," I began.

"OK." I could see the concern on her face as she wondered what it was I was going to say.

As with other events I tried to be as simple and sympathetic as I could. I obviously got it wrong because as soon as I said:

"..... I am a woman born in a male body and can no longer live like this,"

she burst into tears, dashed out of the room, ran upstairs and locked herself in the bathroom. I sat there, stunned into silence. We were all on an emotional high and I had no idea what to do next. I looked at Jean questioningly, wondering if she knew. I had expected a reaction of some kind but this was perhaps more extreme than anticipated. She had shouted "I never want to see you again," as she had stormed out. I was devastated.

I followed her upstairs in the hope of talking to her again. The bathroom door was locked, so all I could do was sit down on the floor and try to talk through it. It was not to be: she refused to say anything, telling me to "Just go away." I had no option but to leave and hope that, once she thought about it, she would realise I was still there for her. I just could not continue to live a lie and was doing what was not just best for me, but would be best for us all in the long run.

I left for the short walk back, feeling a total shit and wondering if she would ever forgive me. I got home and told it all to Chris over a mix of wine and tears. She was sympathetic but could say or do nothing to solve my problem. I was once again an emotional wreck with nowhere to go.

The only positive was that Sophie at least now knew and I could only hope she would be able to come to terms with the reasons behind her parents' separation. On a personal, and perhaps selfish, note it finally opened the door for me to be myself in public. Of course I had no intention of doing so immediately; I would give her some time but I had to move forward as best I could.

I was worried about Sophie but did not want to make contact. She had to make up her own mind and I felt the less I interfered, the better it would be. It was less than a week before I received a text from her asking if she could come to see me. I replied immediately and arranged for her to drop in after school.

In readiness for her arrival I dressed simply in jeans and a blouse; I did not want to be overtly feminine. I was encouraged by her willingness to hug me when she came in. Of course she found it hard to understand what she had been told, but she listened intently as I tried to make it easier for her. It was a start and we have been able to build on it each day since. Our love saw us through and she has come to accept me as Kirstie and is now happy to be seen with me in public, even enjoying our shopping trips together and giving me occasional fashion tips.

Sophie suffered horribly with bullying and nasty comments at school when it became public knowledge. This was to last for almost two years and there was absolutely nothing I could do to help. She was made to pay for my choice in life and I have become so proud of her and of how she dealt with this. Her teachers at school have told me just how protective she has been toward me;

she often had to stand up to others who, in reality, just did not understand and so used it as an easy way to hurt her. She asked me to tell her the correct vocabulary, so that she could explain to her friends' parents about how her father was changing. They were to be told the difference between a transvestite (the first thought of many) and a transsexual. I may not mix with many of the other parents, although I have now, four years later, been accepted by many of her friends and can at least speak to parents on the telephone when necessary. She no longer feels scared to bring new friends home, even though she lives permanently with me, rather than with her mother. It is her choice and I give her every support that I can. It is hard at times for us both but we manage and we communicate. I would go so far as to say that I possibly now have a better relationship with my daughter than many parents do. It has taken tears and pain to get here but I am so proud that we have made it through.

Sophie slowly learned to accept me as I was and got used to seeing me around the village or in the local pub in a skirt or dress, and wearing a wig to cover my otherwise still short and masculine hairstyle. It was always hard for her but she struggled through. She is still too young to really understand but in time I hope that she will do her own investigations and find out what I have also had to face. I hope that this story will be one of the references which she will come to use as she tries to understand what I have gone through in order still to be here and to be of help to all of my children.

I openly used social networks such as Facebook to let her and my other daughters introduce Kirstie to their friends. It was easier for the older two in many ways. They had a degree more maturity and their friends were more open to difference, so they did not suffer the bullying. I am so pleased that my daughters' friends were accepting; it has helped them and has also made my own journey that much easier.

I had at last told everyone in the family who mattered and could move forward on my journey but I still had to build on that foundation and improve the fragile bonds that had been retained. It was worth it: there was only one way to go as far as I was concerned and that was up.

Anyone else would just have to deal with my transition. The problems were theirs, not mine. This is an easy statement to put down now, so many years later, but at the time it was a very scary attitude to have. It was, however, the only approach I could take which would see me through the next four hard and difficult years.

The next decision I needed to make was to find the best way to become known as Kirstie in the village. Chris was more than willing to help and she knew far more people in the village than I did. As the pub was the centre of village life we felt it would be a good idea to tell the landlord that Kirstie would soon be dropping in.

The first step was to meet him and to let him know what was going to happen in the next week or so. Chris came with me for moral support and we chose a Saturday afternoon, which was usually quiet after the lunchtime rush. It was simply done and we sat in a quiet corner as I explained the whys and wherefores of being transsexual and what was to happen. My move out of the marital home was already common knowledge throughout the village but, as with everything else, the actual reason why was still generally unknown, although rumours were starting. I had to stop these quickly before things got out of hand.

The landlord listened attentively and asked a few questions; it helped that he was gay and so understood what it was to be like to be different. He thanked me for telling him before the event and assured me that his staff would be told and that I would be treated with the same respect and attention as I had always had as a regular in the pub.

We agreed that I would arrive to break the ice as Kirstie at a quiet time the following weekend. It may seem that I approached this in a very calculating manner, which is exactly what I did. I planned to make my transition as smooth as I could and to get as much support before the event as was possible. I obviously could not tell everyone in advance so I was still prepared for the shock value when I did step out; but the pivotal people such as the landlord were always warned in advance.

Duality is hard enough to deal with when one side is hidden from the world, as it had been for me all of my life up to this point. Leading an openly dual life was to become more stressful as time went by and it became a real struggle each time I had to change back and become Ken again on a Monday and on each weekday morning. That was to be in the future, though; my challenge for now was to find the courage to face people who had known me for many years as a male. It would be a shock for many and, for a few, a step too far, as they could not, or would not, accept the change.

The week leading up to my open entry to village life went much as always. Sophie started to drop in more often as she became used to my change and there was no longer any shock for her, as I still kept my clothing changes in the evenings low key.

Friday night was the prelude to my public appearance in the village. I did let Jean know what was to happen, as I did not want her to meet me unexpectedly. She was not happy naturally but by this time realised that I was serious in my intentions and that there was little she could do. She arranged to be out of the village on Saturday afternoon, taking Sophie with her, as she did not want to be associated in any way with my first trip out. I can understand her feelings now but at the time felt she was over-reacting.

I wondered what I should wear and discussed my options with Chris. My wardrobe was still, by comparison to today, small and I was also limited in my choice of wig. I stuck to what I felt was most comfortable; naturally I still wanted to look feminine but not overtly "in your face". After all, I wanted to join the community, not scare it. I settled for a blouse and jeans with low heel black court shoes. I felt feminine and, to me at least, I looked the part. I believed I would pass a glance but not necessarily close inspection. Chris gave me all of the support she could but of course had no real idea what was going on in my mind.

How could she? Our new relationship was still forming and she was learning to live with a transsexual who was someone she had known as a man for the best part of twenty years. It could not have been easy for her, although I think she thoroughly enjoyed the experience and was eventually to feel fully involved, even having great 'girlie' shopping days and lending me her clothes for special occasions. It was a great match and one which smoothed my transition so well.

Saturday came like any other in July, warm and sunny and, for me, scary as this was to be my debut in the real life of the village. I had done all I could to prepare others for my introduction as Kirstie. I woke early as I usually did, knowing that I had a few hours to prepare; I started with a hot shower and a close shave. I lounged around in my dressing gown for most of the morning, becoming more and more agitated as the realisation grew that, after today, there would be no going back. I had chosen to go to the pub around three o'clock, after the Saturday lunchtime rush. There would still be some customers there, of course, but I hoped that it would be quiet enough to let me survive this first experience without any major mishap.

I was ready in good time and Chris, like any good friend, sat me down in the lounge, turned on the music and put a large glass of chilled white wine in my hands; it was just what I needed to steady my nerves while we just chatted. Then it was time.

"OK, Kirstie are you ready? Let's go," said Chris, taking control.

I had little choice; I finished my wine, stood up, smoothed down my clothes and headed for the door, picking up my handbag on the way; my heart was pounding. I could not think about this too much. Indeed, I had walked out of this door dressed similarly only a few weeks previously but the circumstances were totally different; I was now walking out in full sight of the neighbours and in the company of Chris. It would be obvious to any who saw who I was, or so I felt.

The walk to the pub was no more than a hundred yards; the day was bright and sunny. Chris kept her own counsel as we walked, guessing that I would be in turmoil inside. She was right: I had butterflies throughout and was so nervous that I was sure anyone could notice me sweating. Going as Kirstie to a location where I was known by many as Ken was entirely different to going anonymously anywhere else.

The walk was uphill along the side of the pub to the junction with the main road; we rounded the corner and stood in front of the entrance doors. I stopped and looked at my goal, not sure that I really wanted to do this. Chris stood by my side and quietly said:

"In your own time Kirstie, you will be fine; it's not busy. Go in and walk straight through to the garden and I will get us both a drink."

I swallowed hard and stood up proud. I pulled open the door and walked into the coolness of the pub interior. Trying not to look around and draw attention to myself, I just walked towards the back of the pub and the door to the safety of the garden. I can't deny it: I was scared. I could not know who was there, or whether any of them would know me.

It was a pub frequented by many from outside the village so could even be full of people who had no idea who I was. I did not care. Luckily the garden was empty and I sat down to wait for Chris to arrive with the drinks. I chose a position as far from the door as possible but from where I could see who came and went. I had made it and without mishap! The relief was immense as all of the stress and tension drained away and I settled into my new life. Choosing this quiet time gave me the chance to settle myself in an environment I had known well for many years.

Chris obviously let the bar-staff know I was there and as they served her I am sure they made some comment, although I never knew what was said of course. I was obviously a topic of conversation now, I was public and the gossip would run through the village like wildfire. I was also very grateful that I was given some time to myself, to regain my composure and to get ready for whatever might happen next.

Chris came into the garden area carrying two glasses of wine. She put one in front of me and sat down. I took a grateful swallow of the chilled wine and sat back in relief.

"They know you are here so don't worry, no one will come and bother us. They know you need some space."

So we sat and chatted and I did my best not to worry about something that may never happen. In fact we were not bothered at all. I couldn't decide what was worse: to be ignored, or to be bombarded by the curious. I suspect that the former was the best for my first time out. We did not stay long and on leaving I did go to the bar and say thank you to the staff.

Unlike my entry, I was calm and smiling as we left the pub and took the short walk home. That was it: it had been so easy, although I knew that harder challenges were to come. It was now public knowledge and I would have to deal with the confusion, misunderstanding and even anger in the days and weeks to come.

My forays up to the pub came more often and in busier periods over the next few weeks. I slowly met the regulars; it was easier now, as the news had spread ahead of me. I was a curiosity, something I was at least used to, and after the first experience the rest fell into place quite easily. Over the months I had to deal with a variety of reactions. I was often stared at, but I could deal with that. Some told me how brave they thought I was – a sentiment I understand, but which is not necessarily fitting. Others wished me well but said that they could not deal with the change, effectively ending our friendship (if we had ever been friends) or at least our acquaintance. There was downright hatred, although never expressed directly to me; the woman in question was a staunch friend of my wife and told others in no uncertain terms what she thought of me.

I eventually found the courage to sit on a stool in the main bar and talk to the staff and anyone who was prepared to come and join me. Chris was a staunch supporter and did all she could to ease the way. I am very grateful for that support at a time of extreme difficulty for me.

Jean even managed once to meet me in the pub for a drink, doing the best she could to be supportive. At that time I believed that she meant it and I am pleased she did so; unfortunately it was not to last.

The only issue I ever had with the landlord was the time-worn problem that all trans people face over which toilet to use. I was living a dual life and so used the pub in both the male and female role, particularly in those early months. There was a degree of confusion among some of the regulars as to who or, indeed, what I was. I have to accept some of the blame for this, given that I visited the pub as both Kirstie and, less and less often, as Ken. With hindsight it would have been better if I had been consistent from Day 1 but, as all transitioners know, it simply is not possible to completely switch identity overnight. There are practical reasons why the 'old' identity has to be at least partially maintained.

One evening the landlord quietly took me to one side as I came out of the ladies' toilet, saying he had something to discuss with me. He told me that some of the female customers were unhappy about me using the ladies'. He was sympathetic and did his best to cushion his request that I did not use that toilet. He understood my predicament but he had his customers to think about. I was not upset and said there was no way I would use the male toilets when openly being Kirstie but agreed not to use the ladies. I lived only a few yards away and was quite happy to go home if the need arose. He also assured me in no uncertain terms that, when the time came, and I transitioned fully, he would support my right to use the ladies', no matter who complained. We parted amicably and, true to his word, when I transitioned fully, I was never barred and no comment was ever made again.

The choice of which toilet to use is a constant problem for a trans person. We should not be discriminated against and for those like me, who were in the process of transition, there should be no reason why one cannot use the ladies'. I did so often when using public toilets. I behaved correctly and was never challenged. I carried a letter from my GP stating that I was transsexual and was living my real life experience which was to become a permanent change. I always carried this letter in case I was ever stopped by the police or anyone similarly in authority; luckily I never had to produce it. In the end common sense is all that is required. If in doubt I always used the unisex disabled facility, if it was available, although there is no legal reason why I should have had to do so.

Life went on and I became part of the village scene. I settled in and eventually my daughters were able to meet me in public and have a drink with me as well. I never forced the situation: it was always their decision. I was so happy the first time that Sophie had the courage to come with me; now it is second nature for her.

There was no way we would ever have a family holiday again and in some ways I felt that my responsibility had changed. My older two daughters were, in most ways, on their own but I was still legally responsible for Sophie, who remained living with her mum. She visited often and stayed over at weekends, so our relationship was improving.

I needed to get away from all of the stress and strain I had just gone through. Going public is a necessity but one which drained every reserve of energy I had. I felt I needed a break away from everyone who knew me, and from all of the questions, sideways glances and comments. I was happy to hear from Chris that there were far more in the village who accepted me than those who could not. I saw this as a positive result when it could so easily have gone the other way and turned out to be disastrous. I could so easily have been vilified and made an outcast.

I had been moderating an online international transgender support and advice group for some months by this time. I learned a lot and also provided my own support and advice to others. My co-moderator was a Canadian who, at that time, was slightly unsure as to where she lay on the transgender spectrum, although has now fully transitioned. We hit it off and, as I had with Linda a year or so before, we explored how we might improve our friendship. We spoke on the telephone and found we had a lot in common. in addition to our transgendered nature.

Before much longer she invited me to visit her in Montreal, an offer which I gratefully accepted. In one way it was another blind leap into the unknown but, having done it before, I felt it worth the risk. I was always so careful, controlling and organised in my working life so it was good to take risks occasionally and they have, I am glad to say, usually had a positive result.

All I had to do was arrange my flight and take some pocket money; everything else would be provided. She lived in the mountains north of the city, by a lake and surround by forest. It sounded idyllic and just what I needed, so I arranged to travel in August for ten days. When my family, particularly my wife, found out about my trip I was not flavour of the month. However, I was learning to look after my own wellbeing and did so without too much guilt. I needed this break in order to be able to continue with my journey. The added bonus was that I would be staying with someone who understood how I was feeling.

The holiday was a wonderful experience, although I had to travel as Ken as that was still the name in my passport. There is no way it would be possible to travel on a male passport when dressed as a female. The security arrangements required at modern international borders is such that it was not feasible. I wished it were otherwise but accepted that I had to travel as a male, although I carried in my luggage only female clothing and accessories. Goodness knows what would have happened had my bags been opened at customs but luckily I was spared that embarrassment.

It was an adventure: I was going to a foreign country, to spend over a week with someone I had never previously met. Was it a risk? Of course it was, but then again I was now taking a risk with my whole life, so why should another be a problem? There was even the chance that, when I arrived, she could have taken one glance and left me stranded at the airport, just as I could have done all those months before with Linda. I'm pleased to say that was not the case, we met, we quickly became friends and I had a wonderful experience over the next ten days, made even more enjoyable as I lived every hour of every day as Kirstie.

Her home was in the wilderness, a mile or so around a lakeside in the depths of natural forest. Within half an hour of arriving we had a swim in the lake; it was wonderful. I had arrived in Montreal at the height of summer and the temperatures were in the low thirties. I lived a wonderful life for those few days. I was taken around and visited the city; I had a canoe trip around the lake to see the beaver dams; I shopped and ate in the local restaurants. I had the holiday of a lifetime and it was a sad day when I had to say goodbye and board the aeroplane back home to the UK.

My life was on track. In only a few short months I had moved into a new home, had openly introduced Kirstie to the local community, had entered the NHS system for transition, and made great progress with my counselling. Most importantly, I had informed all of my family about my intentions; they all knew about my choice and were dealing with it, each in their own way, and each giving me a degree of support – some more than others. It was obviously hard for my children but they were coping; my brother was supremely supportive; my father was learning to deal with it; my friends were getting to know the new me. Jean, however, was another matter. As my life improved so hers deteriorated. I felt guilty for the deception over so many years; it was an inevitable emotion but one I had to confront.

Chapter 12

My 'wake': goodbye to Ken forever. Good times and bad

I returned from my Canadian break with recharged batteries and ready to face life at home once more. Now that I had started my official journey to transition I was anxious to progress as quickly as possible. That said, I had chosen to follow the carefully laid out path of the NHS route, which is slow but sure; it does its best to make sure there are no mistakes. I saw the chief clinician at Charing Cross and, as I had been previously advised, there was no question about my being transsexual: I would eventually be a suitable candidate for reassignment surgery, should I wish.

I was to visit Charing Cross a total of seven times over a two and a half year period. At each visit I moved forward another stage on my journey, some being easier than others, before being able to move on.

My counselling had continued throughout the interim period and we had reached the stage where I was sure what my motives and needs were. I knew that I would cause hurt to others but in the end it was my own wellbeing that had to be satisfied before I could look to helping those close to me once more. I was still attending these sessions as Ken, because I would go during the working day, leaving from the office and travelling directly into London. There was no opportunity to change and I knew that I would have to do something about this.

The months following my return from Canada, through to early 2008, were a time when I settled in to my new life. I became a 'normal' part of village life as the novelty started to wear off. I was always stared at, especially by strangers to the pub, but it was no longer an issue. Those who knew me and could deal with my change remained as friends and acquaintances; and those who could not drifted away, although they were always polite and made sure they said hello. There were also one or two diehards who wanted to remain friends but who could not bring themselves to call me Kirstie. I put up with this initially; after all it was a time of transition, of change, and it takes time. Now, four years later, it is something I do not tolerate. I have transitioned fully and Ken no longer exists, legally or in any other way.

Christmas that year, 2007, was difficult for us all. Relations with Jean were strained but not quite at breaking point, so we decided to try to have as normal a family time as we could manage. My father was invited as always and I agreed to go to the house on Christmas morning, to help cook the dinner. I provided the turkey and other essentials and my dad brought the crackers and other trimmings as usual. The whole idea was a mistake; the day was a strain from start to finish, and 'Happy Families' it was not.

No matter how hard any of us tried, the underlying troubles were never far from the surface. We all did our best, and no arguments ensued, but I know how glad I was when I said my farewells and went home that evening. I suspect it was the same for everyone. Dad stayed at the house, as he always stayed till the afternoon of Boxing Day at least, although I could tell he was not happy about it but there was no way I could put him up with me. We were trying to keep it as normal as we could for his sake and for that of the children but we failed miserably. I went back next morning for the traditional smoked salmon and bucks fizz for breakfast. Dad and I had breakfast on our own.

I was a stranger in what had been my home; the children stayed out of the way of their parents and did all they could to make it as easy as possible for their 'Grampa', but the lie was clear to all. I stayed long enough to ensure that Dad was packed and loaded for his journey home. He set off much earlier than was usual. We all stood at the front door to wave him off, knowing that this was an event that would never happen again.

The marriage and the relationship were over. After a short while I, too, went home. Chris was away with her family so I was on my own. I was sad but knew that there was to be no turning back, my mind was made up and my resolve was strong. I would see this through, no matter how hard and hurtful it would be for those closest to me. I am sure I had one or two more glasses of wine than was good for me before going to bed, unhappy but resolute.

2008 arrived and it was to prove a momentous year in my journey, as it was the year when I left my male persona behind forever; this is a critical time in my, and any other transsexual's, journey. It would be the year in which I would move from living a dual life to one which I had desired for so many years: one of living and working full time as female, as my true gender.

The year started well, with my first visit to counselling in January as Kirstie, instead of Ken. I had decided it was about time that I showed just how determined I was. It was so much easier now that I lived in my own space and now that the neighbours all knew about my life change. I decided to take the day off work and to attend as Kirstie, instead of going directly from work, where I had not yet transitioned.

Like other important dates previously I ensured that I was prepared and looked my best. There was no longer any worry about dressing to go out into the world at large. I was confident and felt comfortable in my new life.

The counsellor's office was in North London. I drove there, parked at a meter and walked the few hundred yards to the clinic door. It was all quite normal; I had no worries, concerns or nerves. I knew this was right and that this milestone was going to be met without incident. I went in and up to the reception window, as I always had. The receptionist did not even look twice; she took my details and directed me to the waiting room; nothing was any different. At the appointed time the reception door opened and my counsellor's face appeared as usual, inviting me to follow him upstairs for our session.

So far, everything had been just as before. The difference began with his small but significant hesitation as he saw me, and realised that I had come as Kirstie. His face broke into one of the broadest grins I had seen in a long time. I could see how happy he was for me to have made this major change and to have come to see him as my true self. We had discussed transition and all that it entailed for some time, so I knew how he felt and he knew that I had made up my mind. He just needed to see it for himself and today, 25th January 2008, was that day.

I smiled in return and followed him upstairs for what was to be one of the last sessions that we would have together. In one sense it was much like the others; after all I had already made my decision and he knew that. The fact that I had arrived in different clothing and now presented my female self was not as significant as you may think. It was, of course, still an important day but, as we had discussed on many occasions, the clothes do not matter as much as the person inside them. The clothes just helped others to identify who and what I was: I was Kirstie and I was female.

The session was very positive as we talked about my feelings and my plans. The next big hurdle in my way was the problem of how to transition at work. With that out of the way my journey would be well-established and I could begin hormone treatment. Unlike the private route to transition, where hormones are sometimes prescribed prior to full time transition, the NHS insists that the patient present a fully transitioned 24/7 lifestyle, including at their place of work if employed, before hormone treatment could be prescribed. I knew this was the case when I made my decision to follow this route; I just had no idea how hard I would find it. The session finished on a high and we agreed the date and time for the next appointment.

I was feeling good at this time as I slowly but surely started to tick the boxes which detailed my journey. As I crossed off each one there was another to take its place but, like all journeys, it was a case of "one step at a time". The next challenge – transitioning at work – was potentially going to be harder than telling my family and friends; when telling them there is hopefully a close bond of love and friendship to lessen the shock. It is no easier for them but they do have that cushion to help soften the blow and to alleviate the emotional trauma. Depending on the employer (for some are better than others) the only protection that is available to the transsexual at work is the legal one. With luck, one can hope that the company is prepared to be sympathetic and supportive in this rarely-encountered situation, where employers and personnel departments can often, like everyone else, be floundering in the darkness. Unfortunately that is not always the case although, as public awareness grows, it is becoming easier; nevertheless overcoming the hostility of work colleagues, if it occurs, is a problem which both the employer and the law find difficult to resolve.

At this time I was a main board director of the architects' practice, responsible for health and safety throughout the company, as well as for the external contracts of my own office's projects. My professional discipline required me to plan ahead, to know each step which needed to be taken, and the sequence of those steps. I had to be able to bring each project to a satisfactory conclusion and within budget. I needed to be adaptable and to marshal the necessary skills should the unexpected happen. I was proud of my professional ability and I applied these skills to the planning of my transition journey. Nevertheless, planning the details of how to make my permanent transition happen at my workplace, as well as in my private life, was a challenge different to any I had previously encountered.

The company was not large: it had about fifty employees and therefore had no separate personnel or human resources department. In bigger organisations it is often easier for transitioners such as I to deal initially with the HR department, whose staff are bound to maintain privacy and confidentiality. In my company I had no option other than to go to the top, to the chairman and owner of the practice. The fact that I had known him for more than twenty years should have stood me in good stead, but he was 'old school'. My work had already suffered, perhaps through my depression and my domestic difficulties, as well as because of the sheer complexity of living a dual life. My performance figures (for everything is measured on spreadsheets these days) were not good but, in my defence, we did not know at that stage that we were on the brink of a major recession – the whole industry was struggling and slowing down.

This was not the best of times in which to drop the bombshell which I planned. Clearly I was aware of the full story, but others, including the chairman, would at best have only known of two out of three factors which were influencing my performance: the whole construction industry was suffering; and my family difficulties might have been picked up by some; but the true reason for those 'family difficulties' was known, within the company, only to me. I now had to summon up the courage to be honest and to tell the chairman the full story.

I had already caused a small stir the previous summer, when I took the decision to have my ears pierced. I was fed up with clip-ons. Earrings for pierced ears simply look better, they are more feminine, and they come in a much wider range of designs. They are also much more comfortable. As I was living an increasing part of my life in the female role I wanted to look my best and that, of course, included the need to wear earrings.

True to my long-term planning skills I had looked ahead, and had decided to pierce my ears prior to going to Canada; I would need to allow six weeks for the holes to heal. I went with my daughter Kat to a studio where she had previously worked. I wanted the smallest studs I could have, which meant that the usual piercing gun could not be used. At the specialist studio my ears were pierced the old fashioned way, with a hypodermic needle, and very small studs were inserted. Unfortunately for me, even the smallest and simplest steel balls are quite visible. I had chosen my time well, with most of my staff on holiday; also, it being summer, most clients were away and my work-days were mostly spent in the office where I hoped that I would not be discovered.

I reached five weeks without discovery and thought I had made it. I would soon be able to take them out during the working day, without the holes closing. I had not reckoned on the Managing Director dropping in on his day off to collect some papers. I could see the double take but he said nothing at that time. I knew I had been caught out but I hoped he would take a modern approach, for a good many men have a single stud or earring. No chance. If I had done just one ear I may have been able to pass; but both ears were a step too far.

A little while later I was asked to go to the London office for what appeared to be a legitimate and genuine meeting. I went, hoping that my little foible had gone undetected. The other staff there noticed, of course, and quite probably were making comments behind my back, but I was senior to most of them, so nothing was said out loud. I carried on with my day until:

"I don't care what you do in your private life but earrings at work for a person of your seniority are totally out of order. Get them out. The staff are all making comments." The MD was very direct.

I admit it: I had pushed my luck. I was also aware of the rules against discrimination and that I could fight the case if I really wanted. However, knowing I had greater battles in front of me, I nodded agreement and said nothing, probably surprising him in the process. I was prepared to risk taking them out a few days early and hoped the holes would not close up; I could always put the studs back in every night and at week-ends.

I don't know what he actually thought about my earrings but, after transition, he did become a supporter of my cause and we never mentioned the event again. I suspect that the same can be said for the majority of the staff, once they had come to terms with the reason why I had done it.

It was now clear to me that I had an uphill task to complete; I began my detailed planning. I knew that I would have the full backing of the law, in principle at least, and if I went fully prepared I should be able to get over the first hurdle. I did my homework and copied a document "Gender Reassignment – A Guide for Employers", produced by the Department of Trade and Industry in 2005. This set out the legal requirements for an employer to follow, gave some appropriate advice on the best way for a company to administer the transition, and provided links to sites with further information.

I then made an appointment to see the chairman on a one-to-one basis; he requested that a second director attend, to which I agreed. I drove to the head office for the meeting at the end of January 2008, where there were just the three of us in the board room. We quickly got down to business. The chairman began:

"Thanks for coming up, Ken. I was going to request a meeting shortly anyway, to look at your figures. However, you have asked for the meeting so it's all yours to start."

I thanked him and opened with a request: "What I am about to say is of a highly sensitive nature. I would be grateful if you would treat it in total confidence."

That got the meeting off to a good start and my colleagues were clearly wondering what the hell I was about to tell them. As always in such a situation, their worst guess did not even come close to the truth.

"Of course. Please continue," the chairman replied.

"I have been suffering from an uncommon medical condition all of my life and find that I can no longer keep it a secret. I have to do something about it otherwise I am heading for a breakdown. I know that my performance has been less than satisfactory recently and perhaps after this disclosure you will understand why."

That set the scene and I was the centre of attention. I was scared to go on, as my whole working life, and my ability to proceed with my plan depended on how the next few minutes went and on how my superiors received the news. I swallowed hard and, as I had on many occasions before, just went for it:

"I am transsexual and have been in counselling for a number of years. I have a formal diagnosis of Gender Identity Disorder and I am now progressing to transition from the male that you see to the female that I actually am."

Shock and stunned silence! If only for a few seconds I could sense both of those reactions passing through their minds. I am also sure they realised that I would not be there exposing myself in this way unless I was very sure of my legal position.

They were quite correct. I was indeed well aware of my legal situation and of just how well I was protected when undergoing transition in the workplace. No doubt an unscrupulous employer could circumvent the legislation but I knew that my employer was an honourable person and would hear me out.

"That's quite a shock Ken, to say the least. Can you please elaborate some more?" the chairman asked.

I spent the next forty minutes or so explaining what it was like to be transsexual and what I now intended to do to resolve the situation. I explained the legal ramifications and presented them both with a copy of the document I had previously printed, with a polite request that they read it through.

"So, what is it that you want us to do and what are you plans?" he asked.

"I wish to transition at work and to be known as Kirstie. We need to agree a timescale which is suitable for me, the company and my clients. I understand how sensitive this is and, that if not treated appropriately, it could damage client relations. I would like your approval, and support, to be able to see the major clients face-to-face and to tell them of my intentions in advance. In this way I hope I can reduce the shock and also explain what is going on."

The obvious next question was:

"What timescale are you considering?"

This was a hard one and even then I had not fully worked out a detailed timetable; there was still a lot to do.

"It is still January, so I will need a few months to sort everything. I must first change my name by deed poll and then all the official documents, my bank account, and such like. I would like to think that April would be a suitable month. The actual date can be agreed closer to the time."

"That seems to be a bit quick but I imagine that you have it all planned. I can't see that you're likely to change your mind. I would like to have time to consider the company's position in relation to our clients and then I'll come back to you," the chairman responded.

"That's fine. I don't wish to be unreasonable but now that I have started this I don't know that I will deal with delays very well," I replied, standing my ground.

"Alright. We will keep in touch over the next few weeks and make our decision then. We have a board meeting next month. Is it your intention to tell the other board members then?"

"Yes. That is my plan. Until then I would ask that this remains entirely between the three of us here in the room." I felt I needed to remind them of how sensitive the information I had disclosed was.

"Of course I understand your position. And please don't worry: this stays here between us," he replied. "If that concludes your agenda there is one point which I had originally wished to bring up but your revelation would appear to put my concerns to one side, for a while at least. I now understand what has been happening for you personally. I had intended to discuss your own performance and that of your office, but I will put that aside for a while until this is resolved."

"Thank you, I understand your concerns and I honestly believe that, when this is resolved and I am back on an even keel, I will be able to recover my position."

I left the office and headed back south to my own offices, knowing that I had not only achieved my goal but had gone beyond the point of no return. The next challenge would be the board meeting, to be held a few weeks later, when I would tell the rest of my colleagues. That was going to be just as hard.

What the chairman and the MD did not know was that I had already told my secretary, who had been with me for the last fifteen years. She knew it all and had agreed to support me through the next very difficult months at work.

It was a few weeks later when:

"That concludes the agenda for the board meeting. Is there any other business?"

"Yes, I have some important news to tell the board....."

I had planned it all, even down to writing a personal letter to each director. To each letter was attached the document I had presented to the chairman. As before, it was a shock to everyone, but they all had the decency to hold back on any immediate comments; some asked for a few clarifications and each promised to read the document and to come back with any questions. I also told them that my secretary had been informed and had agreed to answer any initial questions on my behalf. This was a task she performed exceptionally well for the next few months, while clients were slowly but surely advised of my change in status.

I was feeling very positive and I was now determined to proceed at a pace to suit me. I had laid out my programme, the first step of which was my name change in March. I would then inform the main clients and after that I would complete my transition at work in April. I set it all down, line by line, as I wanted there to be no doubt about what was going to happen. My concession to the company for the support I anticipated, and in order to lessen my profile, was to resign as a director. I retained my own office autonomy though, as well as the responsibility for company-wide health and safety matters. It suited everyone and the meeting broke up a little while later. A few of the others had a quiet word with me saying they would be in touch. It was too much to expect them to even begin to understand what I was facing and so I left it at that and went home.

I took that first step and on 1st March 2008 legally changed my Christian name to Kirstie, retaining my middle name and my surname, although I did not formally use my new name until I transitioned and left my male identity behind. In the intervening weeks I started the long process of changing all of my official documentation, starting with my passport. I used the letter from my

GP to support my applications, along with the deed poll. It was not difficult to do: it was just time-consuming.

I selected a few key clients whom I would personally tell about my change; the rest would have to deal with it as and when they learnt of it. I had known the main clients for many years and so they received my news in much the same way as my work colleagues had done. Their response can be summarised as: initial shock followed by an acceptance of sorts. They, like everyone else, could not fully understand this condition I had lived with for so many years. That was hardly surprising, especially in such a masculine field as the construction industry. The chances of hearing about, let alone encountering, a transsexual were remote, to say the least. They were, though, pragmatic enough to realise that the change did not affect the knowledge that I had or how I could carry out my duties. My work brought me into contact largely with people at middle- and senior-management level. I was dealing with people who could at least look at my transition in an educated way; there was a good chance that I would not encounter the prejudice or discrimination that I know others like me have faced elsewhere.

After transition I still had to visit the building sites occasionally and deal with whoever was working there. I'm glad to say that I never suffered from open prejudice or discrimination. Perhaps my own prejudice toward my work colleagues is unfounded and maybe the macho construction industry is actually more open and accepting than it is perceived to be.

I went to Charing Cross in March expecting to move on in my transition. I had advised the clinic of my name change, with a copy of my deed poll for their records, and of my impending transition at work. All was going well. The consultation was all about the hormone regime I would be on; I was told that the clinic would write to my GP with appropriate protocols. I know I travelled home so happy after that consultation; I felt I was really making progress. Unfortunately, it was not to be so simple and I was to plummet into unhappiness for a time.

I went to see my GP a week or so after the Charing Cross consultation, fully expecting everything to be fine. Although she had been extremely supportive of me throughout the early stages she was also extremely cautious. Perhaps I was just being naive, or perhaps I just expected to run before I could walk.

I had received a copy of the letter from Charing Cross to my GP, so I knew that they were recommending hormone therapy, the only little twist being that they thought I had already transitioned at work, which was in fact still a few weeks away. I thought that would not really be a problem, as it would take a week or so to sort it all out. My GP had received the letter but she was quite adamant that she would not start to prescribe, as there was no medical protocol attached to the letter detailing the expected results and effects of the medication. She went to great lengths to explain just how dangerous the introduction of high doses of female hormones could be to what we both knew was a perfectly normal and functioning male body. There was no way she would do this without proper and authorised direction.

She was prepared to seek further advice by contacting the chief clinician by phone and she also requested another full set of blood tests to set the base line markers. I was unhappy and also distressed at what I perceived to be an unnecessary delay; after all, the letter clearly stated the type and dose I should receive to start with. My GP, however, was unmoved and emphasised that she was doing her duty in ensuring that I was treated safely and appropriately. I left in tears.

I felt crushed, let down and upset in equal measure as I went home, expecting it to take a week or so to sort out. I went for the blood tests and waited for the results and a letter from the practice asking me to return.

A week later the letter duly arrived, asking me to attend the practice. I made the appointment as soon as I could, expecting it all to be resolved. The doctor did not have good news:

"There is a borderline issue with your blood results and I have to ask for them to be taken again, please."

I wondered what on earth was happening to me. Why should there be any further delay to what was a direct request? I had done everything correctly. I had two formal diagnoses of my problem, and every previous blood test had come back normal. Was I fated to fall at the final hurdle? Apparently my kidney function was low and my GP, ever cautious, was unsure what effect the hormones could have. We were both aware of the potential for increased risks to major organs with the introduction of female hormones into a male body. That, however, was a risk I was prepared to take. My doctor felt that she needed to seek advice from a renal specialist. She asked that I take another test but to ensure that I drank sufficient water beforehand, as it could be a simple matter of too little water intake.

The doctor then told me she had spoken to the clinician at the Charing Cross clinic and had received a protocol with which she was having difficulty, due to some irregularities, as far as she saw them. She was waiting for further clarification but in the meantime would like me to confirm that I was now working full time as a woman, and said that a letter from my employer would suffice. After that, nothing more would stand in the way, and she would be willing to prescribe the hormone treatment for me.

By this time I was attending the surgery as Kirstie and my records had all been changed. My GP only saw me in the female role and so had assumed, wrongly, that I was also working as Kirstie. I chose not to discuss my work situation and ended the meeting with doctor as quickly as I could, despite my disappointment. I knew that in a few short weeks I really would be going to work as Kirstie but it was already clear to me that the doctor would not be prepared to negotiate that point – she obviously would not prescribe for me until she had the letter from my company. I was deeply frustrated: despite my previous intentions to abide by the rules and to follow what I understood to be the correct route towards transition, this latest setback made me want to bend the rules, like so many other transsexuals – perhaps not surprisingly – are tempted to do. Unfortunately, it was clear that the doctor was not prepared to do the same.

I was crestfallen once more as I left the surgery empty-handed. For the moment I was also very angry with the system which, despite my willingness so far to adhere to the rules, seemed to be out to defeat me. I had known that it would be strict and difficult, but this new 'roadblock' seemed unfair and perverse. I could not get round it, though, and so I had to wait my time.

Eventually, in May, I obtained the all-important letter confirming that I was working full time as Kirstie. My latest blood tests now showed acceptable levels in all the important areas. The Charing Cross clinician had also clarified the protocol to the satisfaction of my doctor. Finally the green light was given for me to begin hormone treatment.

I was very frustrated by the delays but was all the happier when everything fell into place. My pragmatism helped me through: I reckoned that, after waiting more than fifty years, I could stand a few more months. In the meantime, I had had to begin my full time life as Kirstie without taking hormones. Not that they would have helped me in any practical way with my transition at work, but they would have given me a big psychological boost in those early days of letting colleagues and clients see me for the first time as Kirstie.

My first prescription was not issued until June 2008: three months later than I had hoped. Those three months seemed like an eternity. I can clearly recall the day when I collected my tablets and took the first one: it was like a rite of passage from masculinity to femininity, although clearly one tablet –or even an entire packet – made no noticeable difference to my appearance or behaviour.

However, they did change the way I felt – I felt that I was on the last leg of my journey, which would lead eventually to the surgery I so much wanted and needed.

By the summer I was moving forward every day. Work knew, clients knew. I had legally changed my name and all of my documentation, with the exception of my birth certificate. That would be a much longer process – one which I could not do until my journey was complete. I was researching the actual surgery by this time and had spoken to many transsexuals worldwide, both pre-operative and post-operative. With their help I was making up my mind where I wanted to go for my surgery.

If you speak to any post-operative transsexual they will always say that their surgeon is the best; it's human nature. Those who say otherwise have either made a very bad choice or have had a traumatic incident post-operatively. I always had the option of waiting for the full twenty-four months, to satisfy the NHS requirement, after which I could have my surgery in the UK free of charge. That always remained as my backstop position.

Nevertheless, I wanted to make sure that I really was choosing the best option, so I continued looking. I searched worldwide; there are plenty of surgeons to choose from and I spoke to many people, online and face-to-face. I did my homework well; this was too big a decision to make without doing so. In one sense I already knew where I wanted to go, but I continued my research into the available options until my initial choice was confirmed beyond the slightest doubt. I wanted to go to Dr Suporn in Thailand, recognised as a pioneer for his particular surgical techniques, and considered amongst the best in the world for this particular operation. I reasoned that if I was paying for it then I should buy a Rolls Royce rather than a Mini.

My mind was made up and in June I opened communication with the clinic. One reason for my choice was purely to reduce the preparation and associated pain. Facial electrolysis to remove beard-growth is bad enough, as I can now testify; but genital electrolysis which is required by many surgeons as a precursor to the sex reassignment surgery, was a great leap too far in my opinion. The procedure undertaken by Dr Suporn did not require this and, in fact, he preferred there to have been no electrolysis in this region.

While I was making plans far into the future, I still had to make the transition at work. I set my target as the early May Bank Holiday, intending to make the change over that weekend.

There were two events which occurred within a few days of each other. The fifth of May was a Bank Holiday Monday and I intended to make my appearance formally at work on the sixth. I would leave work on Friday the second of May as Ken and return the following Tuesday as Kirstie. I let this be known to the company directors, so that each office could be advised. The essential clients were also made aware; the rest would just have to take it in their stride as the days went by. My secretary knew what to do and would advise clients as they rang in asking to speak to Ken. She would tell them what had happened, answer any relevant queries and then pass them through to me. A few wished me well and those I knew well asked more in depth questions. No-one refused to be put through and no one was rude. It was a very smooth transition.

I had chatted with Chris and we had agreed on the same idea: that my transition should be celebrated with a garden party. We gambled on good weather and set a date for the Sunday of the Bank Holiday weekend, the fourth of May. Chris had a large garden and could accommodate many guests. I arranged for live music to be played by friends and we put up a gazebo as protection, just in case the weather let us down. I invited friends, both straight and transsexual, and family; I was delighted when both of my eldest daughters and their friends agreed to attend, plus some work colleagues from the local office. Sadly my wife would not let Sophie attend and so she was not there to celebrate my 'wake', as I then designated the day. I was celebrating the passing of Ken and the birth of Kirstie. Everyone, except Jean, could understand this and all were prepared to join me and celebrate this as I had planned.

Before the weekend, though, I decided that I would end my life as a male in my own way and go to the office as Kirstie earlier than advised. I let my staff know (there were only four of us), that this was my intention and they were all happy to let me do this ahead of schedule. My secretary took her duties seriously and went round the other companies who had offices in our building and told them what was to happen the following morning.

Thursday, the first of May 2008, was to be the day I ceased to be Ken forever. It could have been a day like any other, but for me it definitely was not. I got up an hour earlier than usual; after all, I had some extra morning preparations to do. I showered and washed my hair; it was not long, but was enough for me to dispense with the use of a wig. It takes a long time to go from a very short masculine cut to a longer more feminine style and Kat was slowly cutting it so it would grow properly.

The shower was followed by a close shave, of my face and my body; I wanted to feel as natural as I could, so the extra effort was essential. I had yet to start electrolysis so I had full male beard growth to deal with and, without the hormones, still had a lot of body hair to consider. I spent a long time in the bathroom and so had started early as I had to finish in time to let Chris have the bathroom; she also had to get to work.

Back to the bedroom and then the big decision: what to wear? I needed to be comfortable but also respect the position I held in the company. My own staff would accept me, as long as I dressed appropriately, but I felt that I had to make a statement on this first and very important day. I decided on traditional business-wear: a white blouse, black skirt and suit jacket, black tights and low heeled black court shoes. The outfit was smart, traditional and, most importantly, comfortable.

I dried my hair, taking time to ensure I got it into the style it was supposed to be. I dressed slowly, enjoying this change in my morning preparation for work, continually thinking about this first day. I was no longer scared, as I had been living the female role outside of the work environment for long enough to be comfortable anywhere in public. This, however, was a very different situation and as I dressed I realised that I was denying my masculinity for the very last time. I vowed never to wear male clothes again.

I took some time to reflect on my past and on the future. Looking in the mirror as I dressed I still had a flat, male chest and the obvious lower 'equipment'. Both of these would change, I knew that. I also knew that the clock was counting down. Fifty years is a long time to wait, so a few more years should not make any difference; my head knew this only too well but my heart was elsewhere. Dressing, and the application of cosmetics, was no longer a long drawn-out process. Practice does make perfect. Well, perhaps I was still not perfect but I could certainly create the image well enough now not to worry. Earrings and a touch of scent completed the look. I was satisfied and then went to find Chris.

"How do I look? Will I pass for the first day at work?"

"Of course. You look great - there will be no problem," she reassured me with a smile.

"Good! Thank you," was all I could then say. I knew I looked fine but the reassurance was essential.

Chris then left for work and I was on my own. I was getting more nervous as time passed. I went back into my bedroom, checked in the mirror again and then carried out one more very important act in the process of closing down my life as a male.

I took up my wallet and removed credit cards, my driving licence, cash and the other little pieces of paper we all keep. These I then put into my purse where they would stay. I put my wallet in the bin; I would not need it anymore.

That was it; there was no going back. I knew that I would be bagging up all of my male clothes at the weekend and they would either be binned or, if they were possibly of use to others, would go to the charity shop. I did relent for a few months and kept one suit, a shirt and a pair of black shoes. "Just in case," I told myself. However, I never needed to even consider putting them on; I kept my vow.

Walking out of the front door was no longer a problem and I even nodded to a passing neighbour. I got into the car and knew that this was it: my first journey to work as Kirstie. It was only a ten minute drive, which went without incident. I was still on safe ground after all. I arrived and turned into the office car park, reversed into my usual space, turned the engine off and just sat staring at the entrance to the offices. I had deliberately arrived later than usual so that everyone would already be there. I wanted to do this once and once only. I opened the door of the car and slid out, turned and straightened my skirt. I locked the door, glanced in the wing mirror to check that all was as it should be, drew in a breath, and walked across the car park to the entrance.

I have no idea if I was being watched from any of the windows, as I kept my eyes straight ahead and walked to the door. I met no one as I walked up to the first floor where the office was located. I reached the landing and faced the entrance door to the office where 'Ken' had been in charge for the past five years. As from this day, 'Kirstie' would now be in charge. What remained to be seen was how my staff would react.

Well, this was it. I was sure my secretary would be fine but it was all about how the other two would behave. I took a deep breath as I walked into the office. "One step at a time," was all I could think of as my heart pounded. This was not easy but I had crossed so many obstacles previously that I knew that there was really nothing to worry about. That did not make me feel any better and all I could do was walk forward into the main office, where my secretary sat chatting to the other two; no doubt I was the topic of conversation.

"Good morning,"

I said as I passed through to my office. I had no idea how to deal with this one. I thought it best to let them come and say hello to me, rather than force what was a difficult situation for us all. They had seen Kirstie walk in so they knew who was in the office. It was, of course, my secretary who came in to see me first.

"Morning," she said, as was quite usual. "You look fine. How are you feeling?"

"Nervous," I smiled. "But I'll be much better when this is all over."

"Don't worry," she encouraged me. "Everyone is fine and looking forward to working with you. They are fine...honestly."

"OK. Let's get it over with and have an office catch-up over coffee," I suggested.

"Great idea," she smiled and asked the others to join us as she went and made coffee for us all.

That was it. We sat over coffee and discussed various work matters as though nothing was any different. They were fine about it and all said they had no problem; I was after all the same person. They agreed it would take a while to get used to the skirt but they would manage. They all said how happy I looked, and now that I had settled I looked less tense; these were all good signs for the future. After that we just got on with work as always. Once more I thanked my lucky stars just how easily this was actually going for me.

That Friday was just like any other day at work. I never caught anyone saying inappropriate remarks or saw a backward glance. If they had issues I never knew and was happy to leave it that way. Work was now sorted. I had no problems the following week either and each time I went to a client's office I was treated with politeness and dignity. The odd misplaced male pronoun always happened but I never made a comment or issue about it. The perpetrator was always far more apologetic than I ever felt was necessary. It was good to know, however, that they realised their error.

The weekend arrived and the party preparations went on. Sunday promised to be a bright, warm, sunny day which is exactly how it turned out. I was going to say goodbye to Ken and to welcome my rebirth as Kirstie with friends and family on a glorious day.

It was a wonderful day, which went on late into the night. My two eldest daughters were there in support. It was unfortunate that Sophie was not able to even drop in for an hour or so but I bowed to her mother's request. We had good food, wine, live music, laughter and a damned good time. I went to bed late but so happy to be starting my new life on such a high.

I had done it. I had put my male self behind me and could now move forward in life as Kirstie, the female I should have been at birth. My happiness could not be imagined. I looked to the future in a very positive manner.

May passed without further problem and June duly arrived. I now satisfied all my doctor's requirements and so collected my prescription; it was the start of the all-important hormone therapy, which would trigger the outer physical changes to match my true inner self. I was going to go through puberty for the second time in my life, this time in the gender I should have been at birth. It took only six months before the small breast buds were obvious and over time they developed, just as they do on any other pubescent teenager. Of course in comparison to what my own daughters and any other natal female faced, I had it easy. I changed in ways that were all positive, without the down side that natal women also have to face. I also knew that less obvious changes were occurring at the same time. My brain functions were being affected by the hormones. The wiring in my brain, the parts that governed how I thought and behaved, were slowly but surely being adjusted.

I have always been a determined person, and someone who liked to plan things well in advance. It therefore suited my personality to begin the planning for my surgery, even though that event was still a long way in the future. I was in regular contact with the clinic and had completed the initial questionnaires; I also knew what supporting documentation would be required.

I took a leap of faith, backed up by my extensive research and preparation, and booked my surgery for October 2009. I also added the possibility of breast augmentation and upper eyelid reduction to my shopping list. My booking was made and accepted. I paid the necessary deposit to keep that date secure for the main operation, my sex reassignment surgery, or SRS; the other procedures could be confirmed later, prior to my arrival in Thailand. I was looking at a date eighteen months after my transition to living full time as a woman, well in accordance with the international standards of care but six months short of the minimum required by the NHS. By this time I had made up my mind that I definitely wanted Dr Suporn, and not the NHS, to carry out this most important of operations.

I knew I was committing myself to considerable expense: not only had I to pay for the surgery but I also had to budget for the flights and the additional cost of the hotel where I would stay after my discharge from hospital. Sex reassignment surgery is such a major, invasive procedure that a minimum of four weeks' recovery after the operation is advised, before considering flying the long distance back to the UK. I had eighteen months to sort this out. My father was aware of my wishes and he had even brought up the subject of how he could help. He was still struggling with my transition but knew I was on course and determined to make it. I loved my dad and was still feeling guilty about the pain I had caused him. We were working on it together and would see it through as father and daughter.

As for the rest of 2008: on a personal front all went well but, slowly but surely, my work suffered. I had my last counselling session in July. It was short and sweet. I arrived and explained what had happened over the past months. As I spoke I could see the psychiatrist's smile spread as he realised I had crossed the finish line and was at peace with my life. I remember his words clearly:

"I can see just how far you have come, Kirstie. I don't feel we can do any more together and you are able to face the future as you are now doing. Congratulations. Of course I am always here if you should need me. You will always have the option to return at any time should you wish."

The whole session had taken no more than ten minutes. I was elated as I said, with a tear in my eyes:

"Thank you for your help and support. It has made my decisions so much easier, as everything was clarified. I am so happy now."

There was nothing else I could say. I realised he was right. After nearly twenty sessions together there was nothing else to talk about. I had made it to my interim goal. He and I both knew that I had the next target firmly in sight, that I knew how to achieve it, and that I was already well on my way toward it. I stood up, shook hands with him, and left feeling like the happiest person in the world.

Chapter 13

A special birthday card, Australia, unemployment and a disaster

2008 passed. It was a busy and eventful year but the latter half was at least calmer as I settled down to live my new life as Kirstie. I never had a single regret about my transition; after all, it was how I should have been born.

Sophie had overcome her initial disquiet and visited regularly, even bringing friends for weekend sleepovers. She was having problems with her peers at school and that bothered her; she struggled to deal with the hurt she received from those who did not understand the reality of my situation. Naturally I was concerned for her but there was little I could do except talk things through with her, as often, and in as much or as little detail as she wanted. Her mother clearly also did what she could to help Sophie but this was all set against the background of our deteriorating relationship as we tried to settle the divorce.

In October 2008 I moved out of the village with Chris into her new home, where I retained my position as her lodger. Chris was also organising her own divorce, which required the sale of her house. She had made it very clear that I was more than welcome to move with her and so that is what I did. She downsized from a three- to a two-bedroomed house in the next village - only a mile or so away from where we were living. In many ways it was better, as I was away from any immediate contact with Jean but still close enough so that Sophie could easily visit. The only downside was the loss of the extra bedroom; now, if Sophie wanted to stay, there was no spare room. Nevertheless, we found a solution: I always gave up my own room and slept downstairs in the lounge. At first it was not a problem, as it was only every now and then; and if she had a friend with her the two of them used the sofa bed in the lounge. It worked well at first but increasing problems at home meant that Sophie slowly preferred to stay with me more often.

My father did his best to deal with his new daughter but still called me son and wrote to Ken on birthday and Christmas cards. The birthday cards he sent me, though, changed in style from the masculine 'To my Son' to a genderless 'Happy Birthday'. That was hard for him, I know, but it was a start; I could see that he was slowly doing his best to come to terms with my life-changing decision. Whenever I saw him I dressed in an androgynous way, although my hair was significantly longer and was definitely cut in a feminine style. To make it easier for him, when sending him cards I never signed them 'Kirstie'; but I would not sign them 'Ken' either: that person no longer existed as far as I was concerned. I ended any greeting with the simple initial 'K', which seemed to satisfy both of our needs.

My niece in Australia was getting married in April 2009 and in September 2008 both dad and I received the invitation to the wedding. I put it to one side, preparing to send a note of thanks but declining the invitation. I did not feel I would be able to attend, with so many other things happening in my life. Dad would also be doing the same, as he was too frail to make the journey.

I had a telephone call from my father shortly after the arrival of the invitation.

"Hello son. How are you? I expect you have received an invitation to the wedding."

"I'm fine thanks, Dad. Yes, I have an invite. I was just thinking about writing a note to say thanks but I will not be attending."

"Well, I have thought about this. I obviously can't go. How would you like to go and represent the family for both of us?"

I was stunned; this was beyond my expectations, as I knew just how hard this was for Dad to do. He was well aware that it would not be his son attending but Kirstie, his daughter. Even had I wished to do so I could no longer travel as Ken. My passport and all my legal documents had been changed to Kirstie and he knew this.

"You realise what that means, Dad. I can't go as your son. I have to attend as Kirstie and clearly that is what any wedding photographs will show." I felt that I needed to make sure he realised the implications.

"Yes. I'm fully aware of that. I have thought hard about this and it's not easy but I want you to go on my behalf and to represent the UK family. And of course I will pay for the flights."

"I would love to go Dad. Thank you so much for the opportunity." I was almost in tears but held back, as I knew he would struggle with the emotion.

He then became very brisk and business-like:

"Well, that's all sorted then. You let them know you are coming and sort out the flights. Let me know what it costs and we will settle up."

The rest of the call was more about his granddaughters and how they were getting on, plus the usual family news. The trip was an opportunity beyond my dreams. It was going to be another of those trips into the unknown but they were becoming easier each time I took a risk.

My brother and his daughter were due to visit the UK for a brief holiday in November 2008, soon after my move with Chris into the new house. They stayed with Dad but came to visit. My niece had never had a traditional Christmas dinner as she was more used to the Australian summer heat in December and I promised to make her a traditional turkey dinner with all of the trimmings. The new house was small but I managed to fit us all in and cooked for nine. Relations with my wife were strained but at the time I felt it would be crass to exclude her from this event. I was pleased when she accepted the invitation.

I coped well and the meal was a great success. We all made the most of the fact that we were having Christmas dinner a month early. Dad enjoyed the chance to have all of his family around him for a celebration and even Jean was able to feel comfortable.

2008 closed on a positive note for me personally, although life at work was getting worse. The recession was biting hard and the company was feeling the loss of income. The performance of my own office was poor and, to be honest, I was reaching the point where I no longer enjoyed my profession: I was losing interest. My lack of interest was also being noticed by my superiors and I had an idea that 2009 would be a hard year at work, whatever transpired.

The New Year arrived and it was to be another significant year in my life. I was going to Australia in March and then to Thailand in October. Dad's health was slowly deteriorating and he could no longer drive the eighty miles to visit, so I always went to see him when I could. My 54th birthday arrived in February and brought with it a breakthrough which, for me personally and emotionally, was one of the best surprises I had ever had.

I received the usual cards from my daughters and my brother. I also received a card from Dad which I opened and, as always, there was a cheque enclosed as my present. This card was however distinctive in that it was very different from others I had received in the past. It was a floral and very feminine card which I opened, expecting to see the usual inscription "to my son". This time it was very different and brought tears to my eyes. Dad still could not bring himself to write 'Kirstie' but, in the same way I always signed my cards to him, it was addressed to 'K'. To me it was his way of acknowledging my transition and was the best present I could ever have wished for. I have kept this card and will treasure it always.

Plans progressed for my trip to Australia. I had to tell the company and decided that, in the current climate, two weeks away would have to suffice. It was short for a trip to Australia but I felt it appropriate. At a meeting with the chairman, where my office performance formed the main agenda, I finished by telling him of my plans. I was surprised when he said:

"It's a long way to go for two weeks. I think you should take three weeks for the trip."

I was astounded and said my thanks as we parted. I had work to do on figures for the year's projections but was confident I could do that. The meeting had been on a Friday and so over the weekend I searched for and booked my flights. I also paid for them. All was looking good and I was happy.

I returned to work on Monday and received an email from the chairman. The message was clear: he had reconsidered his offer and, in light of the deteriorating market conditions and my poor forecast, he felt that it would be inappropriate for me to be away for so long. To say I was unhappy with this would be an understatement. I emailed back saying that my tickets were booked and paid for; I could not change my plans. With the Easter holiday included I would be away for sixteen working days, so I felt that I had kept to our agreement.

He then asked me to prove that the flights were actually booked, which just made me furious. It was an easy matter to do so and ended the exchange between us. This lack of trust on his part was the beginning of the end as far as I was concerned.

I put the exchange behind me as I shopped and packed, ready for a trip to sunny Queensland. There was one last important thing I had to do before leaving for the wedding. Dad had to agree to meet Kirstie as I truly was, not as the watered-down version that he always met. After all, it would be Kirstie he would see in the wedding pictures and I had no intention of dressing down for that occasion. I intended to enjoy every moment of the wedding as any woman would and had shopped accordingly.

When I phoned him to tell him what we had to do he said:

"I know. I have been expecting this and I am prepared. It won't be easy but we will be able to see it through, for both of us."

I had a business meeting not too far away and so I said I would drop in after that had finished. I dressed for the business meeting as I usually would: a black trouser suit and white blouse, with a little jewellery and light makeup. It was no different to a normal business day but this time I would also be meeting my father…..in a sense for the first time.

My meeting finished at four o'clock and I drove the ten miles or so to my father's house. During the journey I reflected on the past few years and on the trials I had faced. I had already confronted all of the major ones and this was, in many ways, not a great obstacle. Dad had known of my change for over a year now; we had never lost touch and I had always been sympathetic to his feelings and wishes. Nevertheless, this was a major step for us both; it was a meeting that we had to have and we had to put the demons behind us.

I pulled in to the drive. It was early evening and full day light so not only was Dad going to meet me but his neighbours were also able to see his daughter arrive. I got out and stood proud despite the fact that I was shaking inside; I was also sure he would be feeling much the same.

I slowly walked to the door. I had checked how I looked and felt it was right for this first meeting. I rang the doorbell and waited for the front door to open. I did not have to wait long, and there was my dad looking at his new daughter – properly - for the very first time. We both stood silently, just looking at each other; it was only a few seconds but it was noticeable. Then we both stepped forward and hugged, holding on tightly. I could feel the tension drain from him as he held me. He stepped back, had a second look and then he invited me in. We had done it.

"I was not looking forward to this, I can tell you. But now I see you I can see just how happy you are. I love you and I'm very happy for you. We will be fine."

We went in and I made us both a cup of tea. We chatted about the impending wedding and my trip. I made no mention of my difficulties with work: I knew it was not fair to burden him with other issues in my life. I did not want to overstay my welcome on this first visit so, before too long, I took my leave. We had achieved a great breakthrough and I knew that there would be no problem with him seeing me as the full Kirstie in the future

The whole trip to Australia was a wonderful experience. David happily introduced me to everyone as his sister. The wedding was fabulous and I did my best to put on a good show. I felt great on the day and thoroughly enjoyed the opportunity to represent the UK branch of the family as my niece and her husband welcomed me into the new Australian side of the family without reservation.

After the wedding I had the luxury of a relaxing week away with my brother and his wife. It was a week I shall remember with affection for many years. We had the chance to spend time together and catch up on all of the years we had missed. I had a wonderful three weeks but eventually I had to return to the UK, to face the music at work and also to deal with family issues which had deteriorated in my absence.

I returned in April 2009 and started to rearrange my life. Two months later my life began to fall apart and June that year is a month that remains seared in my mind forever.

Sophie eventually fell out with her mum and wanted to move in with me full time. That created all sorts of problems as there was no room for three of us in the house. After all, the house belonged to Chris – I was just the lodger, for all that we were also very good friends. It was becoming a problem for everyone. I eventually knew I would have to find a place of my own where Sophie and I could live comfortably together.

Relations at work between the chairman and me continued to deteriorate, to the extent that I began to feel it was a personal issue between us. The deepening recession had required ever more redundancies throughout the company and I found myself under scrutiny more often, as I struggled to meet budget targets. Finally I reached the stage where I forced my own redundancy, rather than keep on working for the company where I felt persecuted. My last day was on Friday the twelfth of June, when my office was closed down for 'economic' reasons. The company tried to get me to transfer to the London office but I knew that would only prolong the agony. I was within my rights to refuse, and I did so. The company had effectively closed down my job and had no option but to make me redundant.

My father died on the twenty-third of June, after three days in hospital with acute kidney failure.

It's no wonder I hit rock bottom. Ever the planner, though, I had at least used the last few weeks at work to prepare for the financial checks I would need to pass before I could rent a new flat. I made it by the skin of my teeth and was able to move into the perfect flat for my daughters and me on the third of July.

Dad's death hit us all hard, not surprisingly, and of course David came to officiate at the service, just as he had at our mother's ten years earlier. My father was in his eighties and had outlived all of his family and friends, so it was a small service, unlike Mum's. It was no less a ceremony for all that; it was just different. Of course for me the greatest difference was that I had attended Mum's funeral as Ken and now Dad's as Kirstie. I was the same person and grieved in the same way for each of my parents; it was only the outward appearance that had changed.

David and I shared Dad's house for a week as we sorted out the essentials. I was then left to sell the property and deal with probate and the closing of his affairs, as I was the only executor of his will. Unfortunately I was named as Kenneth in his will, so I had to go through the process of proving who I was. It was merely a matter of providing the correct paperwork to prove my change of name but it was another task I could do without.

The country was now in the depths of recession and the housing market had collapsed, so selling the house was a drain on my time and on my now limited resources. I only had enough in the bank to pay one month's rent. I was forced to sign on and apply for benefits, something I had never done or contemplated doing in my life before.

The divorce process had reached a point of open hostility and, in order to make ends meet, I had to contact the hospital in Thailand and cancel my operation, to take back the deposit I had paid. I also had to instruct solicitors to work on my behalf against my ex-employer to obtain the redundancy payments to which I was legally entitled. I was under extreme stress and it showed.

I had been undergoing speech therapy for some months to change my deep male voice to a more feminine pitch and timbre. By that summer I had achieved excellent results and was very pleased with the outcome. The stress hit me hard, though, and ruined the last months of hard work. The effect was such that ever since, even with further therapy, I have never been able to recover the position I had achieved, much to my disappointment.

The next six months to December were extremely difficult. I was living on the edge, only just managing my finances to keep my head above water. Each time it looked as though I would run out I was able to draw on funds from dad's estate as bank accounts were closed or other funds became available. In November I won my case for redundancy and agreed settlement terms. I did go to a few interviews for work in the industry I had worked in for so many years. I learned the hard way about discrimination, although it could never be proven. I only ever received one interview from any agency I signed up with and the interviews slowly but surely dried up. Being transsexual and looking for work is entirely different from being transsexual and transitioning in the work place. As time went by I lost interest in ever getting back into the construction industry and, to be honest, my heart was no longer in it.

As funds from my father's estate slowly became available I knew I had to finish my journey; I needed to re-book my surgery and I needed it to be with the surgeon of my choice. Yet I still did not have enough reserves to pay Dr Suporn's fees. Only the sale of my father's house would provide enough funds. I took a gamble and, in August 2009, I contacted the clinic again. We agreed a date of the fourteenth of January 2010: come what may, I had to get Dad's house sold, to release the legacy he had left for David and me. At the time, though, I could afford neither the surgery nor even the flight to get to Thailand. I scraped together the deposit, knowing the remainder had to be paid a fortnight before the operation date.

I also had to obtain a letter of referral from a medical professional in the UK before the Thai clinic would agree to perform the surgery. I contacted the Charing Cross Hospital, knowing they would not officially support me without the required twenty-four months of living full time as a woman. Although my decision was acknowledged as appropriate I could not obtain the required supporting paperwork from them.

I therefore returned to the specialist I had seen more than a year ago. He had my records and I could provide all of the other supporting documentation to show that I had completed more than twelve months of 'real life experience', including my hormone therapy and the fact that I had been fully employed as Kirstie. It was a forty-minute consultation, after which I had my letter of referral, which was the Holy Grail as far as I was then concerned. I had everything I needed for the surgery except the funds to pay for it.

Life was back on track again as I slowly but surely gained control once more. After the, to my mind, unnecessary legal battle I received my redundancy monies and my father's house was finally sold in December 2009, with the funds available by the end of that month. My gamble had paid off: I could afford to pay for my surgery and, just as important, I could afford to get there!

The last few months before my trip to Thailand were relatively quiet, as I was out of work and unemployable, as no-one would even consider taking me on, given the fact that I needed a month off for the surgery in Thailand, followed by further months of recovery on my return.

I was getting bored doing nothing and needed a new goal in life. I sat back and thought about what I really wanted to do. I now had a golden opportunity to choose a new career that suited me and, most importantly, that I could enjoy.

My experience of gender counselling had shown me just how limited the support was. I had spoken to many other transsexuals and the story was the same worldwide. There are just too few appropriately qualified counsellors to support the needs of the people suffering from Gender Dysphoria. I thought about it and knew that I had to help; I would do my utmost to qualify as a counsellor and to support those who were facing the same trials and tribulations that I had done.

As with everything, I did my research and found a suitable introductory course called "So you think you want to be a counsellor?" It fitted the bill and I signed up for the initial ten weeks at a local college. I loved every minute of that introductory course; I had found my true vocation. I was found to be proficient and I knew I had to sign up for the subsequent course to continue my studies.

The only problem I had was that it started in January 2010, the month which was scheduled for my surgery. I was determined, and had no wish to delay my training, and so I spoke to the head of department. It would mean missing the first five weeks of a twenty-two week course but I could keep in touch via the internet; I could be advised of what reading and coursework was needed and could submit my weekly journals, which were a requirement of the course.

I must have made a good case and I believe my determination must have been recognised. I was accepted and could register for the level 2 course, which I did as soon as it opened for enrolment. I knew where I was heading and once more felt that my life had real purpose. Everything was falling into place.

Chapter 14

Thailand, the culmination of my journey: outbound and reassignment

Christmas came and went uneventfully; the girls spent Christmas Day with their mother and came to me for Boxing Day. I enjoyed the family time and also the peace of Christmas Day on my own, as I was preparing for my trip. I was leaving on Friday the eighth of January, arriving in Thailand on the ninth, giving me a few days before my hospital admission on Wednesday the thirteenth for surgery the following day. The weather in the UK was awful: airports had been closed as were main roads. I was concerned but there was little I could do about it except keep my fingers crossed that all would be OK on the day.

I had arranged for my friend Sarah to take me to the airport, rather than trust to public transport or taxis. She was more than willing to do so as we would be meeting again in Thailand. She would be flying out a week later than me as her surgery was scheduled to take place four days after mine. I had planned everything carefully as usual. It was an evening flight with a ninety minute stopover in Dubai. I would arrive in Bangkok the following evening, when I would be met at the airport and taken to my hotel.

On Thursday evening Sarah rang to say she had a problem: her heating had broken down and, in the depths of winter, she had to get it fixed. She had booked the engineer to come on the Friday afternoon and so asked if I would mind going to the airport earlier than planned, to give her time to get home again. I fully understood her situation and of course agreed.

I had arranged to meet another friend at the airport for a drink before leaving so I hoped I could ring her from the airport to move our rendezvous forward. She lived close by and I had agreed to ring her so she was not left waiting, had I got stuck due to the weather. I would at least have company during the long wait, as Sarah could not stay even for a quick coffee.

Sarah arrived about nine o'clock that morning; the roads were open and the snow was clearing but more was forecast. I had been packed and ready for ages, feeling quite emotional, as this was the start of the final leg of my life's journey. We had a cup of coffee and spoke about the adventure that we were both going to be taking over the next few weeks. Sarah was anxious to get a move on as she had to get back home before the engineer arrived, and we had no idea what the motorway would be like.

We did the journey in forty minutes and Sarah dropped me at eleven o'clock, saying her farewells as she dashed back home to get her heating repaired. We would see each other again in about three weeks, allowing for the time in hospital.

I was at Terminal 3 and walked in, knowing that I would be joined shortly by a friend to pass the hours before my flight at eight o'clock that evening. I rang to hear a very hoarse voice saying that she had come down with flu and would be unable to meet me. I was on my own for the next nine hours!

I was relieved, however, as the weather was looking poor and I didn't want to suffer delays. I had checked-in online the night before and decided to see if they would take my luggage early. This would then allow me to go through security and at least sit in comfort in the departure lounge.

I approached the desk and cautiously asked if I could check in.

"I'm sorry, but not usually this early before the flight is due to leave. I will ask and see if we can do something," was the reply, as she turned to speak to a colleague.

She came back a few moments later to ask if I would like to travel on an earlier flight as there were spare seats. There was absolutely no point in staying in the UK with the deteriorating weather conditions so I quickly agreed. It was now half past eleven and my new flight was leaving at a quarter to two: there was just time to get through security and have a drink before boarding. I realised I would be in Dubai for my stopover six hours earlier than originally planned and would now have eight hours to kill, but better that than risk being stuck in the UK.

I went through into the departure lounge, which was a far better place to spend some time before leaving. I wandered around the shops and had a glass of wine to pass the time. As departure was notified I headed for the gate; I was just about to turn off my phone when it rang. I did not recognise the number but answered anyway. It was a good job I did, as it was the college, calling to advise me that my course had been undersubscribed and was to be cancelled. There were places on the evening course if I wanted to transfer my application. As far as I was concerned this was not a problem and I readily agreed. I had been incredibly lucky: five minutes later and I would not have received that call. It was a lucky break which boded well for my trip.

The trip to Dubai for the stopover was uneventful and the plane was not full. I arrived at one o'clock in the morning but the airport was still surprisingly busy. I found a seat where I could pass the many hours ahead of me before my next flight. I used my laptop to chat with Kat and Sam on Facebook. I also managed to doze for a while on the chair but it was not the best rest I had ever had.

I boarded the aeroplane for Thailand and we landed in Bangkok at twenty to seven in the evening as scheduled. I was tired but glad to have made it; I was only a few days away from the life-changing surgery which would remedy my birth defect.

It turned out that I had been very lucky indeed. My original eight o'clock flight from Heathrow had been cancelled due to a security alert. A passenger on the flight, apparently worse for drink because the flight had been delayed, started to complain and then mentioned the 'bomb' word. With heightened security the aeroplane was stopped, the passengers disembarked, and the gentleman in question arrested. There was no bomb, of course, but there was no way the airport authority and airline staff could ignore his threat. Passengers were put up in a hotel overnight and then flew out at three o'clock on Saturday afternoon. That would have totally ruined my passage and I was so glad I had been able to leave early, despite the resulting eight hour stopover in Dubai. I reflected on how the misfortune of Sarah, with her defective heating, and my other friend's sore throat, had combined to my advantage: I could so easily have spent longer in England and would have ended up on the originally planned flight.

Disembarking from the plane I realised I was finally in Thailand. I had made it to the place of transition where I would finally achieve my dream to change my external appearance to match my inner being. I would lose the masculine sexuality and gain the feminine that I had wanted for so long. I was excited but also very tired as I saw the massive queue I had to join, to pass through immigration and enter the country. I did the British thing and joined the queue and moved towards the entry point, where my passport was checked and stamped. I walked forward into Thailand.

The clinic had provided instructions on how to meet the person who would collect me, although I still wondered how I would know them. In fact it was all made very easy. There is a specific area of the airport for travellers to be collected and I made my way there. Very soon I saw a sign with Suporn Clinic and my name on it, being held by a diminutive Thai lady with a great big welcoming smile. She introduced herself "Hi! I am Cin. Welcome to Thailand. Please follow me."

Cin was very chatty and provided a wonderful end to my journey of nearly thirty hours. Outside the terminal the heat and humidity hit me. Having come from the UK in subzero temperatures and snow, to arrive in a temperature of over 20°C at night was somewhat of a strain, particularly as I was dressed in jeans, sweater and boots. We waited for the clinic minibus to arrive and my baggage was put in the back by the driver as Cin and I got into the air-conditioned interior; I settled back to relax and enjoy the drive to the hotel.

The journey was approximately forty minutes and on the way she asked about my trip and what life was like in the UK. She explained the details for the next few days and confirmed my surgery dates. She gave me a welcoming card with my appointment and contact details for the clinic staff. She also explained that I was almost the first patient to arrive this year and so there were very few others at the hotel where the clinic's patients stayed before their surgery and then after their discharge from hospital. This would change quickly over the next week or so and I would then have plenty of company.

The hotel was a modern business hotel with all the usual facilities so I felt at home, having used similar ones so often during my working life. My room was a standard double with an en-suite bathroom; it was on the third floor, overlooking a roof terrace. It was nine o'clock in the evening when the minibus dropped me off; we parted after checking in and Cin had seen me up to my room.

"Bye, Kirstie. Get some rest and I will see you at the clinic on Monday afternoon."

As far as my body was concerned it was only two o'clock on Saturday afternoon so I had a shower and went downstairs to the restaurant. I was the only customer and was served by a smiling young man whose English was excellent. He welcomed me as he handed me the menu and I ordered a glass of wine. I had a light meal and then felt that a short walk would settle me before I could possibly think of sleep.

I was on my own but felt quite safe as I walked out of the hotel doors into a wall of heat and humidity. I cannot say that it immediately smelled any different but, as I got closer to the bustling pavement cafes which lined the busy main road, I could smell the spices and the aromas of unknown foods quite clearly.

The clinic itself is just a few hundred metres from the hotel and I found it easily. My first impressions of the area were that it was clearly not for tourists. All of the shops were closed but there were dozens of street stalls selling food prepared on ranges and barbecues on the pavement. They were busy as they are the main places where Thai people go to eat every day, taking the place of more formal restaurants. No-one paid me too much attention, for all that I was European, tall, red haired and transsexual. Dr Suporn's clinic is world-renowned and they are used to seeing transsexuals in the area.

I walked around for about thirty minutes just to settle down and to get an idea of the surroundings where I would be living for the next month. The main road was not busy, although I could imagine that it would be during the week. I walked back to the hotel where I went to my room and slept for a full twelve hours.

The cleaner woke me at eleven o'clock on Sunday morning and was surprised to find me still fast asleep. I got up slowly: it was too late for breakfast and I was not very hungry anyway. I had purchased internet access for the month when I checked in, so I sent several messages to family and friends advising them that I had arrived safely. I showered and dressed in light clothing – it may have been January but in Thailand the daytime temperature was above 30°C. I wanted to go outside and explore the area a little more before my confinement in the hospital. Today was Sunday, another free day, as I was to have my consultation with Dr Suporn on Monday afternoon.

I went out of the hotel and walked to the local shopping centre. It was a large covered area and consisted of lots of individual stalls with shops around the perimeter. It was very busy and crowded and thankfully it was air-conditioned. There was a large department store on one side so there was plenty to look at and browse through. I wanted to buy some open sandals if I could and was prepared to try my only Thai: I wanted to see how "Sawasdee Kah" helped me get on, as English was not widely spoken.

My feet are not large – I take a size 8 (42) – but that was too big for the Thai shops. I looked, I smiled, I pointed and I was polite and was well received everywhere, even being asked to try on some shoes. It was all to no avail: I would be wearing my pumps for a month! I was in no hurry so I took my time and soaked up the atmosphere of being in a totally foreign country. Thailand is an Asian culture and was completely different to anything I had ever experienced. It showed in everything that I saw, heard and smelled.

I was enjoying myself and walked for miles around the area. The streets were clean, although I had to dodge the odd motorcycle on the pavement which was used as a short cut to miss heavy traffic.

I just walked and walked all afternoon, returning to the hotel at about six o'clock that evening. As I headed to my room to shower I noted two other Western girls in the dining room. We acknowledged each other as I passed through to the lift. I hurried my shower, hoping to get back down and join them for a while but they had already left when I returned; I found myself alone again for a second evening.

I tried the Chinese restaurant on the first floor of the hotel rather than the general restaurant which was located on the ground floor. I felt that, perhaps, the cuisine may be more authentic than I was used to in the UK. I ordered and sat back alone in the dining room, waiting for my meal. It was clearly out of season and the place was dead. The waitress started to talk with me; she was used to having transsexuals in the restaurant, as were all of the staff, and her English was also good. She extended my knowledge of the Thai language with "khorb khun ka" for "thank you"; another very useful piece of vocabulary. The meal was excellent but I was feeling lonely. I knew that I was amongst the first of this year's patients and that the hotel would be sparsely occupied on my arrival but I still felt the need to talk to someone.

I finished my meal and headed downstairs to see if either of the two ladies I had seen earlier had returned. I was pleased to see that they had and so went over and introduced myself. I had no embarrassment at all about going up to complete strangers in a hotel coffee shop as I assumed we were all there for the same reason.

I met Emily from the US and Julia from Germany. Julia had to excuse herself almost immediately as she had to go and dilate. She had had her surgery just prior to Christmas and had spent the entire Christmas holiday in the hotel with Emily. Julia was by now three weeks post-operative and was heading home on Tuesday. Dilation is the one thing none of us can afford to miss out and I knew that only too soon I would be doing exactly the same. This regular procedure, otherwise known as 'maintenance', is a topic which all post-operative transwomen are well aware of. The newly-formed vaginal canal needs to be kept open; it needs to be maintained. Imagine what happens if you have your ears pierced and don't keep the studs in during the early healing period - the holes close up. It is exactly the same for the new vagina in a post-operative transsexual. We can't however go around wearing a stud with a butterfly clip on the end! We have a series of exercises to undertake, which slowly reduce in frequency over time; but will have to be carried out for the rest of our lives – use it or lose it is so true!

Emily had come to the clinic for facial surgery. She was the same age as me and she was as glad of the company as I was. We were joined by Beyar from the

Netherlands, who was accompanying his friend, who had gone to hospital that morning for surgery next day. We hit it off immediately and were up chatting till after midnight. Thailand is seven hours ahead of the UK so I managed to catch up briefly with the girls on Facebook before going to sleep. It became a routine I was to carry out nearly every night I was there.

I do not, normally, sleep well in strange hotel beds but I nevertheless managed a few hours, as I was still tired from the journey. That was one of the reasons I had arrived a few days early, so that I could recover from the trip before being bed-bound for seven days in hospital. I went down to the breakfast room, where I was pleased to see Emily; we continued on from where we had parted the previous night. Breakfast finished, I wanted to walk again and so we went our separate ways. I left the hotel and walked into an entirely different world to the one I had witnessed the previous day.

It was busy as well as hot and humid. I had dressed minimally in a cotton skirt and light sleeveless top and I was glad I had done so. The temperature was in the low thirties and rising towards mid-day. The shops were all open and the street thronged with traffic: it is a main arterial road from the coast into the city of Bangkok. Cars of all types, buses and motorcycles were everywhere. The road was crossed at regular intervals by bridges for pedestrians: it seemed suicidal to try and cross any other way at this time of day.

I walked for a few hours, just absorbing the fact that I was in a totally different culture. The people were friendly and smiled often; the shops were full of unusual foods and objects; my frequent stops to window-shop were an enjoyable way to pass the time. I managed to get an idea of the geography of the area and of where the main shops were.

The hotel and clinic being located on a very major road made it easy to navigate around. I felt that I could not really get lost and was prepared to explore some of the smaller streets. Many of the shops just opened onto the streets without windows; they just had shutters which were brought down at night. It made it easy to browse and I could do the quick calculation of the currency conversion and see just how cheap goods were in comparison with the UK.

I was also astonished to see the preparation of fresh food to be cooked later that night in the street cafes. Hygiene was not apparently a top priority as whole families sat at the rear of the shops, preparing the food in the open air, with no chilling or refrigeration, no clean surfaces to work on and with shellfish just left out in the sun to warm up. It was, in a way, frightening compared to what we are used to in Europe. However there are no mass episodes of food poisoning of the population so the final result must be safe. That did not mean that I was prepared to try eating out in the cafes; I doubted that my soft European digestion would be able to cope. The last thing I needed was an upset stomach at this point in my trip. I decided I could do without the experience and so would continue to eat at the hotel.

I returned to the hotel in good time to go upstairs for a shower and to put on clean clothes. I wanted to freshen up as I would be examined in the clinic later that afternoon. I had also made up my mind to write a journal of my trip and set myself the target of writing every day that I could, although I was aware that it might not be possible every day, especially immediately after the surgery.

I was sitting in the hotel's reception area before going to my appointment, thinking about what was going to happen, when someone sat down next to me and introduced herself as Maddy. She had arrived late the previous night, and as it turned out, was to have her surgery the day before me. We talked for a while and, since I knew where the clinic was, I suggested that we walk together the short distance to the clinic.

We walked through the doors of the clinic into a busy, bustling waiting room full of people. Dr Suporn was running late, which was not uncommon, as I soon found out. Thai time just happens and appointments are often for convention only.

Still, the surroundings were pleasant and we were offered drinks to pass the time – I chose chilled Thai tea. After a while I was ushered into another much quieter room, to be taken through the formalities. Cin explained the process, which was very thorough. My passport was checked and copied and of course I had to produce the letter of referral from the UK medical authorities, without which my journey would stop right there. There were other forms to complete and disclaimers to sign; eventually all the paperwork was done.

Cin then introduced me to my new 'Thai boyfriends', the name jokingly given to the set of acrylic vaginal dilators, which are needed by all transsexual women. I would probably need them for the rest of my life and the set, in a beautiful presentation box looking like the most exotic of oriental gifts, was included in the cost of my surgery and after-treatment.

I returned to reception to wait for my consultation, which had been booked for half past four, although it was now already after six. Emily was there so we chatted for a while but she left when I went in to see the doctor.

It was my turn: this was it! I was nervous as Cin came in with me to translate should there be any difficulty. Dr Suporn is a pleasant quiet man, typically Thai to look at, with nothing to indicate his surgical genius. The consulting room was longer than it was wide, with a desk and computer at one end. The far end was taken up with an examination couch, with cupboards and a sink running alongside. The walls were a mix of painted plaster and wood with a large, full length mirror in the centre of the long wall at the end of the couch. There was a door opposite which led into an adjoining consulting room.

We greeted each other with "Sawasdee Kah" and he invited me to sit down. We went through a number of formalities and questions about any allergies I might have and about any medication I might currently be taking. Then we got down to the real business I had been expecting all along. Dr Suporn said that he now needed to examine me, and asked me to remove my underwear and get up on the couch. It was a brief and simple request but one which was about to determine how my surgery would work out. A minute at most was all that he needed.

"You have plenty of material to work with. I see no problems and we will be able to achieve an acceptable depth."

That was all it took and I knew I would have my surgery on Thursday. I could hardly believe it. In those few words he had removed any final worries about possibly not being a suitable candidate for surgery. It is rare for anyone to be turned down at this stage, but it can happen, or there can be complications which lead to the need for additional surgery. In short, the female hormones I had been taking over the last eighteen months had caused my genitalia to start to shrink – it happens to all pre-operative transsexuals and is a known sideeffect. This was his reference to "plenty of material", because some patients have lost so much skin and tissue that the surgery becomes much more difficult. This is because most of the male genitalia are restructured or 'recycled' to create the vulva and vagina, so the surgeon needs material with which to work. Without sufficient 'donor' skin, it is difficult to create a vagina of adequate depth.

We returned to his desk where he went through the procedure in more detail, showing me actual pictures of the operation and giving me an idea of the expected results. I had a few queries, which he answered clearly and concisely.

Once the SRS had been discussed we then reviewed my other surgical requirement. Call it vanity if you wish, but I do not see it that way: I wanted to have all of the loose skin removed from my upper eyelids, as they were drooping badly. My eyes looked far older than the rest of me. I was not considering any further facial surgery as I was, in my view, too old for major reconstructive feminisation surgery, which is something that many transsexuals do have. My new friend Emily, for instance, was recovering from a brow reduction operation to remove the so-called 'brow bossing' above her eyes: male skulls have a slight but noticeable ridge of bone above the eye sockets and this is one thing which can be changed to give the face a more feminine shape. She was the same age as me but it was not a procedure that I considered at that time. There is an issue here about what we see when looking in the mirror. At the time of writing, this is one aspect of my appearance that I can live with but time will tell and I cannot discount the possibility of surgery in the future.

As for the blepharoplasty I was considering, Dr Suporn looked me carefully in the face and then demonstrated, with two carefully-positioned toothpicks to lift my sagging eyelids, what the result of surgery might be. The anticipated success was more than enough to convince me and I was happy to go ahead. The whole consultation with him had taken no more than twenty minutes, although I had been at the clinic much longer than that. Soon I was on my way back to the hotel, feeling very happy with life.

I passed the evening as I would most evenings for the rest of my stay: I showered again, for the heat in the streets was still intense and I was sticky from my walk back to the hotel, and then I went down to the restaurant for dinner and to see who else was there. This time I met Emily and Julia again, as well as a new girl from Australia called Kelly, who had arrived only a few hours earlier. I was glad to have the chance to talk to Julia for a while before she left Bangkok, which she would be doing in the morning. However, our chat did not last for long as she again had to go back to her room for the dilation process, which has to be done three times a day in the early post-operative period.

Kelly, too, had already had her SRS operation – quite some time previously. She was actually on her way back to Australia following a holiday in the UK. She had decided to cut short her holiday because of the awful weather and to use the time instead to call in at the clinic in Bangkok. She had had various procedures carried out there in the past and was well known to the clinic staff. We talked until it was quite late, before going to our rooms. Once there I made contact with my family and friends in England, and eventually turned out the light around half past midnight.

The next day started as every day would; those who were able would meet downstairs for breakfast and then each would go their own separate ways until we either met again at the clinic or else back at the hotel, where we would eat in the evening.

After breakfast, with nothing much to do, I wandered down to the clinic. The reception area was empty apart from Kelly, who was using the computer (the clinic provided free internet access for its patients); she suggested that we could visit the others in hospital, which was fine by me. It was to be my first journey in a tuk-tuk three-wheeled motorcycle that serves as a local taxi. The fare was 100 Baht (about £2), which was very reasonable for the distance, so we got in. There were no doors, no seatbelts, no real concessions to safety of any kind – but it was a wonderful part of just being in Bangkok, despite the dense and potentially dangerous traffic.

The hospital was a short journey away - about fifteen minutes. It was a modern, multi-storey building which was very clean and efficient looking. I felt I would be happy having my surgery in such a place. Kelly knew that Dr Suporn's patients were all on the ninth floor, so that is where we headed. We very briefly visited two patients, Amelia and Ellie, who had had surgery on Friday and Monday respectively. It became obvious that boredom and loneliness were the greatest issues for patients to deal with. Both were glad of the company, even though it was only for a few minutes. While we were there one of the girls from the clinic arrived and offered us both a lift back, which we accepted; the offer of air-conditioned comfort won out over the excitement of the tuk-tuk.

My walk that afternoon was just along the roads as before. I found municipal buildings, offices and of course more shops. I was still out walking as the schools came out and it was interesting to note that a lot of children actually stopped and said "Hello." I, of course, replied "Sawasdee Kah." One boy, I would guess of about twelve, even went so far as to ask me my name in English and I told him. I cannot imagine a child in the UK saying hello to a Thai tourist in his own language: it just would not happen.

The hotel was very quiet and no-one was around. I had an early meal at about seven thirty and was joined by Beyar. We chatted for a while but I had things on my mind, as I would be admitted to hospital in the morning. Later Emily joined us but by half past ten I was feeling tired so I made my excuses and went to bed. I still checked the emails and spoke to all three girls via Facebook, just to reassure them that I was fine and that they should try not to worry. It was especially good to chat with Sophie, as I had kept missing her previously. She seemed fine when we said goodbye but I am sure she was still concerned about me and she admitted that she missed me. I determined to ensure that I did my best to make contact with her on a regular basis. I turned the lights out and slept well.

I woke early for a change, at about seven thirty, and went for my usual shower. As I did so I looked down and realised that this would perhaps be the last time I would perform this particular routine of genital cleanliness. After tomorrow I would look, and feel, completely different, although it would be a good many days before I stood in a shower again. This led to a brief reflection about my life and whether my path had been the correct one. Of course I was doing the right thing! My life had been a lie for so long and I had to finish what I had started. It was a brief reflection but, I think, an important one. My course was set, my mind was made up and I was determined to see this through and become the person I should have been from birth.

I dressed and went down to breakfast at nine o'clock, where I was joined by Kelly then Bayer and finally Emily. We chatted as though we had known each other for a long time. My impending trip to hospital was a major topic for us to discuss, as was my farewell to Emily: this was probably the last time I would see her as she was going home on Saturday.

It was impossible to stop thinking about the surgery, about all that it entailed and about what the final outcome would be. I was a bit pensive and quiet but the others respected that and let it be. I made an early exit in order to return to my room and pack the few essentials I would need for the hospital. I did not need much: my laptop, phone and chargers, my sponge bag and toiletries, creams, lotions and books. I knew I was going to be bored and lonely as I was on my own and also would not be able to see clearly for a few days following the eye surgery. I also had to take my 'Thai boyfriends' with me, as I would learn how to use them properly in hospital before I left.

I went down to reception at about twelve o'clock as I was due to leave for the hospital at a half past twelve. Emily and Beyar joined me as they were heading for the clinic and we left the hotel together. As we walked toward the glass doors I was struck by a change in the song playing on the hotel's background music: the new tune was Louis Armstrong, singing 'What a Wonderful World'. I could not have asked for anything better to sum up my happiness at that time, and I left the hotel with a broad grin on my face.

Jib, one of the lovely assistants from the clinic, was with me the whole time I was going through admittance. My passport was checked and then I went on to the medical tests. It was all carried out smoothly and quickly and we then headed to the 9th floor, and to room 905 that was to be my home for the next seven days. My weight and blood pressure were taken again by a nurse and then that was it: I was left on my own to settle in. I had not checked out of the hotel: the room remained mine, though unoccupied. I had left most of my things there so that there would be no delays on my return. The room was as large as my hotel room with the same facilities, not that I would be able to use them as I would be bed-bound for most of the time. One plus-point, though, was that it had a view of the sea in the far distance.

During the next few hours I was visited by both the anaesthetist and the psychiatrist. This was another formal requirement: although I had provided a letter of referral by a British psychiatrist, Thai hospital standards insisted that I also be checked by a Thai psychiatrist, to make sure that I truly wanted to go ahead with this irreversible procedure, and to be certain that I knew exactly what I was doing, that I was approaching it in a calm and considered manner, and that I knew beyond a shadow of doubt that it was absolutely right for me.

I felt at peace with life, now that everything had been done. I had been formally admitted and the hospital psychiatrist had confirmed that I was able to undergo the surgery in a little over seventeen hours' time. I reflected on all that had happened over my life, the last five days and, most importantly, on the twenty-two months since my transition and the beginning of my full-time life as Kirstie. They were significant times indeed.

There had been many before me to reach this point in their lives and I knew many more would follow. We all have similar stories to tell but each of us is also unique. We understand what we each have sacrificed to get to this time and place, for all that those sacrifices differ from person to person, and for all that the outcome of our decisions and actions is different for each one of us.

I had no regrets about my life so far or about the burden I had carried. I had done so alone for most of that time. I reflected that, for the majority of my life, I was unaware of the particular needs of that burden. I had lived in denial and had fought against the pressures that kept rising, in order that I could be seen as 'normal'. I had not willingly or knowingly hurt anyone but, unfortunately, there were still casualties, the most obvious being my second wife, Jean, who had probably had to deal with the hardest situation of all.

Before his death my father had reconciled himself to my change. My brother and children had all come to terms with the new situation and each, in his or her own way, was dealing with that change. I would remain the same person, albeit the outer appearance would change. I felt that I had become a much better person as I embraced my femininity. I thought back to how I had been comforted, before making my journey to Thailand, when talking to my daughter Kat. She had said, in answer to my question about how she now saw me: "Yes, you are the same person; but you are also a better one than before." I had to take that as a great positive statement and one that reinforced my decision to become what I have always believed to be my true self. I trusted my daughter's insight; her honest comment back then had strengthened my resolve to continue, despite the obvious costs and pain to others.

Later in the evening I caught sight of the logo for Dr Suporn's clinic on some of the paperwork. It shows a chrysalis and a winged female resting beside it. The imagery is, perhaps, a little obvious for some, but I found it very meaningful and very appropriate for me: I could imagine that my male body had been my chrysalis and that, in the morning, my female self would emerge complete and whole.

I had one last challenge before surgery the next morning. It is one which those who have already passed through the surgery are only too keen to tell to those who follow behind. I was due to have multiple enemas at about nine o'clock in the evening. My digestive system had to be completely clear, not only for the more obvious reason that the surgeon, working in that area, wanted to minimize the risk of cross-infection; it was also important to be 'empty' in order to have several days of healing time for the whole area before possibly putting strain on the stitches by going to the toilet. It was not something I was looking forward to but as the anesthetist had joked earlier, when telling me about the impending procedure:

"Just look on it as a significant detox; it won't be so bad then."

She was laughing at the time and I could do little but defer judgment until afterwards.

The enemas, I hardly need to say, were not fun; nor was the shave of my whole genital area, which was also required in preparation for the surgery in the morning, but I survived both. For a change I agreed to take a sleeping pill before retiring and I slept right through until six o'clock, when the nurse woke me and asked me to shower. I was then transferred to a gurney for the trip down to the operating theatre. I had been told that I would still be awake on entry as Dr Suporn was to do my eye surgery first and I had to sit up for the markings to be made. It was only a few moments but at least I can say I have seen inside the place of magic. Once I lay down I was unconscious in a second and knew nothing until I awoke back in my room, more than ten hours later.

I had plenty of time for reflection over the next few lonely days and realised the significance of the number fourteen. I had had my surgery on the fourteenth of January, the same day that fourteen of my peers had started the counselling course. I was thousands of miles away and was to miss five sessions in total but I was determined to catch up and to succeed with the course and the new direction in my life.

Memories of those days are blurred to say the least. One of the clinic girls stayed with me overnight on the first night, sleeping on the couch in my room, but I was barely aware of her and could not remember who it was. The one thing that stands out more than anything is my obvious bad reaction to morphine, which was introduced intravenously to combat the postoperative pain. In less than ten seconds I had vomited all over myself. The nurses tried twice more but with exactly the same result; it was obvious that morphine would not form part of my recovery pain management.

I could see nothing for the first few days. I was wearing a chilled gel pad over my eyes to limit swelling. This was regularly changed for me but, for most of that time, I didn't see anyone except when the pad was being changed. I was bored and very lonely; no one had come by to visit.

Pain was not an issue as far as I was concerned but boredom was. All SRS patients are kept in bed for the first five days to prevent any damage to the stitches, so I was visited regularly for blood pressure, temperature and pulse-readings. My health and recovery were certainly closely monitored. After five days the dressings were removed but the internal packing had to remain in place for another two days. As I was not allowed to sit up I could not even use the laptop or read easily, as my eyesight was still very blurred. Nevertheless, the hours and days eventually passed and I reached the next important stage: the removal of the internal packing by Dr Suporn. A day after that and I would be free to leave the hospital, as long as I was well enough, and I could then return to the hotel. Small things come to mean a great deal when your horizons are very limited and I began to long for the chance of a shower. During my enforced horizontal stay in bed I had been given a bed-bath every day by the nurses, which was fine, but I longed for a proper, hot shower.

Seven days after my surgery Dr Suporn arrived in my hospital room. He removed the final dressings and checked that everything was as it should be; I was passed as fit and could be discharged. One of the clinic staff came in and helped me shower, wash my hair and generally make myself presentable to the world. The hardest part was the facial shave. I had stopped taking hormones two weeks before the surgery, to reduce the risk of blood clots; my self-produced testosterone had once more taken charge of my body until its permanent removal. I had not shaved for seven days and I looked and felt awful: I could not have looked less feminine had I tried. It was just another timely reminder of the other issues I had to deal with – I would almost be glad to get back to facial electrolysis.

There was one last thing I had to do before being allowed to leave and that was to pass water normally, following the removal of the catheter which I had relied upon for the duration of my post-operative stay. I drank plenty of water and went to visit Sarah who had arrived and had had her surgery while I was confined to bed. She would still be in for another five days. We talked about any number of things and discussed the operation but I just did not need to urinate; I eventually got through three litres of water before I performed and could be discharged.

Chapter 15

Thailand, the culmination of my journey: recovery and home

The journey back to the hotel was not long and I went straight up to my room, slowly but confidently. I had left the hospital with a large holdall full of essentials and medications, which were unpacked by Jib who had accompanied me throughout my discharge and return to the hotel.

One of the more important items was the rubber cushion, which I had to take everywhere as it was the only comfortable way to sit for the next month or so, until the swelling and tenderness had subsided. My first duty, once I was settled back in my room, was to carry out my own first dilation, with a member of the clinic staff staying with me to ensure that I was doing it correctly. The nursing assistants from the clinic were wonderful and no praise is too high; they have seen it all and nothing fazes them. They act as intermediaries between the patients and the clinic, bringing supplies to the hotel where most patients stay after surgery, monitoring blood pressure, answering questions, checking that medication has been taken, and dealing with minor medical matters. They are a vital line of communication, too, for they all speak excellent English as well as other languages, as the majority of Dr Suporn's patients come from outside Thailand. I passed my test and it then became my responsibility to ensure I did it correctly without fail thereafter.

I was mobile and not in any great pain. Walking and sitting down were sometimes uncomfortable, of course, but life went on and I settled into a daily routine. I was visited by one of the clinic representatives each day to check on my progress and to take my temperature and blood pressure. They also checked how I was managing with my dilation, as it was a task I had to carry out conscientiously twice each day.

The morning after I returned to the hotel I had a meeting at the clinic, during which the full post-operative procedures and possible problems were set out in detail. I received a full manual of do's and don'ts: it made interesting, if scary, reading. Later that afternoon I had my first post-operative check up with Dr Suporn.

I first saw the nurse, who removed the stitches from my eyelids, as well as some from the site of my SRS. I then had my consultation and everything was pronounced to be satisfactory, although I had some small areas of necrosis, or dead tissue, which was not unusual and I was told not worry.

I improved each day and my dilation-routine became second nature: everything seemed to be falling into place. Each day I walked a little further and ensured that I did all of the required exercises. I also continued writing my journal. More patients were arriving and morning breakfast was becoming a social event as numbers slowly rose.

It was my daughter Sophie's birthday on the twenty fourth of January and I was still away. I had worried about this even before I set off for Thailand. I felt it important that I manage to speak to her on her birthday. Making allowances for the time difference I knew that if I tried at seven in the morning, when I got up, I could perhaps catch her at midnight as she turned fourteen. I got the timing right and was the second person to wish her a happy birthday: one of her school friends had beaten me. We managed to talk for a while over the internet and I was so pleased to have done it: it cheered us both up.

My recovery moved on and, although my healing progressed, I unfortunately suffered a bit more than was normal with necrosis of the tissue around the operation site. I also over-exerted myself with walking one day. I crossed the busy main road by using the pedestrian bridge, which I soon learned was a big mistake. The effort of climbing the stairs caused me to lose some stitches and it undid some of the surgery which I had spent so long in wishing for.

I simply knew that something was not right 'down there' but I did not panic: I was not bleeding nor was I in any additional pain, so I waited for the usual morning visit from a member of the clinic staff. She asked if all was OK and I explained my worry. She looked at the operation site and told me not to worry: the swelling had changed but that could be normal. Dr Suporn would be seeing me next day and he would let me know if I had anything to worry about. I rested for most of the day and had a light evening meal on my own. I did not feel like company and was lost in my own thoughts; I was worried about the outcome of this incident and just wanted to take it easy on my own.

The next morning I felt better and went down at my usual time for breakfast. There was already a table of five: Kelly, Ellie, Beyar, plus two new girls I had not seen before. The table was full so I headed for an adjacent table just as Kelly shouted out:

"Don't sit over there! Just pull the table over and join us."

That was easier said than done, but once she realised that I could not manage she came over to drag the table across the gangway; the staff had also cottoned on and rushed to help. There were no objections from the hotel staff to me rearranging their furniture and I suspect they were glad of the chance to see some fun.

Just as I was settling in Sarah and her partner Michelle turned up: we were now eight for breakfast, although the first five had mostly finished and were just chatting over coffee or tea.

I sat next to Liza, one of the new arrivals, and introductions were made. She was here to support Becca who was having some revision surgery that afternoon. Both girls were from San Francisco and therefore very cosmopolitan: introductions were quick and easy, and before long we were chatting like old friends. We three latecomers went and got our breakfasts and then settled down. Conversation was varied and then I remembered something from the previous day:

"Kelly! It's Australia Day. Have a good one!"

Kelly grinned and then offered to make us all Vegemite on toast to celebrate the day. She went to the buffet and came back with two plates of toast, which she then liberally spread with Vegemite; laughter and hilarity ensued. I had already tried Vegemite at the first breakfast with Kelly and hated it; it's just like sweet Marmite as far as I am concerned. However everyone joined in the fun and most, strangely, liked it.

The breakfast party just got better and better: discussions ranged from evolution vs. creationism to religion of many creeds, from Dr Who and the Cerne accelerator, to black holes and the Big Bang Theory, to name but a few. We stayed for over an hour. However, some of us had to prepare for a clinic visit and so went back to our rooms, while the discussion raged among those who were free to stay at the table.

Cin arrived at about eleven o'clock to see me and we went through the usual routine. She confirmed that I had an appointment with Dr Suporn at about four o'clock and said that I should arrive at the clinic in good time. Although the dead skin around my genital area had fallen away there was still extensive swelling and a change in the shape of one of my labia indicating that all was not as it should be. Cin advised me not to worry, to take it easy and to await the doctor's diagnosis.

I had full confidence in both Dr Suporn and his staff and so did my best to rest. Nevertheless I was a little agitated and so decided on a short walk at about mid-day. I met Becca in the foyer as I was leaving the hotel. She, too, was passing time, as she had to see Dr Suporn at two o'clock for a small surgery which would still require a general anaesthetic. We decided to take the short walk to the clinic and back together, just for the exercise.

I felt wary but the need to exercise is essential for recovery. In the twenty-minute walk I told her about myself and she, in return, filled me in on a bit of her own history. At the clinic Becca said:

"Shall we see if the cat is at home? He was here last year, when I was here."

I had not noticed one before but as we entered the clinic garden, and as if on cue, a ginger Tom was there, mewling for some love. He proceeded to perform for the pair of us, even moving into a sunlit patch for photographs, which we both obliged him by taking.

We concluded our walk back to the hotel and I went to my room to rest. I was then collected by a driver for the short drive and duly arrived at the clinic at about quarter to four, in good time for my appointment. Dr Suporn was running late, which was common: he is, after all, a very busy man and treats each patient according to their needs rather than to a timetable. Liza was there, waiting for Becca to wake up from her operation, and we spent time together. The clinic has a fully functioning operating theatre on the first floor, where revisions and small surgeries are carried out. After a short time Liza was told that Becca was awake and went up to see her. I was called in for my consultation a few minutes later.

I went into the consulting room and lay on the table as usual; Jib was there to assist. Dr Suporn was in the adjoining room, so we had time to talk about nothing in particular but just chatted like any two women with time to spare.

Dr Suporn came in and, after a few words with me and with Jib, inspected the damage. Sure enough, I had torn some stitches, partly because of the weakness of the necrotic skin. It was disappointing but it was not an unexpected diagnosis. Skin necrosis is a fact of life with grafts. Some of us will suffer to a greater or lesser degree and I had been unlucky, although I also suspect that climbing the stairs had not helped.

His next comment, however, certainly came out of the blue:

"I will repair you this afternoon. Go with the nurse, she will sort you out and get you prepared."

That was a shock! On the one hand I was pleased that he would take care of my problem almost immediately; on the other hand I would be lying if I said I was not concerned, as the repairs would be done under a local anesthetic. Jib held my hand as we left the room and she took me to the bathroom: she asked me to shower and clean the area thoroughly. I was also provided with a peach coloured theatre gown.

My thoughts as I showered were in turmoil. I was upset that I needed a repair so soon, and over the fact that it could have been me at fault, partially at least. On the other hand I was also very pleased that he could repair the damage there and then, especially as the whole area was still badly swollen.

I came out of the bathroom, my personal belongings were placed in a locker and the key safely tied to my gown. I was led back to reception and sat with Kelly to break the news.

"I have lost some stitches and Dr Suporn is going to repair the damage this afternoon. It will be done with a local anaesthetic and I'm scared," I told her.

"Hey! Don't worry. You are not the first where this has happened. Dr Suporn is great. You won't have any problems," she said, cheering me up.

I was then called back into the consultation room where the nurse checked me over and applied a topical anaesthetic, which had to be left for at least thirty minutes to work. I went back to the reception where Kelly was just heading back to the hotel.

"Don't panic," she said, "We'll see you tonight back at the hotel."

I sat and thought about what was happening to me. New girls were coming in for their first consultations, the clinic was busy. Jib came over and sat next to me holding my hand. She asked how I was feeling.

"I am nervous and scared but I have confidence in the doctor," I replied

Jib smiled, which lifted my spirits and we sat quietly for a few moments before she said:

"It's time to go."

She helped me to stand and then we walked together towards the staircase which led up to the operating area. Not everyone made this journey so it was a step into the unknown for me. I removed my shoes as is the custom and we walked up the stairs together, Jib still holding my hand. There were two couches on the landing and Jib directed me to one so I could wait in comfort. Just as I was about to sit we were told I could go straight into theatre.

This was it and my pulse rocketed! We walked past a recovery room on the way and I noticed Liza holding Becca's hand. We nodded to each other in silent acknowledgement; she smiled and quietly wished me luck.

I approached a pair of timber doors with frosted glass panels and was led into the theatre. Jib left me at the door - she had duties downstairs - and another girl took over as she led me to the operating table in the centre of the room, which was about twenty feet square. There were units around the perimeter, sinks and all the paraphernalia of a modern operating theatre; there were also four staff, all fully gowned and masked.

I was asked to lie down on the table. The nurses adjusted my position and I noted that the table could split, enabling my legs to be spread to give access to the all-important area. I lay down and all I could see was the ceiling. Not much else was visible and I would be looking at this for some time.

I waited and it became obvious that Dr Suporn was delayed for some reason. The ladies in theatre chatted away in Thai so all I could do was listen and think about what was going to happen. It was perhaps not the best way of passing time under the circumstances, but I had no choice.

There was a flurry of activity as Dr Suporn came through the door and he apologised for the delay; suddenly it was all action. My legs were lifted, as the bottom of the table was split, and each one was strapped into a cradle to hold me in the right position. This was it and I was scared: the wait had added to my worry. I was going to be awake the whole time that I was being repaired. I was covered with the heavy green surgical cloth and was quietly told to put my hands underneath.

Everyone obviously knew the routine and it all just seemed to slot into place.

"This will feel cold," I was told, but I could not see who was speaking.

I lay there with my legs wide apart as I was swabbed with an antiseptic wash. I stared at the ceiling, hearing nothing but rapidly-spoken Thai and the clatter of instruments.

"This may prick," came another voice, before I felt a short pinprick as a local anesthetic was given; the topical cream had done its job of partially numbing the area but a proper anaesthetic was needed to obliterate the pain of the procedure. There is not much I can say about the next half hour, other than I felt pulled and prodded. The repair was evidently not as straightforward as I thought it might be but, then again, what did I know about such things?

Finally it was over and Dr Suporn gave me a mirror so that I could see between my legs, as he explained what he had done. The whole area was swollen of course but it looked so much better than when I had arrived. He then told me to be careful and not to walk too far; he would see me again in two days. I was given an injection of antibiotic and, after a brief discussion, we decided upon an injection of pain relief rather than relying on oral tablets; the Novocain, used during the operation, would wear off in an hour.

"Thank you so much," was all I could say.

It seemed too little but I am sure Dr Suporn understood just how much this meant. I would not be going home with a total disfigurement and my gratitude must have shown on my face.

Before leaving I asked if I would still be able to go on the clinic trip to the beach house in the morning. This was one of two trips organised by the clinic to give patients and their supporters the chance to see some other part of the country.

"Yes you can go, but do not do too much walking. No visit to the temple: too many steps."

I was disappointed that I would miss the temple visit but so glad that I would still get away from the hotel for a day. Like many others, I was going stir crazy.

I was helped down from the table and out through the doors into the reception area, where I meet Liza and Becca who were just about to go downstairs. We smiled, each knowing that we had undergone a similar experience and that our lives could now move forward once more. I noticed that Becca was also wearing the same fetching peach gown as I. We were asked if we would like to change or go back to the hotel in the gowns. There was no contest! We agreed to go back in matching dresses!

We went slowly down the stairs, one step at a time, and out to the waiting transport which would take us the few hundred yards back to the hotel. The step up to the interior of the minibus was difficult, with both of us needing some assistance which Liza was more than willing to provide.

Two minutes was all it took to reach the hotel entrance. The hotel doorman saw us slowly and gingerly disembark and opened both entrance doors wide. Becca and I took one look, nodded to each other, smiled and made our grand entrance to the hotel. Two very groggy ladies in matching peach gowns made a grand entry through the busy hotel reception lobby. There were a few stares, perhaps, but neither of us was in the least concerned.

We made it to the lifts where Becca and Liza headed for the seventh floor but I was getting out at the third. I murmured quietly to Liza that this was where I missed having a companion, as Becca would have her help. Liza just turned and smiled sweetly, saying that they were in room 711 and that I should give her a call if I needed anything at all for the rest of the evening or during the night. It was a lovely feeling to have just met someone who understood in some way what I had just gone through, having supported her friend Becca, and was so selfless in offering help if it were needed.

"Thank you," was all I could say as I smiled gratefully.

I said my good night to them and headed to bed where I soon fell asleep, while looking forward to a trip out in the morning. I and my fellow-travellers in the hotel were not in Thailand on a tourist holiday. We had gone for surgery of one kind or another and so were largely confined to the hotel, the clinic and the immediate surroundings. However, as we each began to recover from our operations we began to need a little more variety – we were all affected by cabin fever and longed for a change of scenery. The clinic is well aware of this and arranged supervised trips out, for those who were mobile, so that we could at least get away from the hotel, even for just a few hours of 'holiday'.

The 'Beach House' belongs to Dr Suporn and is a substantial mansion overlooking the Gulf of Thailand. It is set in its own landscaped grounds which slope some one hundred metres from the rear veranda down to the low rear wall of the property, where there is a gate leading out onto the public area. The garden is perfectly kept, with shrubs, trees and palms everywhere to give shade. There is an area of soft white sand along the bottom boundary and a number of small covered areas, where one can just sit and watch the world go by. The interior is comfortably air conditioned, and we were able to go inside whenever we wanted if it became too hot outside.

There were twelve of us – patients, companions and staff – and we travelled in two minibuses. One of the vehicles stopped at a temple on the way for some sightseeing. However, I and two others recently discharged from hospital were not allowed to go, and with good reason: the climb up to the temple involved hundreds of steps. That was an experience I had no wish to repeat so soon after my repair, and I was cautious about climbing any stairs for a long time to come.

There was almost a party atmosphere once we all gathered at the beach house. Some of us were admittedly a little subdued as we were still recovering from major surgery, but we were all looking forward to a pleasant and relaxing time. I was mindful of the instruction not to walk too far so I took it easy. I walked slowly down the lawn to the bottom of the garden and onto the area of soft white sand. I then walked through the gate to the beach and into the Gulf of Thailand for a paddle. I was obviously not allowed to swim but I thoroughly enjoyed the feel of the sand between my toes and the warm water lapping around my calf muscles. It was a wonderful feeling.

The beach was not really public: it was no more than ten or fifteen feet from the garden wall to the high water mark and there were no others there, apart from our group. Later on that day I sat for an hour in the shade and watched a local Thai family dredging the sand for shellfish. The parents worked, while a small toddler just behaved as any child anywhere in the world would do and played in the sand. It was a peaceful scene to watch and I felt gloriously happy.

The whole tempo of the day was relaxing. I took my time as I moved from one area of the garden to another, sometimes happy to be on my own, and at other times joining in the conversations. There was absolutely no rush.

We stayed until early evening and watched the sun set into the sea. I had some photographs taken with the sunset in the background, one of which is a favourite and will always remind me of that special day at the beach. I was not necessarily looking my best at that stage, as it was only thirteen days since my operation. I had also had the revision surgery only the previous day. I was, however, very content with my life and I like to think that that shows through in the photograph.

We returned to the hotel and parted company in the lobby, tired but happy. I went up to my room for, like several others in our group, I had my dilation routine to complete. It hurts, and it is a chore, but we all know how absolutely essential it is. I doubt there is anyone who, having had the anguish of gender dysphoria, and who has finally achieved the longed-for surgery, would compromise the success of the outcome by not doing the dilation exercises. After I had finished I was tired and could not be bothered to go back down for an evening meal. An early night called and I slept well.

The second trip was different and more active. We visited a gem factory where I purchased a bracelet and matching earrings as a memento of my trip and also in memory of my father; I wanted something of value to keep as a reminder of his love and support. We then moved on to a theme park where we were to see traditional dancing and elephant displays. It was a nice day out but without the peace and contentment of the Beach House trip. I did at least get to do 'the tourist thing' for a while!

Each day was much the same as every other. We got up, had breakfast and returned to our rooms to wait for the clinic visitor to come and take our blood pressure and temperature and to check how we were. I was seen at the clinic every other day to monitor my progress after the revision surgery. I was still suffering from necrosis and there was a slim chance that further surgery may be required. Luckily that was deemed unnecessary but it was a close call and that decision was made only a few days before I left for home.

Patients came and went: I met so many people from all parts of the world and it was an illuminating experience to realise just how many people suffer from this condition known as Gender Dysphoria. It knows no international boundaries nor does it discriminate between race, gender or sexuality. It is however a very cruel and often misunderstood condition.

We all had different stories to tell, yet they were also similar in many respects and there was always a bond between us, no matter where we came from or what language we spoke. I became even more determined then to succeed in my decision to become a counsellor and to specialise in gender issues. The lack of support was, it seemed, a worldwide problem and anything I could do to alleviate the shortage of suitably qualified help would be worthwhile.

I was due to leave for the UK on Saturday the sixth of February and had my final consultation at the clinic on the Thursday. I was healing, slowly but surely, and I was passed as fit to travel. I was told that, because of the revision surgery, the appearance of my vulva might be a little 'lopsided', but that I should not worry as the healing and functionality would be fine. However, if I felt after some months that it was still unsightly I could always return for further cosmetic surgery (labiaplasty is a perhaps surprisingly common operation), although that would be my choice as it was not medically necessary.

I was given various letters to confirm that my surgery had been conducted in accordance with the International Standards of Care for a transsexual and that I was now anatomically and sexually female. I also had a letter confirming that the various medications I was carrying were needed and were for my own personal use – I did not want complications with a suspicious customs official to interrupt my journey home. Finally, I was also given a letter on the clinic's notepaper, requesting wheelchair assistance through the airports; this proved to be of huge value to me.

I was keen to get back home but my farewell to the doctor and the clinic staff was a sad occasion. They had been my surrogate family for the last month and I liked and respected them a great deal - but I had also had enough. I was missing home and, most importantly, my daughters. Still, we had at least managed to keep in touch on an almost daily basis so they knew I was alright.

I was becoming impatient to be on my way now. I had almost reached the end of my journey and, despite the upset with the torn stitches, was recovering well. I still followed the same daily routines in the hotel and the clinic, including the twice-daily dilation, as did everyone else. Others around me were gradually leaving, either because they had arrived before me, or because their surgery did not need such a long stay for recovery afterwards. As each person reached the end of their stay farewells were said and new people arrived. Many of the people I met I would never see again but that bond of shared experience would always remain. I had email and Facebook contact details for the few I had bonded with and, of course, I would see Sarah on her return to the UK, which would be a little later than mine.

The others were passing acquaintances: I was glad to have met them and to have learned about their own journeys. There were now almost twenty post-operative girls in the hotel at various stages of recovery. The clinic assistants who visited each and every one of us tended to see first the patients who had most recently left the hospital, or who had more need of attention; the morning visit could therefore be as late as mid-day, so long periods were spent on our own, just waiting. This was the time I usually caught up with the family and wrote my journals. I had finally been in touch with the course tutor and had confirmed my arrival at college for the Thursday following my return; she acknowledged my mail and told me that everyone was looking forward to my arrival.

My last day in the hotel was Saturday the sixth of February; I would be collected at eleven thirty that night to be taken to Bangkok airport for a two o'clock in the morning flight on Sunday. There were ten of us round the table for breakfast, including Liza and Becca, who would be leaving at ten o'clock for their flights back to the USA. Of all the people I had met over the past month, Liza was someone with whom I seemed to have connected on many levels. She also agreed that we were very similar in many ways.

It may seem unusual that, of all the people there, I connected best with a genetic female who was there to support her partner and friend Becca, the transsexual. Unusual? Perhaps, but then who knows how we choose friends and what makes us connect? We hugged and said our goodbyes and then Becca and I did the same; I knew I would miss them both.

I was still under the care of the clinic and so still had to undergo the usual morning routine, along with everyone else who was post-operative. After breakfast I returned to my room to wait for the visit. Luckily I did not have long to wait before there was a knock at the door. I was pleased to see it was Aei from the clinic. She came in and we went through the standard medical questions. Then she said:

"It's your last day today Kirstie, isn't it?"

"Yes," I replied, "and I will miss you all but I have to say that I'll be glad to get home again."

"I'm sure you will. I wish you the best for the future and perhaps we shall see you again one day," she said as we parted.

"I'm not sure," I replied. "But you never know. Thank you for all you and the others at the clinic have done for me, I am very grateful."

We said good-bye and hugged before she left to continue her rounds. She was the last of the clinic staff I would see: it was a sad and reflective moment.

I suspect that the sadness had a part to play but I really did not feel like doing anything for the rest of the day. Most people would be in their rooms, waiting for Aei's visit and of course Liza and Becca had left. So I lay down on my bed, linked up to BBC Radio 2 online and continued writing my journal. I had to complete my college journal first and it is that, perhaps, which best reflects my thoughts, as it had to be a concise and short statement of how I felt. I sent a copy to my tutor, for her comment and to let her see what I had been writing for the last four weeks. I knew my group would be at college later for a Saturday workshop and I wondered what I would be missing.

I spent the rest of the afternoon with Sarah; she was staying for a longer trip and intended to make a holiday of her time in Thailand. Eventually I went back to my room, as we would be meeting each other again at the evening meal.

My bags were fully packed: I had done that in the morning, and my travelling clothes were all laid out. They included the sweater I wore on my arrival, as I was heading back to the cold and wet of England in February. The only difference was that this time I would be wearing a skirt: it would be a long time before I could wear trousers, comfortably, again.

I used the time before dinner to do my last dilation before leaving, then I dressed in my going-home outfit and packed the last of my bits and pieces. All that was left out were my phone, laptop and cables plus the essential travel documents and the letters from the clinic. I wondered how well the wheelchair service would work in the three international airports (Bangkok, Dubai and London Heathrow); the thought of walking the huge distances, in my present condition, was more than daunting. I checked the room for a last time and headed down for dinner, not feeling hungry at all. I also had very mixed emotions; I was sad to be leaving but also glad to be finally on my way home.

There was the usual crowd for dinner, a number of whom were also leaving on Sunday but none on the early flight I was taking, so I was to leave the hotel on my own. I was not in the least hungry; my last meal in Thailand was a plate of French Fries. I realised I was not much company so I made my goodbye's which took a while and was emotional for us all. I spent a few extra moments with Sarah and made a promise to keep in touch while she was away.

It was about 8pm but I was not being collected until after 11pm and I was tired. The room was mine until Monday morning as I was leaving a day early to catch the flight. I went to reception and ordered a wake-up call for ten thirty that night. Once the staff realised I was leaving there was no problem and the system set up. I went up to my room and lay down to doze, but not before I had set the alarm on my mobile, just in case.

I slept and was woken first by my mobile alarm and then by the automated wake up call from the hotel. I felt refreshed as I dressed and made my way out of the room that had been my home for the past month. I was glad to see the back of it but also sad because of the memories which were attached. I went down to reception where there was no one else around but the staff. All of my new friends were well tucked up in bed so I was on my own.

It was ten past eleven when the bus drove into the hotel foyer area. Danny, the driver, got out and came into the hotel to take my luggage and to help me into the minibus.

Well, what else can I say? The journey back to the airport was a repeat of when I was collected except, of course, I had some lovely company then: Danny's English was very limited. I was left to my own thoughts this time, which tended to be sad at leaving and curious about what I would return to in the

UK. The weather was not high on my list of pleasant thoughts but I would manage.

The journey and arrival at the airport were uneventful; Danny unloaded my bags and took me straight to the correct counter. I suspect he knew the location of every check in desk at the airport, due to the number of times he did the journey.

So here I was at midnight, standing in front of the business check-in counter at Bangkok airport. I had made a conscious decision to fly home in business class, for the comfort afforded by the bigger seats and the ability to have a flat bed. It proved to be a very good decision. There was no queue, unlike at the other desks, for which I was very thankful. The first thing I did was to hand over my passport, my travel document and the all-important letter from the clinic, requesting wheelchair assistance.

The clerk checked through the letter:

"May I take a copy?"

"Of course," I replied.

She disappeared for a few minutes, returning with my original and a copy in her hands. It all then just happened. Someone turned up and put my luggage on the weighing scales. I turned around and a wheelchair was just arriving; the whole process worked like clockwork. I was told my details would be sent on to each airport and that I would be well looked after.

I was sped through departures, using a priority route where there are no queues or delays, and into the departure lounge. I asked my 'driver' if I could do a bit of shopping first before going to the business lounge, where I would wait the hour before boarding.

"That's no problem, Madam," he said.

I directed my driver to the perfume counters, where I handed over a list I had prepared of perfumes I wanted for the girls. A helpful young man went and did my shopping for me and we met at the checkout; it was all civilised and very easy. I was then wheeled to the Business Lounge, where I could wait in comfort for my departure. I passed an hour on my laptop before the wheelchair driver returned to take me to the plane avoiding all the queues, just as before.

I boarded and was directed to my seat. Once we had taken off I laid the seat flat so that I could sleep in comfort, which I did with great pleasure. This was the whole reason for paying the extra fare and I can confirm it was money well spent.

The rest of my journey and transfer at Dubai was just as easy. I was met, avoided all queues, and delivered to the new aircraft in good time. Business class in the Airbus was a wonderful experience and one that has probably tainted my ability to fly economy ever again! I slept a lot and watched a few films until landing in Heathrow.

I was the last to disembark but with the priority wheelchair passage I was almost first into the baggage reclaim where, wonder of wonders, my case had just arrived. It was all so smooth. We went out through customs into the arrivals hall. My wheelchair driver knew exactly where to take me, as I had told him I had a chauffeur-driven car ordered. It was part of the business class package and another reason for my choice on the return journey. We arrived at a desk where I gave my name.

The desk clerk called out:

"Bernie. Please come here. This is Kirstie and you are to take her home."

Listening to someone use the female designation felt good, even more so now that my body matched.

I looked up into a smiling face and we followed him out to the car park, where I transferred to the car. Soon we were out on the motorway and almost before I knew it I was back home, which I had left thirty days earlier to set off on my special journey. I was now, physically at least, an entirely different person. I opened the front door to be met by the aroma of a roast lamb Sunday lunch, prepared for my return. A good omen, I thought, as I entered the kitchen to see my three daughters waiting for me.

It was a quietly emotional reunion. One thing was very clear, they were glad I was home and well, but they definitely did not wish to know anything about my surgery and what I had undergone. This was to be a difficult time for us all: after all they had lost a father figure, although I was still there as a person. We sat down to our first Sunday lunch together in a month. I was tired and so did not drag out this first reunion; I made my apologies soon after finishing the meal and went to bed.

My journey was over. I was home after thirty days during which time I had undergone irreversible and life-changing surgery so that I could feel whole and true to myself. I had the rest of my life in front of me to learn to live as I had always wished to do. Would it be an easy ride from here? I doubted it very much but it would be a journey where I was in control and could at last be honest with the world around me and live as a female in all respects.

This was the culmination of my life's wish and one that I will be forever grateful to have achieved. I have no regrets about my decision to have the reassignment surgery; or, in fact, about my decision to admit to the world at large that I am transsexual and had been hiding behind the masculine façade for fifty years. There had been casualties along the way but they were fortunately very few. I had retained the love and support of my three daughters for which I will be forever grateful. They would undoubtedly still have difficulties with my transition, especially Sophie who, at fourteen, was struggling with her own changes, never mind those which I had imposed.

My surgery made the change public and irreversible and I suspected that it would give rise to feelings in my daughters which neither they nor I could guess at, so soon after my return. Time would tell how we resolved those unknown issues and how we continued with our lives. My daughters no longer had a male father figure in their lives and I felt that this may become an issue for them at times, whether consciously or unconsciously; we would have to wait on that.

My grandchildren will not have a 'grandfather', my daughters will not have a father-figure to take them down the aisle, should they have a traditional wedding. I am sure there will also be plenty of other issues which I have not even begun to contemplate at this time. Nevertheless, I will always be there for them, just not in the traditionally accepted role. I was sure we would work around it and would hopefully reach sensible compromises to each issue as it arose.

I must not feel guilt for my decision, although I am sure there will be times when that emotion will raise its ugly head. I steadfastly remain without regret and will face the future head-on to resolve any unforeseen issues that will fly in the face of tradition but which, in the end, will boil down to nothing more than 'names'. I hope, and believe, that my daughters will continue to show the inner strength that they have already demonstrated and will rise above any difficulties that may be forthcoming; after all, I will always be their Dad.

Chapter 16

Endings – Just One Letter

I was home a week before my fifty-fifth birthday, it was winter and I had a long way to go to heal fully. My emotions were mixed. I was, of course, happy to be home and back with my daughters but there were a lot of unspoken issues to be resolved between us.

The resolution of these issues would not happen overnight. It would take time and extends beyond the ending of this narrative. I'm glad to say, though, that it is a happy ending, although we faced many difficulties along the way.

Home life settled into a routine quite easily but it took a while for Sam and Sophie to understand that I was recovering from major surgery. They kept asking why I did not do various tasks as I usually did. I could not discuss the details with them so all I could repeat was:

"I'm recovering from major surgery. Please give me a chance."

They learned not to ask questions or to disturb me when, twice a day, I shut my bedroom door to do 'my exercises'. The healing was going to take time and in these early days was to impact on my ability to do much around the house. I was glad I was still unemployed; to have to consider going to work in a week or so was beyond comprehension. It was still winter and cold, but I had just returned from temperatures in the thirties with high humidity where my body had acclimatised over the last month. I kept the heating on and turned up high, only slowly reducing it after a week or so. Both girls were continually complaining about how hot it was in the flat, so I just told them quite directly:

"I pay the bill. I will keep it as hot as I feel it needs to be," and left it at that.

I was looking forward to Thursday evening, four days after I got home, when I would attend my counselling course and get on with my life and my new goal.

Thursday duly arrived; I had not healed sufficiently to drive my car so arranged for a taxi. I then vowed it would be the first and last time, once I found out just what it would cost for the return journey! However, at this stage I had no alternative and made my way to college.

I entered the common room where only a few months previously I had tasted this experience for the first time and had now chosen this route to my new career as a counsellor. I was aware that this would not be an easy journey as it would cause me to explore once again many of the issues I had already questioned during the years of gender counselling. I was, however, determined to give this my best effort and was sure that my determination would carry me through the next few years of training.

As I went into the room I saw some familiar faces from the previous course, who were aware of my whereabouts for the last few weeks. My introduction to the group was low-key; I introduced myself, made my apology for joining the course late and left it for the rest of the group to wonder about what may have been the reason. They eventually all discovered my little 'secret' anyway: it was inevitable on a course of that kind. When and how I told everyone was entirely my choice and eventually I selected an appropriate moment; after all, open honesty goes with the territory when on a course learning how to counsel people's deepest, most personal problems.

When they found out, many applauded my courage at following my own path to self-fulfillment. I however saw it as an essential journey for my own survival which we all, ultimately, have to travel in life. My journey was just a little more drastic in its final outcome as not many individuals have to undergo a major surgical procedure to achieve a major goal in life – contentment and self-acceptance. I can only report that the course was a wonderful environment in which to be able to be open with those around me, who were prepared to listen to what I said without prejudice or judgement. It did, in many ways, make my reassignment and recovery just that bit easier, as I had a safe place to be as honest as I needed to be. That is after all why we were all training to be counsellors, and it felt good to be back and on track.

I was lucky attending for that first night and then having a week off for half-term. That evening was surprisingly tiring and the extra week for recovery made a great difference. By the time of the next class I was able to drive myself there. Attendance and homework became the tasks that kept me occupied over the next months until June, when we all finished. There was little else to occupy me as my body slowly but surely healed and I regained my strength.

Life at home went on much as usual sharing a rented flat with two of my daughters, Sam and Sophie; I could not do a great deal and in truth for the first few months after returning did not feel like doing much. I often reflected on the bittersweet situation that had allowed me to take as much time for recovery as I required: the death of my father. His legacy to me meant that I could take my time, for a short while at least.

Eventually I needed stimulation before becoming totally bored with the relatively empty days and found myself a job as a home carer; a job so far removed from my previous career that there was no comparison. Financially, of course, it could not possibly compare but emotionally it was so rewarding that I found it to be a perfect match for my new lifestyle.

I still had two issues to complete before I could consider that I had finally arrived at the end of this part of my life's journey. The first was quite straightforward. I had an outstanding appointment at the Charing Cross Gender Identity Clinic, which had been arranged long before my departure for Thailand. It was essential for me to attend, so I looked forward to early March, only a month after my return.

The appointment was with the head clinician and, under normal circumstances, would have been to decide whether or not I could be referred as a suitable candidate for surgery. This was, of course, now completely unnecessary but I still had to be formally discharged from the system. Even after discharge I could return to the clinic should it ever become necessary either due to unforeseen complications resulting from surgery or to clarify any issues that may arise with my medication. My doctor would continue to dispense the prescription for the hormones but G.P's are not qualified to deal with any significant changes that might arise following my annual blood screening. My blood has to be monitored annually to ensure the oestrogen is kept within safe limits and that my kidneys and other major organs continue to work effectively.

It was a short and very rewarding meeting. There was no displeasure that I had gone ahead and had my surgery elsewhere, nor even that I had not completed the NHS requirement of a 24-month real life experience. I had, after all, only shortened the requirement by a few months. My reasoning that it was better to do it when I had the time and the funds (following my redundancy) was accepted as appropriate. I was clearly happy with the outcome and this was noted in the discharge letter to my GP.

That was it, as far as the NHS was concerned I was discharged and, therefore, in my opinion, no longer a transsexual but a female. I was satisfied.

The last task to be completed was the change of my birth certificate to officially recognise the error recorded at my birth and to confirm my reassigned sex in every way. The change of a birth certificate is not undertaken easily and nor is it a given fact that it will be granted. It also requires some consideration by the person requesting the change. Once done it is irreversible and the applicant is recognised as having the acquired gender as if from birth in all respects such as retirement age, pension entitlement, National Insurance liability, and so on.

In fact, in some ways I actually became worse off, particularly with my pension rights and that is an issue which prevents some post-operative transsexuals from taking that final step and applying for a Gender Recognition Certificate. Yet, without the certificate, the state would continue to regard me as male, to the extent that I could theoretically be sent to a male prison if I committed a sufficiently serious crime; and I would certainly be recorded as male on my death certificate and in the national register of deaths. The legal reason for this is that the death certificate has to 'cancel out' the birth certificate and so the details have to match. The Gender Recognition Certificate and, with it, a new birth certificate showing my sex as female, would allow my death, when it came, to be recorded properly. I would not be around but nevertheless it was important to me. It was a clear-cut decision for me: of course I wanted to correct what I saw as an error on my birth certificate, formally and forever.

The process is quite straight-forward. It is a collection of papers and proofs, along with appropriate letters of support from the medical profession. Even though I had undergone surgery I could still be turned down, as the medical certificate received from Thailand was not considered adequate proof because the surgeon is not a member of the British Medical Association.

One letter of proof had to come from a member of the Gender Recognition Panel's list of approved practitioners in the gender field, as well as an additional one from my own GP. Luckily the specialist I had seen privately, and who had provided my letter of referral for surgery, is on that list and so I was able to provide all necessary supporting documentation.

I made the application in April and then had to wait, as the Gender Recognition Panel only met once a month. Four weeks later I was thrilled to receive the letter stating that my application had been successful and enclosing the all-important Gender Recognition Certificate. On the twenty first of May 2010 I was formally recognised as a female and would remain so for the rest of my life. I openly acknowledge that I shed tears of happiness when the letter and certificate arrived – as life-changing moments go, this was one of the very best.

This was followed a few days later by a letter from the Registrar General in Scotland, where my birth details were held, asking me to confirm the details of my new Birth Certificate before it could be issued. This was very easy as there was only one change I wished to make: that was my Christian name. It would be changed from Kenneth, which my parents had chosen for me fifty-five years previously, to Kirstie. It was now more than five years since I had chosen this name, the one I had been using formally for the past two years, and the one which I would now happily be known as, in every aspect of my life and death, whenever that might be.

My new birth certificate is dated the twenty fourth of May 2010 and the only other change on it is the one I had struggled with all of my life to resolve. In the column headed Sex it was the simple change of just one letter, from M to F.

I also shed tears when that document arrived, just as I am doing now, while writing this: tears of joy and happiness. My struggle had lasted throughout my life; yet the time from when I told Jean about 'the problem' to the date of my legal recognition as female was a short four years and seven months. Have no doubts about it, those last few years, and the last steps of my journey, were traumatic for all concerned: for my family, for my friends, and of course for me. I was often asked if I felt I was doing the wrong thing, but I never doubted myself. Once I had taken that first step to be honest with the world there was no chance to go back; my mind was made up. Every step thereafter just reinforced my resolve and confirmed that I was doing what was right for me.

I could finish my story at this point and there would be nothing wrong with that. However, there was one small but important event still to come where I could safely disclose my feelings and where I knew others would understand just what this meant to me.

The twenty fourth of June was the last day of my course at college and I already knew I had proven myself proficient at level 2 counselling skills. I was happy about this but knew there was still a long way to go before I could achieve my goal of becoming a gender counsellor and help others who were going through a journey similar to the one I had just completed.

The tutor had asked that we each do a 'show and tell' to the rest of the group. It could be absolutely anything we liked: there were no restrictions. I remember we had left the previous week, wondering what we should each do to entertain and interest our peers. My mind was made up almost as soon as the request had been made; I knew what I would take.

The course was coming to a close as we drew our chairs into a circle to finish the evening. Some of us were not going to go on to the next level, either for personal reasons or because they had reached a level at which they were satisfied. Training to be a counsellor is not easy and not everyone can deal with the self-awareness which has to be achieved.

We had each brought into the room something personal and unique, ranging from a voodoo doll to a photographic mosaic, from pictures of a garden to a diary extract from a Mount Everest trip; one person even demonstrated a Zimbabwean dance, which we all joined in with.

Then it was my turn and I held up two pieces of paper, with the blank sides towards the group.

"As you all know, these last few months have been a journey for me. I have been struck by the parallels between my personal journey and this course, which I would like to share with you all. For a start, the first day of this course, and my reassignment surgery, were on the same day."

I had everyone's attention.

"As part of the course we had to provide a portfolio of documentation, illustrating our ability to understand what we have learned and undergone. We have done so. As we progressed through the course we were also examined and had to prove to an external examination board that we were proficient at this level of counselling skills. Again, we have done so."

"To achieve my transition I also had to provide a portfolio of information, to prove that I understood who I was and to prove that I am truly female. I did so: my proof was examined and found to be appropriate; it showed that I knew what I was doing. At the same time I also had to prove to an external examination panel that I was proficient in the role of being a female. I did that too: I'm pleased to say that the panel agreed, and I have the certificate to say so."

I held up my Gender Recognition Certificate as I explained its significance. I have no idea what the others in the room were actually thinking but I had their attention and the room was silent.

"This certificate has allowed me to progress even further and to conclude this part of my journey. But I have also received a second and possibly even more important certificate."

I was openly crying as I held up my newly-received birth certificate.

"This is my new birth certificate which contains two differences to the one issued at my birth. One is my change of name. The other is a very small and apparently simple correction but for me it is also the most important acknowledgement in my life."

I pointed to the column which designated my sex at birth: it now showed F for female and not M for male.

"So simple… but so important: the correction of *Just One Letter*. Thank you all for listening," I said as I sat down.

Tears of happiness were running down my face for all to see and I know that others in the group joined me as they expressed their happiness for me in completing my journey. I was content that I had had the opportunity to express my feelings openly in a safe group of people who could empathise in some way with just how I felt.

We moved on and finished the evening with music and a farewell sentiment from our tutor who played a recording:

"My Wish" by Rascal Flatts

Verse:

I hope your days come easy and your moments pass slow

And each road leads you where you wanna go

And if you're faced with a choice and you have to choose

I hope you choose the one that means the most to you

And if one door opens to another door closed,

I hope you keep on walking till you find the window

If it's cold outside…show the world the warmth of your smile,

But more than anything….more than anything…

Chorus:

My wish for you is that life becomes all that you want it to;

Your dreams stay big your worries stay small

You never need to carry more than you can hold;

And while you're out there getting where you're getting to…

I hope you know somebody loves you…and wants the same things too…

Yeah this is my wish

Verse:

I hope you never look back but you never forget

All the ones who love you and the places you left;

I hope you always forgive and you never regret;

And you help somebody every chance that you get.

I hope you find God's grace in every mistake,

And always give more than you take.

But more than anything…more than anything…

It was an emotional and appropriate ending to the evening and the course. This song expresses my wish for anyone embarking on a journey similar to the one I have travelled. It has not been an easy journey but the end result is worth every bit of pain and hardship that I faced.

I have a whole future in front of me now and I intend to live my life as it should always have been – as a female.

Chapter 17

New beginnings

It has been five years since I wrote my story, and four years since its first publication in paperback form. This opportunity to review and re-edit the story has been welcome and I hope that new readers have found it easier to read and, as a result, easier to understand what I have faced during my life.

My investment in writing this book has been rewarded by positive feedback from around the world, associated of course with sales, limited though they may be. This will never be a bestseller but that is not why I spent a year in writing, revising and publishing it. I wrote this primarily to understand myself better and to inform anyone who was interested in what it meant to live a life which was incongruent with how I felt.

I have been fortunate over these past five years but, I also believe, my good luck has been greatly enhanced by my ability to plan ahead and to adapt to unexpected change. My life following my SRS in January 2010 has not all been plain sailing. It has, however, been much easier than many others have faced, and for this I am very grateful.

A lot happens in five years, particularly in this modern world of instantaneous communication by news services and, of course, through social media. As I write this final chapter, in late 2015, the 'trans' issue has become a significant news item in many parts of the world. Celebrity trans persons are making an impact and coming out publically, in ever greater numbers. Some are attempting to improve the visibility of gender variance and are seeking greater acceptance by society in general for those living in this way. In my opinion it should also be acknowledged that these high-profile revelations benefit the individuals themselves: the publicity seems often to work to their advantage, even though this may not be the prime reason for their vocal support.

I applaud their actions in doing this and I recognise their wish to seek greater acceptance for trans people in general. However, there are both positive and negative issues surrounding these disclosures. I am concerned because the celebrity lifestyle does not reflect what the rest of us have to overcome when living in our own communities. The positives are all about raised awareness of trans and gender variant people and what they have to face in order to live in today's society. The negatives are all about self-promotion by people who are cushioned from the hardships that many face just to survive and to live as normal a life as they can.

Those who openly oppose trans and gender-variant people are always quick to point out irregularities in presentation and to find fault where, perhaps, none exists. The use of social media such as Facebook and Twitter enables instant publication worldwide with little opportunity for the accused to respond in their own defence.

Unfortunately violence is also all too commonly experienced by those who just wish to live and let live. Instant media coverage has made the world more aware of this but I am not sure just how much notice is actually taken by society at large. It also has to be acknowledged that, in many parts of the world, young trans people work in the sex industry, which is a far cry from the way of life of the celebrities whose disclosures hit the headlines. They do so as a means to support themselves and to finance the necessary surgeries to which many of them aspire. These people do not have the luxury of wealth or publicity machines to promote their image, nor do they have access to the best medical and psychological support that money can buy. The violence experienced by this portion of society ranges from verbal abuse up to and including murder; something which no one deserves, especially when they are just trying to live their life as best they can.

This is not to say that celebrity disclosure is entirely bad and should be condemned. Anything which raises the public's awareness of the difficulties faced by trans people has to be seen as positive. However, this type of disclosure has to be accepted cautiously.

Social media does allow others such as me, when writing blogs or articles, to promote positive issues which influence how we relate to the world at large. It also allows worldwide distribution of the good, the bad and of course the naively stupid by anyone who believes they have something to say about anything!

****

I originally ended my story with the disclosure to my peer group of counselling students that I had received my Gender Recognition Certificate and had then had my birth certificate changed to show my true birth gender – female. At that time I felt that it was indeed the end of my journey and that life would then carry on, just as it does for any other woman of fifty five.

In some respects it did; but in others I think I can say that I have experienced and achieved more than might be expected by the 'average' person in such a short period of time. I have no wish though, to just list my achievements over these last few years. I would, however, like to share some of them and to show that life can go on even after major upheavals and changes of the kind I have shown.

I eventually gave up being a personal carer after four years of hard but rewarding work which, for most of the time, was also a very enjoyable experience. I was grateful for the opportunity to work in this field and for the chance I had to meet many people, all of whom needed support of some form or another. Their needs ranged from personal care and medication through to a cup of tea and a chat – all of which were very important to the people for whom I cared. I was appreciated for the help I was able to give and to many I became a friend whom they looked forward to seeing every day. This work was also emotionally demanding for me as many of my 'friends' died of old age or terminal illnesses during this period. I learned a lot about myself during this time and I feel it was a necessary interlude in my life. I also learned more about people's emotional needs and the help that they required in order to live fulfilling lives in today's busy world. My training as a counsellor eventually progressed to a point where I could give up my job as a carer and could then start my new profession. On completion of my clinical training I was given the opportunity to take a position as a counsellor at the agency where I trained. I was happy to accept it and am pleased to say that I still work there.

In addition to qualifying as a general therapist I completed a further two years' specialist training to become a psychosexual and relationship psychotherapist. This, along with further training directed towards diversity and sexual minorities, means I can now confidently work with trans and gender-variant members of society. I can help those who wish to journey through transition to become the individuals they have always known themselves to be. I am also able to help people who just wish to explore their own identity, whether that is caused by gender or sexual confusion, or by something else. My experience, at the time of writing, is still limited but those I have met and with whom I have worked have all said it has been a positive experience for them. I also work with individuals and couples, of all sexualities and gender-expressions, dealing with the day-to-day issues of relationships and sexual difficulties. I have reached my goal and I consider myself very lucky to be able to say that I have achieved professional recognition twice in my life. This second profession, however, is one where I feel much more valued and where I can perhaps make a significant difference to the lives of others.

As for my own personal life, that too has been very busy in the five years since my SRS. Eighteen months after my initial surgery I returned to Thailand, and to the clinic. I had fully healed by that time but, as expected, I was not entirely happy with the cosmetic outcome, following the repair to my labia shortly after my SRS. This was to be a shorter trip of fifteen days and was more like a holiday than a surgical visit. I had arranged my return with the clinic: the routine was the same as before and I stayed at the same hotel. My corrective surgery was very simple and was carried out under a local anaesthetic in the clinic, much as the original repair had been - it took no more than thirty minutes! The result is, in my opinion, much better and I am much happier with the final visual appearance. The daily routine at the hotel was the same and I once more had the opportunity to meet other girls from around the world, and even their mothers or fathers, during my short stay. My heart was warmed by the way the younger transitioners, in their twenties or thirties, were being given such positive support by their parents. Going to Thailand for first-class surgery is one part of the equation; but having the emotional support of one's family is an additional factor which will contribute immensely toward a successful outcome, in every respect, for the transitioner.

The opportunity to just rest and do nothing much was a welcome break between college courses and also from my work as a full time home carer. I used the time well and worked on the final draft of this book, so that I could publish the paperback version on the first of November 2011. This is an achievement I shall always be proud of; I never thought I would be able to write so much and see it right through to publication.

In 2012 I met Dawn, a wonderful woman, and we were married in 2014, taking the opportunity to have a same-sex marriage, which became legal in the UK that year, rather than a civil partnership. We met on an internet dating site in May 2012 and love blossomed quickly. One of my greatest fears following my transition and SRS was that I would end my life as a lonely old spinster. I am very happy to announce that this was not to be. Dawn, whose own career was in publishing, has since told me that one of the attractions which caught her eye in my online profile was that I was a published author. I have one more reason to be thankful for writing my autobiography and sharing it with the world - it may well have turned out to be the best reason imaginable.

Within eighteen months we had decided to marry. Some may say this is not very long but at our age I think we were able to make up our minds quickly and knew we were doing the right thing for our happiness. We have a lot in common, both professionally and personally, as well as sufficient individual preferences to make our relationship interesting and diverse. We love to travel and have promised each other that we shall do our best to see the world – for example we have enjoyed our first cruise together, with a promise of more to come.

Perhaps her greatest demonstration of her love for me (other than marriage of course!) was her willingness to accompany me on another trip to Thailand, while we were still just friends. After much deliberation, and despite my stated feelings about facial feminising surgery when I had met Emily all those years ago, I decided that I would undergo this surgery myself and once more contacted Dr Suporn's clinic.

I had changed my mind. I can't say when I did but I was becoming more aware, and therefore more critical, of the masculine features on my face. I felt it made me stand out and allowed me to be 'read' more easily – this was something I was not comfortable with any more. I still had no intention of living in total stealth, trying to hide my past and to deny it. I did, however, wish to present myself as best I could in day-to-day interactions with society at large. So it was in November 2013 that I returned to Thailand, this time with Dawn for support, and underwent cosmetic facial reconstructive surgery. Primarily the surgery was to remove the brow bossing above the eye sockets, which is a feature of the male skull and produces that deep-set eye socket visible in many men. Removal of this bossing opens up the eye area giving a wider-eyed, more feminine structure and appearance. The alterations are, in one sense, minimal, requiring a very skilled surgeon to make such fine and detailed changes; yet the difference in perception by others (once the swelling and bruising has gone) is quite dramatic. Human beings identify the sex of another person not just from the 'big' clues, such as clothing, hair, voice, and body-shape; but also from a subliminal recognition of 'small' clues, such as the brow-bossing I have mentioned, the shape of the nose, the presence of an Adam's Apple or the curve of the eyebrows. It was these almost imperceptible modifications to my facial appearance that I wanted Dr Suporn to provide; I wanted to cut down as much as possible the signals that might give others cause to question my female status.

I had also chosen to have a face-lift at the same time, thinking that it was likely to be the last opportunity I had to consider any further cosmetic procedure. There was also undeniably a part of me that wished to enjoy being younger and to show a more youthful feminine appearance. I had, after all, missed out as I grew up and had been unable to experience being 'a younger woman'. The surgery itself was significant in its extent and invasiveness and required nearly eleven hours in theatre. Recovery was difficult for the first few days as I could not see, my hearing was muffled by dressings and I still had drains in the wounds to allow fluid to escape. It also took much longer to recover from the anaesthetic than on the previous occasion for SRS, having been a much longer procedure. I was so happy to have the support and help throughout this period that Dawn was able to provide.

We were in Thailand for a month, the same length of time as for my SRS in 2010. I had been told that recovery from the facial surgery was likely to be quicker than that from SRS, despite the length of the operation, and that I would be mobile sooner. This proved to be true: my recovery was actually very fast, which was commented on by the clinic staff. The bruising and swelling reduced quickly and I can only put this down to the additional personal care I received and the regular badgering to drink water and keep my fluids up! I was also able to sleep a lot on my return to the hotel, in the knowledge that all of my needs would be met. I was very lucky.

My progress was a good sign, as Dawn and I had decided to take the opportunity to get away from the city and have a holiday, provided that Dr Suporn cleared me as fit. We had booked a hotel at a resort located on an island, Koh Samet, about a hundred miles further south from the clinic. The island was a forty minute boat trip from the mainland and was a regular weekend resort for the people of Bangkok.

Dr Suporn did indeed pass me as fit to travel and agreed to me having a three day holiday before a final clinical discharge and my return to the UK. It was a wonderful experience; made even more adventurous by us having to catch a bus down to the coastal town, and arrange tickets for the boat across to the island itself. Catching a mini bus from the bus station located about half a mile from the hotel, sharing this with local people who got on and off at regular stops, just added to the whole experience. We had a fantastic holiday, on a tropical island get-away, and we still have many happy memories of our time there together.

Our return flight home went without mishap but was nevertheless memorable for one special incident: Dawn asked me to marry her! I had also been thinking about asking her and was just waiting for the right moment. She beat me to it and I, of course, said yes. A number of friends have since commented on the timing of this proposal. We had spent almost a month in very close proximity as she nursed me through recovery. We then had an idyllic time on a beautiful tropical island, complete with romantic walks and candle lit meals together on the beach. There had been many perfect opportunities for that 'romantic' proposal. It was then left to a moment at 35,000 feet over the Indian Ocean in the economy class cabin of an Airbus 320, for the question to be popped – not the most romantic atmosphere, perhaps, but a lovely experience all the same. The cabin crew got wind of our excitement and helped us to celebrate, providing champagne and a photograph as a memorable keepsake!

Life for me, and for Dawn, just went from good to better as we prepared for our wedding later in 2014. She put most of her belongings into storage and moved in with me until the refurbishing of our new home was complete – the last major project was finished two days before our wedding. It was a busy year!

Our wedding was not a large affair. Good friends and family shared our day at a lovely country hotel, now sadly closed. It was an opportunity for me to re-experience one of those magical moments in my life. Ours was not a traditional wedding and the music we chose would not be considered as mainstream. I had the great pleasure of re-living my experience in Thailand as I left the hotel to go to the hospital for my SRS. This time I walked down the aisle, to meet my future wife, to the haunting voice of Louis Armstrong singing 'What a Wonderful World'. I don't think anyone else can imagine my feelings on hearing this song, it is just so emotive, and I now have two excellent reasons for it to be such an important piece of music in my life.

We now live in a small village community and, I am pleased to say, have been accepted as a same-sex couple. I have experienced little discrimination during my life – not even during my transition - and not now either, I am free to live as my true self. The few events I can recall have been recorded here in my autobiography; together with a few other minor experiences. I can honestly say that my transition and entry into my new life have been comparatively easy.

My relationship with my daughters has remained strong and positive. They will actively defend trans rights if challenged on social media and have done so, on more than one occasion, when either I or perhaps others like me have been a target of ridicule, or even hate. I love all three of them dearly.

There are two other major events which happened during the five years, following my SRS, which I wish to share. Both of these are in connection with my daughter Kat, who was the first of my daughters to know about my gender dysphoria; she immediately offered me her understanding and her support. Her sisters, first Sam and later Sophie, were just as supportive when they learned of my distress, and throughout the unfolding of my story.

Kat has never been one to take the easy route through life and I have shared some of this during the telling of my own story. While I was in Thailand and was in the early stages of my recovery from the SRS she disclosed that she was pregnant. This was a shock not only to me but to her as well, for the pregnancy was not planned. I immediately gave her my full support for whatever decision she made. She faced many problems including being told by many 'friends' that a decision to continue with the pregnancy would be wrong, primarily because she was so young. Nevertheless, she chose to have the child, and to bring it up alone if necessary. In some ways her experience of judgement, criticism and anger was similar to my own, when I disclosed my transsexualism and my need to transition. I was, perhaps, able to empathise with her situation more easily than many others.

We still had our 'ups and downs' but I always stood with her in support of her decision. In September 2010 my grandson was born and has been a joy in our lives ever since. His mother is bringing him up to be aware of diversity and not to judge (as much as any five year old can understand) and I am pleased to say that he is a credit to her in this. I am a genderless "Bumps" to him. I am content with this as I am not, nor would I ever pretend to be, a grandma – that identification is for someone else; I am however very happy not to be a grandpa! The questioning of my status has started and it is too early to say how it will turn out. I do believe, however, that we will be fine together and that he will be part of the new generation who will understand and not be judgmental of difference. I hope I am there to help as he grows into adulthood.

The second event also involves Kat and in its own way is further proof that with the right attitude, all things are possible and that labels are just that and can be misleading and unhelpful at times. Some years after the birth of her son Kat met a young man and then accepted a proposal of marriage from him. The wedding took place in October 2015 but, back at the planning stage in the spring, Kat and her fiancé had wanted to discuss with me my role in the ceremony. They had already decided to ask a close male friend to walk her down the aisle. I was pleased that they wanted to talk about it, even though the decision was already made. I was not disappointed: this was their day and it was my place to acknowledge this and to let their wishes take precedence. I would have loved to have had that privilege of taking a walk down the aisle with my daughter but I understand that perhaps some traditions are best left alone. Besides, I had a different role to play.

I was asked if I would give the 'father of the bride' speech at the reception. This was a task I relished, for it was not a task but an honour, and I believe I performed it to the best of my ability. My only proviso was that I should not be introduced as "the father of the bride" and that the Master of Ceremonies should instead say "Kirstie will now respond on behalf of the family." This suited everyone and that is exactly how I was introduced on the day by the toastmaster.

I do not pretend that anyone there was unaware of my true position in our family. I was, however, proud to undertake this task and I made everyone laugh and smile, just as any other proud father would do under similar circumstances. As well as the family and close friends, I was also accepted by many I had never met before, most of whom I would never meet again. I was simply Kirstie and I was supporting my daughter and her new husband; what else mattered in a situation like this?

In the end, being trans has been a life-changing experience for me in so many ways, beyond the most obvious. I am proud to have achieved my transition, to have succeeded in my new profession, and to have a loving and supportive wife. In addition, my children are still with me, living close enough for us to see each other almost weekly; they treat me as a person and not a freak, as happens to some others in a similar position. I am happy and content in my new beginning and look forward to a long and purposeful life ahead. I will endeavour to do what I can to improve awareness and to promote knowledge about what it means to be trans. I am happy to be part of the ever increasing gender-diverse society we live in today. If my openness can help in even some small way then I am content.

Printed in Great Britain
by Amazon